PRIMITIVE MODERNITIES

PRIMITIVE MODERNITIES

▌ Tango, Samba, and Nation ▌

FLORENCIA GARRAMUÑO

Translated by Anna Kazumi Stahl

STANFORD UNIVERSITY PRESS ▌ STANFORD, CALIFORNIA

Stanford University Press
Stanford, California

English translation ©2011 by the Board of Trustees of the Leland Stanford Junior University. All rights reserved.

Primitive Modernities was originally published in Spanish under the title *Modernidades Primitivas. Tango, Samba y Nación* ©2007, Fondo de Cultura Económica de Argentina, S.A.

Printed in the United States of America on acid-free, archival-quality paper

Library of Congress Cataloging-in-Publication Data

Garramuño, Florencia, 1964- author.

[Modernidades primitivas. English.]

Primitive modernities : tango, samba, and nation / Florencia Garramuño ; translated by Anna Kazumi Stahl.

pages cm

"Originally published in Spanish under the title Modernidades Primitivas."

Includes bibliographical references.

ISBN 978-0-8047-6249-6 (cloth : alk. paper) -- ISBN 978-0-8047-6250-2 (pbk. : alk. paper)

1. Tangos--Argentina--20th century--History and criticism. 2. Tango (Dance)--Argentina--History--20th century. 3. Sambas--Brazil--20th century--History and criticism. 4. Samba (Dance)--Brazil--History--20th century. 5. Music--Political aspects--Argentina--History--20th century. 6. Music--Political aspects--Brazil--History--20th century. 7. National characteristics, Argentine. 8. National characteristics, Brazilian. I. Kazumi Stahl, Anna, 1963- translator. II. Title.

ML3465.G3713 2011

784.18'8850982--dc22

2011011919

Typeset by Bruce Lundquist in 10/14 Minion Pro

O tango e o samba

Chegou a hora, chegou chegou

Meu corpo treme e ginga qual pandeiro

A hora é boa e o samba começou

E fêz convite ao tango pra parceiro.

(repetir)

Hombre yo no sé porque te quiero

Yo te tengo amor sincero diz a muchacha do prata

Pero no Brasil é diferente yo te quiero simplemente

Teu amor me desacata.

Habla castellano num fandango

Argentino canta tango ora lento, ora ligeiro

Pois eu canto e danço sempre que possa

Um sambinha cheio de bossa

Sou do Rio de Janeiro.

The Tango and the Samba

(Portuguese) The time has come, it's come it's come

My body trembles and moves like a *pandeiro*

The time is good and the samba has begun

And has invited the tango as a partner.

(repeat)

(Spanish) Man, I don't know why I love you

I feel sincere love for you says the girl from the Plate

(Portuguese) But in Brazil it's different, *(Spanish)* I simply love you

(Portuguese) Your love does not obey me.

(Spanish/Portuguese) She speaks Spanish in a fandango

(Spanish/Portuguese) The Argentine sings tango, sometimes slowly, sometimes fast

(Portuguese) But I sing and dance anytime I can

A small *sambinha* full of *bossa*

I'm from Rio de Janeiro.

Composed by Amado Regis. Performed by Carmen Miranda (1937)

TABLE OF CONTENTS

ACKNOWLEDGMENTS

This book is the result of my postdoctoral research, conducted in the context of the Advanced Program in Contemporary Culture at the Federal University of Rio de Janeiro, Brazil, a program I was able to participate in thanks to the invitation of Heloisa Buarque de Hollanda. During the years in which I was carrying out this work, I participated in a research group that functioned as a space for extremely enriching intellectual discussion. From those exchanges, my intellectual desire drew its nourishment. For all that I wish to thank the "Márgenes" group—Adriana Rodríguez Pérsico, Álvaro Fernández Bravo, Andrea Giunta Eneida Leal Cunha, Eneida Maria de Souza, Maria Antonieta Pereira, Mónica Bueno, Raul Antelo, Reinaldo Martiniano Marques, Silviano Santiago, and Wander Melo Miranda. Thanks to Wander Melo Miranda, I was able to spend a semester at the University of Minas Gerais, Brazil, enjoying the library's valuable collection related to that university's School of Music. The House of Rui Barbosa and its library gave sustenance to this research effort on numerous occasions, thanks to the assistance and kind support of Flora Süssekind, Rachel Valença, and Tania Dias.

Different versions of certain segments of this book were presented at diverse conferences and professional meetings. I thank the institutions and individuals that invited me to participate in those gatherings: in Brazil, Beatriz Resende, Fred Goes, and Marildo Nercolini of the Federal University of Rio de Janeiro, and Maria Antonieta Pereira of the Federal University of Minas Gerais; Jens Andermann and William Rowe of Birkbeck College in England; Adrián Gorelik of the University of Quilmes in Argentina; and, in the USA, Josefina Ludmer, Luz Horne, and Rolena Adorno of Yale University; Arcadio Díaz Quiñones of Princeton University; Julio Ramos and Natalia Brizuela of the University of California, Berkeley; and Juan Carlos Quintero-Herencia of the University of Maryland.

For their careful, lucid, critical, and deeply committed review of my work in progress, I would like to thank a few loyal and steadfast friends: Adriana Amante, Andrea Giunta, David Oubiña, Josefina Ludmer, and Silviano Santiago. Together with Álvaro Fernández Bravo they have been a most powerful and constant source of intellectual support.

I would also like to express appreciation for the commentary that I received on numerous occasions from Alejandra Laera, Gonzalo Aguilar, and Idelber Avelar.

The CONICET (Consejo Nacional de Investigaciones Científicas y Técnicas; National Council for Scientific and Technical Research) incorporated me as a researcher under their aegis; I thank María Teresa Gramuglio for the warmth with which she oriented me in the now distant beginnings of this project. By the same token, I would like to extend my thanks to the other institutions that supported me in diverse research projects related to this book: the Antorchas Foundation of Argentina, the Argentine National Agency for Scientific and Technical Promotion, and the Flora and William Hewlett Foundation from the University of San Andres.

Many thanks also to my colleagues and friends in the Department of Humanities at the University of San Andrés, in Argentina, for the discussions and intellectual wealth of the seminars and conversations we have shared: Claudia Torre, Eduardo Zimmermann, Flavia Fiorucci, Laura Isola, Lila Caimari, Mario Camara, Pablo Ansolabehere, Paula Alonso, Paula Bruno, Robert Barros, and Roy Hora. The former director of the Max Von Buch Library, Mariela Frías, as well as the personnel working in the library, gave me their collaboration and solidarity in seeking out rare sources or patchy references.

At certain times over the course of the research, I received valuable collaboration from students Belén Hirose, Edgardo Dieleke, and Marina Larrea at the University of San Andrés. Edgardo not only wrote a thesis on tango in the avant-garde that was extremely enlightening but also, from Princeton, collaborated with my search for bibliography and references. Euclidia Macedo of the University of Minas Gerais Press in Brazil effectively and quickly helped me obtain the rights to publish the images, for which I would also like to thank the Pettoruti Foundation, Guilherme do Amaral, and Alexandre Teixeira.

I wish to express an additional word of thanks to Celia Pedrosa, who showed me today's samba. And to Álvaro, Ignacio, Alejo, and Maite Fernández Bravo, for accompanying me with their *reboleos* in so many carnival *blocos*, real as well as metaphorical, lending thereby a special brightness to my life.

This book is dedicated to three old *tangueros*: Carlos, Reyita, and "El Negro" Amestoy.

On the occasion of publishing the English version of this book, I am deeply grateful to Anna Kazumi Stahl for her dedicated and enlightening translation of this work. I would like to thank Norris Pope and Sarah Crane Newman for their help with the English edition. I am also thankful to the University of San Andrés for its support.

Finally, I would like to express my deep gratitude to Diana Sorensen for her enthusiasm and support for this book.

PRIMITIVE MODERNITIES

INTRODUCTION

Primitive Modernities

Musically, the tango ought not to be important; its only significance is that which we impart to it. This insight is valid, but can perhaps be applied more widely. For example, to our own mortality or to the woman who disdains us.

Jorge Luis Borges

In the 1920s and 1930s, when the drive to construct a local, autochthonous modernity was at its peak, tango in Argentina and samba in Brazil began to be perceived as national forms of music and dance. In those decades of intense modernization the more primitive and exotic traits of these genres were emphasized in order to highlight their national characteristics and flavor. Not only in the music—samba accentuating the syncopes and the nonmetricality of African rhythms, and tango lingering in that nostalgia for a bygone world—but also in contemporary novels, essays, films, paintings, and iconographic representations, the primitive and exotic character of tango and samba stands out. While that primitive aspect became precisely the reason for barring tango and samba from the national cultural landscape, at the end of the nineteenth century, once their acceptance was consolidated it was primitivism itself—now discernibly elevated in the cultural hierarchy—that was brandished in order to highlight them as national symbols.

The paradox of primitive modernity is not confined to tango and samba. It can be observed in the work of Tarsila do Amaral and Oswald de Andrade, in Mário de Andrade and Jorge Luis Borges, in the *Martín Fierro* group and the *Revista de Antropofagia*, and in Oliverio Girondo and Heitor Villa-Lobos or Radamés Gnattali. Like a sinuous and at times self-conscious movement, that paradox defines a knot of problems in relation to the nationalization and modernization of a Latin American culture for which tango and samba function as ambivalent and contradictory modalities. I have termed this paradox *primitive modernity* in order to represent the unity that underlies apparent contradictions. The paradox manages to cancel the one-way character of an unmistakable meaning: inasmuch as "primitive" can be understood also as "originary," its connection to other modernities generates a syntagm that enables a decentralizing of the supposed temporal breach and chronological delay in relation to Latin American modernities. A cultural critique of these primitive modernities is what this book proposes.

There is an anecdote that, like a kind of Borgesian aleph, condenses the intricate web of problems that entangles this process. The setting is Paris, a cold winter's evening, in the first decade of the twentieth century. In a cabaret in Montmartre, managed by Antonio Lopes Amorim, "O Duque," a group of Brazilian musicians starts to play a tango. In the audience there is a group of Argentines who, when the piece is announced as *"un tango brésilienne"* (a Brazilian tango), react with indignation: "Tango is Argentine!" Brazilians and Argentines, face to face in a dispute over an element of their national identity, come to blows.

I was unable to find out how the anecdote ended, nor to ascertain its veracity beyond its inclusion in a book on the history of samba.[1] What is certain is that in 1910 tango was considered Argentine in Paris and in Argentina, and perhaps in much of the rest of the world, but not in Brazil, proof of which is provided by the numerous tangos composed by Ernesto de Nazareth or Chiquinha Gonzaga. The corresponding scores had started circulating in different social classes and zones in Rio de Janeiro and, later, in Paris as well. Even today, those works remain in the repertoires of eminent Brazilian musicians. The Brazilian tango's itinerary is an extremely complex and winding road; its numerous forking paths led to the constitution of other musical genres, including samba itself, which was to become Brazil's national musical form.[2]

Nonetheless, tango was always principally Argentine, samba always Brazilian; each an element of national essence that would make itself pristinely, luminously manifest. Yet, judging by some musicological studies that the nationalistic histories of music have tended to discount, the first faltering articulations of tango and samba emerge from the same root: the *habanera* genre, present in the origins of tango, is also present in *maxixe,* or the Brazilian tango that later, around the 1920s, intervened in the transformations of the urban samba from Rio de Janeiro, known as the carioca samba.[3]

By 1937 the landscape had changed; Carmen Miranda was able to record a samba titled "O Tango e o Samba" (The Tango and the Samba) in which each of these musical forms is treated as characteristically national. Not only do the lyrics of this song mark the difference between Argentines who sing tango and Brazilians who sing samba, the music itself also slips sinuously from the opening bars with sounds that clearly reference the world of samba—the whipping *batida* (beat) of samba on the guitar, the percussive instruments keeping the beat—to the tango sounds introduced by the *bandoneón* (a type of concertina popular in Argentina and Uruguay). Carmen Miranda alternates an even sharper, faster modulation—one could describe it as cheerful—when she sings the samba rhythm (in Portuguese), and uses a deeper-voiced modulation with markedly elongated vowel sounds when she sings the tango rhythm (in Spanish). It is true that both of these musical forms served, in 1937, to define national identities, but each is manifested with such specificity in the song (to distinguish one form from the other) that in the end it is an outright fandango of cultural differences, especially when, in the second part, the tango is sung in Spanish with an instrumental backdrop of samba *batida.* The song, which the record's informational insert calls a "samba-tango"—a genre whose only register, as far as I have been able to uncover, is itself—was made the emblem of the relationship between Brazilian and Argentine music as well as, by extension, Latin American music sung in Spanish. Decades later, two prominent Brazilian musicians used it on separate occasions as a metaphor for a relationship of proximity. In 1995 Caetano Veloso chose "O Tango e o Samba" to open the concert presenting his album *Fina Estampa ao Vivo* (Fine Figure, Live), on which he performs popular Latin American songs in Spanish.[4] In 2003 Elza Soares used "O Tango e o Samba" in the presentation of her new album *Do Cóccix até o Pescoço* (From the Coccyx to the Neck) on a stage in Buenos Aires—even though the song is not part of the album, which was produced and released the previous year in Brazil.[5] In both of these cases, however, the musical arrangements differed, thereby creating diverse meanings via those same harmonies.

In the case of the performance by Caetano Veloso, who sang songs of his own repertoire in Portuguese along with compositions in Spanish, the musical arrangement of "O Tango e o Samba" tends to erase the marks differentiating the tango rhythms and the samba rhythms, proposing thereby a sort of similitude formulated as an alternation between Brazilian music, of which Caetano Veloso would be a typical representative, and Hispanic American music—all of which tends to be included in a single undifferentiated category (it is possible to observe here a rereading of Tropicalism's relationship with Latin America in the 1960s, especially as from Gilberto Gil's song "Soy Loco por Ti América" [I'm Crazy About You America]).

Among the musicians accompanying Elza Soares for the show in Buenos Aires was a *bandoneón* player, who preceded "O Tango e o Samba" with a few bars of "Adiós Nonino" (Farewell, Nonino) by Astor Piazzolla. Elza Soares introduced "O Tango e o Samba" with a short commentary on the similarity between Piazzolla and herself, both of whom were accused during the 1960s of not performing "authentic" tangos or sambas.

The comparison between Caetano Veloso's version of the song and Carmen Miranda's is illuminating regarding the divergent historical perspectives on tango and samba: whereas Miranda's shift in register from samba to tango is manifested as a strongly marked departure, in Veloso's version, and as frequently happens in his music with the incorporation of other sonorities and rhythms, the difference is only barely marked by an acoustic bass, bringing in sounds that are particular to Brazilian music.

How does a cultural form come to be transformed into a national one? What, on the one hand, does it mean to "be national," and what are the operations that make it possible for determined cultural forms to be thought of as symbols of a national identity? These questions, rather than others that could be asked about tango and samba, indicate that the scope of this book is not to seek or explain the national identity that tango and samba represent via their exclusively formal features, whether in music or lyrics. As opposed to a hermeneutics of the hidden, I prefer pursuing threads in the cultural network that have made it possible for tango and samba to be conceived of as national forms of music.

The study of tango and samba, as in that of so many other cultural practices, usually springs from an idea of culture and cultural practice as pure positivity. When viewed negatively, tango and samba are perceived as arenas for the domination of the masses by State policy; when perceived positively, they appear as authentic expressions of the lower classes.[6] Despite the opposite value that each of these readings ascribes to tango and samba, they share a vision of cultural forms as an unequivocal taking of sides in the face of a conflict that would remain always external to the cultural form itself. The form—the music, the body, the movement, the instruments, and the materials with which these cultural practices are conducted—in these readings is something like a stable, static, essential, and immutable map. That map would be seen as enclosing, like a magical cipher, representing either strategies of manipulation and interpellation or the transparency of an "authentic" identity (social, cultural, or by gender) that would be perfectly expressed through that form, either form-mirror or form-trap. What is certain is that in diverse contextual placements tango and samba reveal often-divergent assemblages of a shared mechanism. Just one example, and a quite abstract one: the syncope and the nonmetricality of tango exert at the beginning of the twentieth century a primitivist fascination that fits in with typical, autochthonous instruments and "obscene" lyrics; for the 1930s that syncope and that "obscenity" are assemblages of a modern sensibility that can be associated, then, with the avant-garde music of a Milhaud or a Stravinsky. How, then, to interpret that syncope? For a study of tango and samba and how these forms are transformed into national symbols, it is possible to dismantle that positivity and study the constellations of meanings that are apportioned to cultural practices and that these practices articulate in dialogue with others. Likewise, one can examine how the practices evolve in relation to those constellations of meaning, be that in favor of or in reaction against them, and finally also the operations by which history pervades those practices and leaves its mark on them.

In addition to the social, political, and musical causes affecting the transformation of tango and samba, the construction of a national sense associated with these musical forms is a complex, tension-filled process involving a mesh of discourses that altered the cultural meaning of certain connotations previously associated with tango and samba. The construction of that sense of the national cannot be contained within rigidly instituted boundaries. Tango and samba, in addition to being musical genres, are objects of the most wide-ranging cultural representations, including paintings, caricatures, album and sheet-music covers, essays and novels, poems, and musical compositions that in a sort of self-referential replication comment on these same rhythms.[7] All of these influenced the construction of that sense of the national in tango and samba, and study of this subject demands that one cross, constantly and irreverently, the boundaries between disciplines.

If on the one hand the ubiquity of tango and samba lends a quixotic quality to the study that addresses those continuities, on the other hand "O Tango e o Samba" stages the construction of the senses of the national that cuts across crystallized forms and performance and thus transcends both musical expressions. Central to that construction too are such international players as Darius Milhaud, a member of the group Les Six, who "exported" samba to European avant-garde music, or Blaise Cendrars who lent authority to the avant-garde modernists' search for popular roots, or Paul Poiret, the French haute couture designer who created "tango fashion" in Paris.[8]

The proliferation of objects, materials, and problems in relation to the construction of tango and samba as national musical forms makes an exhaustive study on this problematic practically impossible. Abandoning such a notion was not difficult given its connection to ideas of totality and its Lukacsian implications. As Adorno said: "the concern with precision becomes a fetish with which the researcher conceals the irrelevance of his conclusions."[9] Yet, I was concerned with defining the object of a study of this kind in order to avoid confusing detours, which often amounted to excluding previously elaborated research material. The scars of those extirpations should be read as the marks of an approach to the problem of the nationalization of tango and samba.

This is not a matter of seeking out preconditions to a way of thinking of the national; in fact, just as tango and samba were thought of as national, other subjects and forms disputed that place of honor within the same historical horizon.[10] The thought of the national, like the construction of a national culture, as Gramsci already showed, implies a hegemony that does not pacify subaltern forces, though it may dominate them to the point of blocking their open expression. Even so, one can read in those cultural discourses the operations that made it possible to think of tango and samba as national forms. Those zones of visibility created by the interplay in diverse cultural discourses make it possible to replace an analysis of culture based on forms (styles, movements, works, or groups) with an analysis of constructions in the relationship between various disciplines and forms. These operations entail thinking of culture as a series of passages and thresholds rather than as a positive object of assured localization. Replacing a history of forms with an analysis of systems of meaning as a way of historicizing must be understood as an exercise in cultural criticism, where *cultural* defines a mode of questioning in search of the contemporaneousness, polemics, and interconnections of discourses and images. It is not, in that sense, the analysis of a culture but rather of the cultural meanings constructed in the intersections of different and heterogeneous cultural objects, the helm, only barely compliant, of the person steering this book.

The Parisian anecdote is interesting also because of its illustrative and even physical quality, that the nationality of a certain kind of music is less a matter of an intellectual or formalist debate and more the figurative embodiment of a fistfight. I pick up on the violence in that incident for its illustration of the cultural conflicts spearheaded by tango and samba from 1880 to 1930 or 1940. That violent clash imparts a certain image of culture as a field of conflicts, as a space of symbolic polemics and struggles, which cultural forms condense in their formal traits, in their divergences, in their contextual situations, and in the ways those forms are used.[11]

Even though the idea of a culture as a homogeneous whole whose opposite would be anarchy has long been called into question, viewing culture as a field of negotiations has not always led to a study of differences. Indeed, what is frequently studied is how that conflict is resolved and how, in order to penetrate into the culture, it ceases somehow to be a conflict. Versus the study of the expressive unit of a culture, which tends precisely to impede and assuage the conflicts that construct it, I consider it important to describe the articulation of those conflicts, not their suture. Only in that way is it possible to apprehend the contingency that resides in those forms, confront the ambiguities and the stealthiness of texts and practices, and abandon a thinking that would consider texts, images, and discourses as pure positivity.

The study of the *expressive unit* of culture not only impedes and effaces the conflicts that construct it, but also supposes culture to be a place of consensus and a "site of reconciliation," as Lloyd and Thomas put forward in their influential book *Culture and the State*.[12] Observing these itineraries via cultural criticism allows one to view the history of tango and samba from multiple perspectives. Thus the debates about tango, for example, are not simply about its different styles, but rather reflections of varying types or networks of cultures. The two musical expressions under study expose broader cultural conflicts that appear, according to specific articulations, in other zones of culture. I am thinking, for example, of the different modernisms and the battles they embodied that could, in the case of Brazil, also be explained in terms of the conflicts that samba, and popular culture in general, would articulate for Brazilian society and for the Brazilian avant-garde of that period. The Argentine avant-garde of the 1920s and its wars for position are also viewed differently according to the positions that these different groups adopted in relation to tango.

This is a matter of discerning the nationalization of a culture through the intersection of its different practices, a process fraught with tension and ambivalences, but of which some residue of those national cultures can be pursued, in the analysis of the *documents*. In the passages and thresholds between different cultural forms—literature, music, popular expressions, film, visual arts—problems are revealed that cut across each form and allow scrutiny of the processes of nationalization and modernization in relation to a Latin American culture in the very materiality of its discourses, its dialogues, and its polemics.

Although perhaps it would be possible to examine the conversion of tango and of samba into national musical forms as one episode in the invention of a tradition, that is not the path this book will pursue. According to what has been set out by Eric Hobsbawm and Terence Ranger, the idea of the invention of a tradition supposes a quite direct relationship between the intention of cultural agents and the crystallization of those intentions into the forms thus produced, annulling not only the contingency but also the radical ambiguity of cultural practices, whose elusive coagulation of meaning is frequently the most interesting attribute.[13] In the case of the history of tango and samba, the intervention of the State is in itself an important episode, but posterior to the process of tango and samba's "formation" in a more traditional sense. It will be with Getúlio Vargas and Juan Domingo Perón in power—not coincidentally, both examples (albeit with substantial differences) of populist governments—during the decades of the 1940s and 1950s that samba and tango will come into contact with State power more immediately. Though the cultural nationalization of these forms can be deemed complete prior to State intervention, it is clear, principally in the case of samba, that a State role is more influential than in the case of tango, and was simultaneous with the process of nationalization that occurs spontaneously. Tango, in contrast, loses celebrity during Peronism. In the case of Argentina, nationalization is not confused with the process that made listening to these musical forms generalized and popular, even though the former may encompass the latter.[14]

Supposed Dialogues

The samba composed by Amado Regis and sung by Carmen Miranda speaks of a relationship between tango and samba that was much more fluid and complex during the years that these musical forms gelled into national symbols than what the recent history of these rhythms would suggest. As the song itself indicates, this is not a relationship of similarity or mutual contact, although many more points of contact emerge than might be expected.[15] But the confluence of tango and samba, or samba's predecessor, maxixe, on some historical stages allows one to think of a comparative study that would be grounded in a series of stories and formal operations that the two music forms have in common.

When in 1913 the rumor spread that Pope Pius X intended to excommunicate the tango, the Brazilian magazine *Cá e Lá* (Here and There) published the following quartets:

If the Holy Father knew
The taste of tango
He'd come from the Vatican
To dance maxixe too.[16]

Not only do both dances coincide in Paris, but also the anecdotes and stories told about one of them are often confused with those told about the other.[17] Vicente Rossi suggests, already in the 1930s, that it was in Rio de Janeiro that the ladies of the Argentine upper class, on seeing the Brazilian elite dance the maxixe, decided that they, in turn, would be able to dance tango.[18] Those convergences of tango and maxixe and the nationalization processes of tango and samba tell one possible story of a peripheral and Latin American culture and its constitution as modern and national culture around the 1930s in the twentieth century.

The comparison between two countries in the construction of a national symbol is proposed not only as a way of avoiding national exceptionalism by finding similar functions in another national space, but also because it allows for certain perceptions that a concentration on national traditions can overlook: the role of internationalism, the transfer and interchange of ideas and aesthetic proposals, and the function of the gaze of the other, for example. That gaze is proposed also as a way of avoiding the essentialism of identity politics that marked certain studies on national traditions in Latin America and especially the study of popular music.[19]

Not only did tangos and sambas in that chronology evince diverse cultural and ideological connotations, but many of them also were explicitly opposed to other contemporaneous forms, constituting themselves in privileged spaces of dispute and polemics. In the 1930s as well, for example, a well-documented debate between Noel Rosa and Wilson Batista took place on the issue of the *malandro/otário* (malefactor/naïve fellow) antithesis, and Borges disputed the various theories on the origin of tango as a matter of cultural legitimacy.[20] In the same period, the two different orchestra styles of Francisco Canaro and Roberto Firpo not only coexisted but were even contracted to perform in the same venue and thus expose audiences to multiple interpretations of tango, such diversity being specifically sought after.[21] At a certain point in that chronology, however, not only were tango and samba constituted as forms of cultural intervention, but they also generated still greater polemics that went beyond music to pervade their cultures. What were the discursive networks that came to be woven into these forms in order to allow them, despite inassimilable differences, to be constituted nonetheless as representative forms for an entire nation? What strategies were invented in order to make those forms documents of a culture? In sum, how was the articulation of those differences conceived? How could they be coordinated so as to build a sense of belonging *in spite of* them, taking those same differences into account or even as point of departure? Those cultural conflicts are inscribed in these forms with a fundamental ambivalence, the study of which enables a complex vision of both Argentine and Brazilian cultures.

The tradition in Latin American Studies, the majority of which are in fact Hispanic American, has created a corpus of study that frequently excluded research on Brazilian culture because of the presumption that Brazil's distinct language and colonial history contradicted a supposed homogeneity. This type of thinking prioritizes epistemological issues (that which can be compared) over political issues (that which requires comparison), as if epistemology were not itself tinted by ideology. The forced, nonconformist incorporation of research on Brazil can serve as a way to oblige studies to reflect on difference.

Key to the comparison between Brazil and Argentina is the way in which Latin American culture is read. The differing cultural traditions of those two countries tend to isolate that which is characteristic of the historical, political, cultural, and even formal problematic to which each culture has been subjected and to expose ways in which those national traditions have been constituted. At any rate, its greater effectiveness will lie with the possibility of conceiving of a Latin American culture pervaded by radical difference and comprehending a shared history.

In recent years Area Studies as well as Comparative Literature have received criticisms that suggest the shared foundation of these disciplines: that there exists a common ground whereby differences would be merely a matter of degree in a kind of spectrogram in which all the cultures of the world would be organized on a hierarchical scale.[22] To these criticisms of comparativism could be added its tendency to highlight a Latin American difference that was overdependent on the unique character of local cultures, which in many cases obstructed differences between diverse national contexts in the pursuit of a shared theory. If in some cases the advantage of a shared theory, such as the case of Ángel Rama in *Transculturación Narrativa en América Latina* (Narrative Transculturation in Latin America), would excuse historical errors (such as Rama's vision of Brazilian regionalism), what is certain is that in other, less honorable cases the damages have outstripped the gains.

The separate criticisms of these two disciplines become even more complex regarding Latin American Studies. In an article on Brazilian literary criticism, Antonio Candido proposes a series of arguments that, like many of his illuminations concerning Brazil, can be extended to other zones of Latin America.[23] In that work, Candido sees Brazilian literary criticism as marked, over the course of its history, by a comparativist design: whether due to its search for influences and plagiarisms, or as a tool for conceptualizing Brazilian literature, the comparativist mindset was always present in Brazilian literary criticism.[24] His argument can be extended not only to other areas of Latin America but also to other disciplines such as Latin Americanist history or political science, usually markedly pervaded by comparison with Europe. In its beginnings and for most of its history, with rare exceptions, thinking on Latin America made use of this comparison in order to construct Latin American identity.

In some cases that collaboration between comparativism and Latin American Studies could lead to studies that would be the object of a double criticism: because of a homogenizing of difference (owing to the Latin Americanist focus) and because of a dependency on a notion of Central Europe as model (resulting from comparativism) from which Latin American cultures would be a sort of deviation.

I believe, however, that it is possible to use both disciplines as a way of interrupting those identity-centered and normative intentions. I would like to think that it is possible to propose a collaboration between comparativism and Latin Americanism that can function as a non–identity-centered and counterhegemonic practice. Because even if tango and samba are thought of as national symbols, a comparison of how they were constructed reveals that they are not simple reflections of a previously constituted identity, but rather crystallizations of complex processes in the negotiation of cultural differences. In that sense, an analysis of the cultural genealogy of that crystallization allows one to displace the problematics of identity and difference and to pursue the study of cultural differences, finding in the nationalization of tango and samba—and, more generally, in the process of nationalization in Argentine and Brazilian cultures—a complex process of cultural disputes.

Nation and Modernity

There is an idea that is quite common in the histories of tango and samba that asserts a progressive transformation from their humble origins on the poor outskirts of their cultures to their canonization in the 1930s and 1940s. According to those histories, that process would have been possible because tango and samba, together with the cultures that gave rise to them, would have become "civilized." There is a very similar modernist and evolutionary teleology in the traditional histories that study these forms of dance and music from a supposed primitive origin—essentially nearer to the authenticity of the lower classes that produced those sounds—to a greater sophistication produced by the intervention of other classes and their appropriation of those forms. Various research analyses have questioned these hypotheses, from Hermano Vianna's studies demonstrating that whites participated in the formation of samba even before its supposed "whitening" took place, to the musicological studies of Carlos Sandroni demonstrating that the samba that was canonized after the 1930s has marked characteristics associated with African or black music, above and beyond the ethnic or social origin of its composers.[25]

The meanings constructed by the diverse discourses elaborated on tango and samba also do not give credit to the hypothesis of its progressive, linear "cleansing." In the work carried out by Argentine and Brazilian artists and intellectuals immersed in modernization and the avant-garde movements of the years between 1920 and 1930 (such as Afonso Henriques de Lima Barreto, Emiliano Di Cavalcanti, Jorge Luis Borges, Manuel Bandeira, Manuel Gálvez, Mário de Andrade, Martínez Estrada, and Oliverio Girondo), one can read a shared strategy, despite their differentiated expressions. It is a matter of elaborating the "primitive" and sensual character of those products as a mark of the most elegant modernity. That same characteristic that during the earliest years had served as sufficient proof to imagine operations of expulsion from those lascivious dances (as occurs in the texts of Aluísio Azavedo or Leopoldo

Lugones) is now resignified as the sign of modernity. Though it should be said that this primitivism is no longer the same as that earlier one, given that in the 1930s it will connote, due to a series of national and international issues that this book sets out to investigate, the national and the modern simultaneously. From the analysis of tango and samba, an ambivalent coincidence can be drawn that will make them seem like amphibious products, aiming simultaneously at the national that would come from an originary past and the modern of a form that has had success in Paris and in the international environments that dictate modernity's fashion and propose its modes. The transformation of the meanings of the primitive and its progressive association with modern traits, the contingent character of primitivism, and its functionality for a Latin American culture in the midst of constructing a particular modernity is what is read upon reconstructing the network of cultural meanings that were ascribed to tango and to samba.

In paintings and drawings by Cecilia Meireles, Emiliano Di Cavalcanti, or Emilio Pettoruti, one can read a strange combination of avant-garde artistic languages and a return to regionalist visualities. Taking distance from the *costumbrista* (mannerist) and realist representation that had been predominant in the nineteenth century, the mixing of apparently contradictory elements—a modern avant-garde language and the insistence on representation in national and primitive ways—was its clearest expression.

The filmmaking industry will have decisive importance in that association of tango and samba simultaneously with the national and the modern. The first Argentine full-length feature film (*Tango*, by Luis Moglia Barth) takes as its theme tango and the world of the poor marginal zones in order to establish in the cinema—which in that period can be considered the epitome of the modern—a national tradition: the tango movie. Samba, too, will be central in the creation of a Brazilian cinematographic tradition, the carnival movie. Many of the first Argentine and Brazilian films took inspiration from tango and samba, their histories and their worlds, their autochthonous characters. The continuity between the world of popular music and the world of film, in that primitive filmmaking, is seamless and easy: musicians, singers, and songwriters frequently crossed over between one world and the other, becoming actors, set designers, screenwriters, or film directors. As figures of an alternative modernity, or, as in the title of the book by Francisco Foot Hardmann, as metaphors of *A Modernidade na Selva* (Modernity in the Jungle), these problematics pervade the films featuring Carlos Gardel and Carmen

Miranda. Key steps in the nationalization of tango and samba, these productions also narrate, in their own way, a possible history of each of those forms.

That perhaps paradoxical or contradictory coincidence of the primitive and the modern is understandable when one recalls that in Latin America modernization does not merely coincide temporally with a strong period of the nationalization of its cultures, but is also identified with that nationalizing process. The conversion of tango and samba into symbols of a national identity is a product of the degree to which this process was tied in with the modernization of Argentine and Brazilian cultures. This book investigates both sides of that transformation: the primitive and the modern, and how both come to converge.

PART I

PRIMITIVES

1

THE PARABOLA OF PRIMITIVISM

The primitivism ascribed to tango and samba in the nineteenth century is markedly charged with negativity: a synonym for *savage* in the most denigrating sense, *primitive* is in many texts and iconographic representations of the era a mechanism for isolating, fracturing, and breaking a cultural fabric, extirpating from it a perceived sickness on behalf of the nation. When tango and samba are read via those coordinates, the tendency is to associate them with the kind of community that is frequently opposed to the community of the nation, and both primitive tango and primitive samba are seen on the basis of that almost ritual community function.[1]

Nevertheless, in those negative representations a certain fascination with the primitive also shines through, which will transform a few years later into a self-exoticism that will lend foundation to a national culture. At the other extreme, the primitivism associated with tango and samba is framed within opposed signifying coordinates: in its association with the savage, it is now cloaked in affinities with the modern; in its foreignness, national characteristics are now preached on its behalf.

For the moment it is of interest to concentrate on the mechanisms that enabled the transformation of one extreme to the other in that mutation of meanings, and to explore how the unresolved ambivalences in the primitive in a Latin American culture toward the end of the nineteenth century are later woven into the modern and the national.

It is possible to describe a parabola from that impulse to expel the savage and exotic primitivism that is not recognized as one's own in favor of a more familiar one. That parabola does not speak only of the primitive's contingency or, as Marjorie Perloff pointed out, the existence of multiple and diverse primitivisms.[2] Inasmuch as the primitive is recovered by revealing the national identity as a demand for distinctly modern content, that parabola also depicts a coincidence and a confluence of mechanisms of modernization and nationalization in Latin American cultures. The trajectory from the *exoticization of the nation* to the *nationalization of the exotic* turns out to be neither a simple nor an immediate operation.

An ironic poem published in 1913 in the Argentine magazine *P.B.T.* describes tango's primitive characteristics, associating them with its possible African origins:

> In France they have transformed it
> and they call it *le tango*
> maybe there it would seem
> deserving of Madame Argot
> who was one to dance
> the March of Ituzaingó
> Richepin defended the tango
> even in the Academy
> (if you ask me, he's mad
> from tip to toe).
> Let them dance the tango
> in its birthplace: the Congo![3]

The poem unveils both the negative and exotic connotations of primitivism, on the one hand using *tango* in association with *mango* (a word in Lunfardo, the argot associated with the world of tango and its lower-class contexts) and *Congo,* evoking the supposed Africanness of the music and the world of delinquency represented by Lunfardo at the time;[4] and on the other hand playing on the association of the dance with all that is foreign and French, by juxtaposing *Argot* with the strongly national and military implication of the *March of Ituzaingó.*[5]

One of tango's many genealogies, perhaps best represented in the essay by the Uruguayan Vicente Rossi titled *Cosas de Negros* (Black People's Matters), effectively proposes tango's origin to have been the Afro-Argentine and

Afro-Uruguayan *candombe* dances toward the end of the nineteenth century. That Africanness is always alluded to simultaneously as proof of this musical form's nonnational, non-"Argentine" character. Antonio Chiappe, one of the first *bandoneón* players, pointed out the following, in an article published in *La Razón* in 1919:

> Tango isn't ours either, the only thing that belongs to us are the new "cuts" in the dance moves, since everyone is well aware that this is a black people's dance. In Africa it was danced in tribes of different types and there was also the Mexican, the Cuban and the Brazilian tango that they called "Condesa" [Countess], "Pasa Mi Sargento" [After You, My Sergeant]. Who, of a certain generation, doesn't remember those candombe clubs?
>
> To the beat of the drum and other instruments, the blacks went right on ahead twisting sharply and wiggling, executing the timing of tango to that music's beat.[6]

The oscillation between a denigrating as well as comical and caricaturesque representation of tango's primitive origin and an iconographic, modernizing representation is evident in the contrast between a poster about tango published in 1890 and any of Pedro Figari's paintings on *candombe*.[7]

The simian features and animalistic postures of the poster emphasize the savage side of primitivism, and the typically rapid pen strokes of caricatures lend, moreover, a representation with both comical and critical intentions. In Figari's paintings on *candombe*, in contrast, the basis of a national language emerges and will be taken up also by the avant-garde group associated with the journal *Martín Fierro*. The paintings' accentuated primitivist features as well as an insistence on primary colors, fauvism-inspired lines, and treatment of the canvas surface not only underscore the primitivist association of tango's origin but also initiate a polemic about national art, its approved themes and preferred materials, that continued through the first decades of the twentieth century in Argentina.[8]

Figari's paintings are useful to the avant-garde: in relating *candombe*, the espoused origin of tango, to "the past of the patria," his works show the possibility of a *criollista* (American-born and possessing Spanish extraction, with close cultural ties to colonialism) genealogy of the tango, an idea whose most conspicuous patron was Jorge Luis Borges, as evidenced repeatedly in his work. Invoking the genealogy theme, Borges's texts on tango describe a rebound from the nation's past of primitive tangos, effectively neutralizing

FIGURE 1.   "Blacks Dancing," *La Ilustración Argentina* [Argentine Illustration], issue
33 (November 30, 1882). Garramuño, *Modernidades Primitivas*, p. 50.

the role of immigration in the composition of more contemporary tangos,
something Borges rejects as a corrupting agent of authentic, primitive music,
and the invention of a criollo (American-born of Spanish descent) past for
tango.[9]

Although the African legacy plays a radically different role in the cultural
imaginary of Brazil today, particularly after the process of reevaluation led by
Gilberto Freyre,[10] things were quite different toward the end of the nineteenth
century. Like their Argentine counterparts, members of the Brazilian elite
were strongly resistant to considering the African legacy part of their national

tradition.[11] The vision of the samba of Bahia and other forms of popular music that formed the urban carioca samba is based on a discourse that associated African descent with savages and sensual primitivism, and was seen not only as negative but also as emphatically dangerous for the formation of a national identity. Clearly, this thinking is a reverberation of Brazilian attitudes about the positivist profile, which sees in its population of African heritage a threat to the constitution of a "healthy" national identity, something Roberto Ventura analyzed so well in his *Estilo Tropical* (Tropical Style). Considered African and savage, samba is also rejected as representative of the nation. Rui Barbosa, at the time a minister of Brazil, complained before the senate that he had heard a *cortajaca*, a sibling to the samba, at a national reception in the presidential palace: "But the *cortajaca*, about which I heard so much talk a long time ago, what is it, Mr. President? The lowest, the tackiest, the most vulgar of all savage dances, the twin sister of the batuque, the catereté, and the samba."[12]

Yet, Rui Barbosa himself participated in the bohemian carioca gatherings, where samba was undergoing the process of transformation that would, by the mid-1930s, convert it into a national symbol.[13] There is in Rui Barbosa an ambivalent attitude, of appreciating samba for personal entertainment but rejecting its capacity to represent the Brazilian nation.

The opinion of Enrique Rodríguez Larreta, then Argentine ambassador in Paris, on tango is similar:

> Tango in Buenos Aires is a dance that is peculiar to houses of ill repute and low-class taverns of the worst sort. It is never danced in salons of good taste nor between distinguished persons. To Argentine ears, tango music awakens truly disagreeable ideas. I see no difference at all between the tango being danced in the elegant dance schools of Paris and the one being danced in the low-class nighttime venues of Buenos Aires.[14]

The twists and turns of discourse in these pronouncements, in which the primitive is constituted as something savage, sensual, and dangerous, show the historical conditions of a process of nation building guided by an internalized European gaze. The yardstick by which national culture and customs were measured in the late nineteenth and early twentieth centuries did not correspond to the demands of European modernity, and the ubiquity of tango and samba in Argentine and Brazilian cultures by necessity narrated a uniquely Latin American process of nationalization.

Cracks in the Civilizing Discourse

The parabola of tango and samba, originally scorned because of their primitivism and later adopted as national symbols, clearly contradicts the idea of a completely civilized and modern culture. Yet, that is precisely the image Brazil and Argentina were striving for as they grappled with a modernization frequently interpreted to entail the imitation of Europe. How was it possible, then, for tango and samba, widely considered savage and primitive, to be converted into symbols of a national identity precisely at the time when both countries were struggling to show the world a modern identity?

The process at work in this transformation is a *civilizing mechanism*, in which tango and samba became progressively more sophisticated and polished after being submitted to a process of cleansing and modernization. Thus over the course of history the original tango and original samba—both popular, exotic, and with evident African characteristics that are more obvious in samba but also figure in early tango—would have been made more sophisticated through combinations with other musical forms and the intervention of composers from the middle class and the elite.[15]

An advertisement that also appeared in *P.B.T.* in 1914 depicts tango from this new perspective. The ad displays a drawing of a dance hall full of young people dancing tango and an older woman, seated to one side observing the dancers.

The caption reads:

> The majority of the dances seen in aristocratic ballrooms are of popular origin and not a little barbarian and savage. [. . .] But tango has evolved, and just as primitively it belonged exclusively to low-class people, who washed neither their faces nor their hands (which are the ABC's of cleanliness), except for Passover, today it prevails in luxurious ballrooms and is danced by people who bathe and wash themselves with sumptuous Reuter soap, whose evocative influence has lent tango, like that languid and poetic abandon that distinguishes it, a delicious "glissage" type of movement, making it seem Reuter soap itself is directly involved.[16]

Personal hand soap factors in this advertisement for a product typically associated with modernity and which appears on the Argentine market in the first decades of the twentieth century.[17] Tango's association with a modern product effectively elevates it from the formerly unsophisticated realm of popular dance to the fashionable circle of modern, middle-class consumers.

EL TANGO DE SALÓN

La mayoría de los bailes que se usan hoy en los salones aristocráticos, son de origen popular y no pocos primitivamente bárbaros y salvajes.

El vals, por ejemplo, el prototipo eterno de las danzas universales, es genuino de las antiguas razas escandinavas, que lo bailaban en sus bacanales y en estado de embriaguez, degenerando las más de las veces en actos licenciosos.

La polca es un baile de origen polaco, absolutamente popular, como la chacona del siglo VII, que luego degeneró en la mazurca, la varsoviana, etc., abolidos hoy de nuestros "carnets comme il faut".

Ahora, el "cake-walk", la "matchicha", la "danza del oso", etc., llevan en sus mismos nombres y en sus modalidades simiescas, el sello más expresivo de su genealogía, y en cuanto a nuestro tango, difícilmente se podrá encontrar nada que exprese su procedencia plebeya, como su designación onomástica y el quebrajeo lascivo de sus movimientos.

Pero el tango ha hecho su evolución, y así como primitivamente fué de la exclusividad de las gentes de baja estofa, que no se lavaban la cara ni las manos — que es el A B C de la limpieza — sino por Pascua Florida, hoy impera en los salones lujosos y es bailado por gente que se baña y se lava con riquísimo jabón Reuter, cuya sugerente influencia ha transmitido al tango, así como ese lánguido y poético abandono que lo distingue, un delicioso movimiento de "glissage", en que parece que el mismo jabón Reuter tuviera una inmediata participación.

Y vean ustedes cómo el tango decente y el inevitable jabón Reuter tienen sus puntos de contacto, cosa en que no hubieran pensado jamás los que empezaron a leer estas líneas.

FIGURE 2. "El Tango de Salon" [Ballroom Tango], *PBT*, 1914. Garramuño, *Modernidades Primitivas*, p. 56.

The illustration is framed clearly by the older woman seated on the margin with her gaze turned toward the ballroom. She is substantially older than the dancers and, by her facial expression, clearly does not share the young people's joy. A second older woman, with feathers in her hair and who is also not dancing, is positioned in the same frame. The women's age would place them closer to the era of tango's "shameless" past, and their attitude of suspicion is evident. The primitive traits of these modern dances are negatively noted in the text: "Now the cake-walk, the *matchicha*, the bear dance, etcetera, display in their very names and in their simian conduct, the telling mark of their genealogy. As regards our tango, it would be difficult to find anything that would express its plebian origin more than its onomastic denomination and the lascivious twists and turns in its movements."[18]

In the *P.B.T.* advertisement, tango is literally cleansed by the soap that is associated with it. The fact that this ad appeared merely a year after the quartets analyzed a few pages earlier speaks to the coexistence in the national mindset of tango's cleanliness (civilization) and dirtiness (barbarity and indecency).

A similar story occurs in the evolution of samba regarding modernization and civilization. H. Dias da Cruz tells it this way: "That classic fellow—with long trousers, wood-heeled shoes, and his hat cocked at an angle—has disappeared. He has been civilized. Instead of the neckerchief, a tie. He no longer sits outside his shack composing sambas. He comes to the Avenue. He writes them at a table at Café Nice. He wears clothes that are tailor-made."[19]

Or witness the clear association of samba and the modernization of Brazilian culture that is present in José Ramos Tinhorão's argument:

> The genres of urban music that were recognized as carioca, or typical of Rio de Janeiro, the samba and the marcha, arose and were fixed during the sixty-year period that runs from 1870 (when the decline of coffee in the valley of Paraíba began to release slave labor that would later swell the lower-class groupings in Rio de Janeiro) to 1930 (when an urban middle class generated by the process of industrialization announced its presence with the Estado Novo).[20]

The similarity between these narratives is obvious: tango and samba accompany and register, like faithful thermometers, civilization and modernity in the Argentine and Brazilian cultures. Yet, in all these discourses the residues of a previous primitivism seem to reverberate with insistence, as if the modern and sophisticated symbols were remembering their primitive origin; as if still within them, hidden, there remained the embers of a vile past, dragged along like a burden.

By 1920 that process of converting the primitive into the modern seems to have been completed for tango. An issue of *Caras y Caretas* runs a cartoon under the title "Foreigner Humor" in which a man is interviewing a pretty young woman:

> Man: I suppose that in applying for this secretarial position you must know typewriting and languages, etcetera.
> Woman: None of that! Tango, foxtrot, jazz . . . and what you can lay your eyes on right here!
> Man: The job is yours![21]

Tango, as a mark of the contemporary, replaces the old standards of professional updatedness. Its association with sensuality—"and what you can lay your eyes on," says the shapely secretary—is, as shown by the man's answer, the most convincing argument for hiring the applicant for the secretarial position.

The print media of the period also registered tango and samba's progressive transformation. During the first and second decades of the century, and despite tango's triumph in Paris, tango appears in the Argentine press only in advertisements for tango records and scores, in other ads, in cartoons, and in crime reports.[22] But its progressive association with the objects with which it is affiliated—a brand of cigarettes named Tango; that innovating object of modern technology, the record album; or the stylish forum for shows and entertainment that were the cabarets and *cafés danzantes* (dance hall cafés)—spin tango as an up-to-date cultural product and firmly place it in the context of Argentine modernity. What was called *Tango fashion* would end up making the tango modern.[23]

A similar process occurs with samba, though somewhat inversely. Samba is completely excluded in newspapers in Rio de Janeiro during the first decades of the century, even during carnival seasons, when an appreciable number of articles chronicle the festivities. The texts that predominate are reviews of the elegant carnival at the Casino da Urca and in the ballrooms of the elite, ignoring the popular carnival taking place in the city streets. Mention of the popular carnival is confined to crime reports or admonishments of "low-class customs."[24] Only in 1930 do articles begin to appear about the popular *carnaval de rua* (street carnival) that will become Rio de Janeiro's hallmark, to the extent that newspapers begin to publish samba lyrics prior to the festivities so that the crowds can sing along.[25]

In the transformation of samba into a symbol of national character, its purely national representativity ultimately secures its association with modernity. An article published in Rio's *O Globo* in February 1931 emphasizes a carnival *bloco*[26] called "Gente do Morro" (People from the Hill), composed by "a large group of *foliões* [revelers], all dressed like convicts" and specifies: "The soul of the carioca street carnival is the '*choro*.' Who does not feel instant pleasure when he hears, at his very doorstep, the suggestive beat of samba, that purely national music, coming from a group of well-tuned instruments played by anonymous musicians who shine as they perform our national folklore?"[27] It is the "purely national" and anonymous aspect of folkloric culture that makes it possible to confuse choro with samba; both become effigies radiating a national essence that fuses one genre with the other. That national essence catapults samba to the most conspicuous expression of Brazilian modernity, the *Manifesto Antropófago* (Cannibalist Manifesto), in which Oswald de Andrade cites the title of a maxixe, "Fizemos Cristo Nascer na Bahia" (We Made Christ's Birthplace Bahia), in a reference to Sebastião Cirino's composition titled "Cristo Nasceu na Bahia" (Christ Was Born in Bahia):

> They say Christ
> was born in Bethlehem
> history is wrong
> Christ was born in Bahia, my dear,
> and into a Bahian he grew
> in Bahia there was *vatapá*
> in Bahia there was *carurú*
> *moqueca* and *auçá* rice
> mango, orange and cashew
> Christ was born in Bahia, my dear,
> this I believe
> Bahia is a sacred place, and
> the Bahian must be a sacred man.[28]

The maxixe's lyrics echo with the *Manifesto* like a condensation of some of the more obvious features of Brazilian, and especially Oswaldian, modernism; its resolutely national character seems to identify rupture and transformation as specifically Brazilian traits.[29] By inverting any negativity toward the primitive—galvanized here in the signifiers that point to African descent: *vatapá, moqueca,* the Bahian Christ—the lyrics also reveal the cracks in the civilizing discourse and lay exposed the limitations of this kind of "cleansing" or modernizing operation of the primitive.

Only a complex, supple process that uses the ambiguities of the concept of the primitive and its functionality within a Latin American culture as origin of an intricate map of meanings will make it possible to dodge those risks in the conversion of tango and samba into national forms of music.

Musical Primitivism

Traces of that primitivist scheme can also be found in tango and samba's musical rhetoric. One of the richest tones of musical primitivism is the accentuation of the syncopated rhythm recognized as coming from African musical forms, which was a clear tendency in music in Latin America at the beginning of the twentieth century. According to Mário de Andrade, in reference to the music of the 1930s:

> It is not because of jazz that the current phase is one in which rhythm predominates. It is because the current phase is one in which rhythm predominates that jazz is so appreciated. Indeed, to cite just a single case, Stravinsky's *The Rite of Spring* is previous to the expansion of jazz in Europe and it is already a predominantly rhythmic piece, with developed percussion that . . . prophesied the coming of jazz.[30]

In that rhythmic predominance, according to Mário de Andrade, jazz, tango, and samba are equals. Rhythm predominated in that particular musical phase perhaps for the same reasons that color and language predominated in the visual arts and literature, in which emphasis on the material itself comes to define the genre. Adorno, in his *Philosophy of New Music*, also signaled the coincidence of a shared primitivist impulse at the irreconcilable extremes of modern music seen in Stravinsky and Schoenberg.[31] Interestingly, he identified musical primitivism as a historical trend during the early decades of the century, which precipitated in diverse and even opposite forms, such as the music of the avant-garde versus popular music.

The musical renovation that came about during the early decades of the century drew intensely on popular and folkloric sources, which tended abundantly toward national musical forms[32] while also pushing in the opposite direction, toward a pronounced cosmopolitanism. Frenchman Darius Milhaud, a member of the group known as "Les Six," lived in Brazil for a few years at the beginning of the century and not only took rhythms and musical methods from the music of carnival and from maxixes and Brazilian tangos to the music of Europe, but also gave testament to the powerful fascination that this music instilled in him. In *Notes sans Musique* (Notes without Music), for example, he writes:

> The rhythms of this popular music intrigued and fascinated me. There was in the syncopation an imperceptible suspension, a *nonchalante* breathing, the slightest arrest, that was very difficult for me to capture. I then bought a number of maxixes and tangos; I made the effort to play them with their syncopation that passed from one hand to the other. My efforts were recompensed and I was at last able to express and analyze "that little nothing" that is so typically Brazilian. One of the best composers of the music of this genre, Nazareth, played piano in the entranceway to a movie house on the Avenida Rio Branco. His sound—fluid, sad, impossible to capture—helped me too to become more familiar with the Brazilian soul.[33]

In tango it is possible to perceive a progressive instrumental sophistication, from the first guitar, flute, and violin trios to the sextets. While the piano worked as an ambassador for tango in the more "decent" circles of society in the early twentieth century, the *bandoneón* introduced a slower pace and added to tango a clearer connection of the sounds.[34] On a rhythmic level, however, the more sophisticated execution of a *staccato picado* (choppy staccato) on the bandoneón (in the hands of Aníbal Troilo, for example) produced a lively tango known as "*saltarín y compadrito*" (jumpy fellow and swaggering braggart). Such innovation marked a much stronger accentuation on rhythm than was possible with a guitar, flute, and violin trio in which no single instrument played a solo.

The bandoneón is a modern instrument that arrived on the scene in the nineteenth century. Its keys are not ordered chromatically, making it possible to play chords of a three- and even four-octave range with a single hand, a counterpoint technique that is nearly impossible on other instruments and which creates an effect of "musical chaos."[35]

Another curve of those primitivist mutations can be pursued in the lyrics of tangos. In the evolution Gobello attributes to those verses in *Las Letras de Tango de Villoldo a Borges* (Tango Lyrics from Villoldo to Borges), tango dispensed with its primitive lyrics—mere "whorehouse couplets"—at the moment of its expansion toward other classes and neighborhoods. According to Gobello, at that time "tango was condemned from the start because of the lowness of its origins; it was not intelligent, thus to irritate its aggressors with the obscenity of its verses."[36] Even so, starting in 1917, when the great development of the tango song begins and marking the beginning of tango's acceptance, its lyrics could not be considered a compendium of bourgeois morals. Though perhaps not reaching the level of obscenity that might be implied in "whorehouse couplets," it is possible to trace a perception of indecency infiltrating the discourse: now the lyrics, in addition to the dance, are articulated as being outside bourgeois morals. The shift of the onus from the tango dance to the tango song deflects amorality from the body to discourse.

Another argument regarding tango's civilization process is that the shift in criticism from the dance to the song effectively displaced the lasciviousness of the dance, and its participants, by converting them from dancers to passive listeners. Yet, the supposed indecency of the danced tango that preceded the tango song must also be questioned. Savigliano states:

> Tango does not perform an "instinctive" sensuality (like the dances of "primitives"), a lascivious excitation (like the peasant dances), or outright impropriety, cynicism or defiant aggression toward the upper classes (like the dances of urban marginals). Nor does it focus only on the erotic powers of the feminine body, like other "traditional" erotic dances. The sexual politics of tango were centered on the process of seduction. A seductive man and a femme fatale who, despite their proximity, hold their erotic impulses in check, gauging each other's power. In its choreography, tango seems like a chess game in which mortal rivals take turns to move invisible pieces with their feet in motion. Their mutual attraction and revulsion are prolonged in an unbearable, infinite tension. And everything takes place, apparently, under the male's control.[37]

Vicente Rossi seems to affirm this attitude in *Cosas de Negros* (Black People's Matters): "One did not dance for the momentary contact with a woman, but rather for the dance itself. The female partner was the other half of the couple; that is why she was required no greater attractiveness than her skill as a dancer."[38]

Cleansing and Whitening

Whereas the supposedly lascivious dance is in fact the restraint of eroticism, the tango song expresses an excess of that eroticism. That was Martínez Estrada's view of tango lyrics in 1933: "Still today the lyrics speak quite clearly of [the tango's] lineage. It features the woman of the streets; it speaks of villainy, adultery, escape, cohabitation out of wedlock, emotional prostitution, the weeping pimp."[39] In novels, essays, and poetry during the 1920s and 1930s, tango continues to be conceived of as primitive and sensual. Borges as well as Lugones insist, in the 1930s, on seeing that savage or barbarous side in tango. Though for Borges tango is a "music of Greek rhapsodists" and for Lugones it is "that reptile from the brothel," both authors coincide in depicting tango as something primitive.[40]

Tango lyrics, on appealing to the world of the poor city outskirts and that milieu's most characteristic individuals, the *milonguita* (loose woman) and *compadrito* (braggart), for example, established a link between the primitive aspect of tango and a kind of self-referential poetic structure that is a strictly modern trait. The nostalgia often associated with tango derives from the almost ritual invoking of a primitive past from a position of loss or absence of that past. Tango lyrics mark a tension between the reference to a past and the ascertainment of its disconnect with the present.

Samba's history is delineated by similar transformations. Given that white, middle-class composers (Noel Rosa, for example) began to intervene in the production of a new kind of samba, the transformation was read as an episode of *branqueamento* (whitening). "Pelo Telefone" inaugurates in 1917 (note the exact coincidence of the year for the first tango song) a type of samba recognized today as older, which during the 1930s suffered a radical transformation to the degree that for many it ceased to belong to the same genre.[41] The rhythmic pattern that identifies that new samba accentuates syncopation and counterpoint, which are blatantly associated with music of African and "primitive" origin. According to Carlos Sandroni:

> on numerous occasions emphasis has been given to what would be the whitening of the genre, its progressive assimilation into the status quo. However, if we admit, with most researchers, that nonmetricality is, in the music of the Americas, a trait of African origins, then, on the contrary, it will be necessary to see in this passage an Africanization, since Estácio's paradigm (the new one, the one with which samba will be nationalized) is much more nonmetrical than the samba of the *tresillo* tuplet (the one prior to the 1930s).[42]

For Sandroni that paradigm remained repressed in Brazilian music even beyond the paradigm of the *tresillo* because its more evident nonmetricality made it less agreeable to the ear and social prejudices of Brazilian culture. Furthermore, nonmetricality would have been repressed aesthetically because it was assimilated excessively into the music of the blacks.[43] Yet, the acceptance of samba coincided with an accentuation of the primitive traits that had been repressed up to that time.

Moreover, samba, in its evolution, accentuated the characteristics that identify it with an African tradition: wind instruments ("European" instruments) are complemented by such percussion instruments as the *pandeiro, surdo,* and *cuíca*; samba's rhythm speeds up; and the lyrics become much more self-referential in relation to the world of samba, making mention of the *batucada* (percussion), the *morro* (hill), the *malandro* (rascal, rogue) lifestyle, and other elements of the social world of samba.

Interestingly, samba lyrics are often surprisingly similar in nature to tango lyrics. Many can be grouped into a subset of themes dealing with the tension between characters, environments, and stories situated at the margins of modernization and negotiating a balance between modernity and primitivism. Lyrics in the subset of *malandro* sambas, exhaustively analyzed by Cláudia de Matos and Carlos Sandroni, refer to a primitive world on the verge of disappearing and whose resistance is eulogized in the samba; "Recenseamento," "Gente Bamba," "Adeus Batucada," and "Voltei pro Morro" are elaborations on the authentic tradition of the *morro* (poor settlements in the peripheral hills of Rio de Janeiro) that was not so present in the early sambas. In "Recensamento" (Census),[44] by Assis Valente, references to modernization in the city, on the one hand, and to the music and the world of samba, on the other, meet in initial opposition that is ultimately resolved in the form of a negotiation:

In 1940
up on the hill they started taking the census
and the census taker
dissected my life which was a horror
and when he saw my hand without a wedding band
looked at the boy sleeping on the floor
and asked if my man [brown/black man] was decent,
if he was hard-working, or if he was the partying sort.

Obedient to everything pertaining to the law
I stayed calm and told him then:
my man is Brazilian, he's a soldier
he's the one who carries his battalion's flag!
Our house doesn't have a whit of splendor,
we live well without owing a cent
we have a *pandeiro*, a *cavaquinho*, a tambourine,
a *reco-reco*, a *cuíca*, and a guitar.

I got to thinking and started to describe
everything, everything of value
that my Brazil has given me
a blue sky, a Sugar Loaf without crumbs,
a green and yellow cloth
it's all mine!
I have holidays that to me are worth a fortune,
the battle of the Retirada da Laguna, worth a ton
there's Pernambuco, São Paulo, Bahía,
a harmony band that can't be beat.[45]

The rhymed pair of "*recenseador*" (census taker) and "*horror*" in the Portuguese lyrics can be said to symbolize the State and State intervention in everyday life, signaling a kind of violent and discriminatory early biopolitics portending something strange and ominous whose actions are feared.[46]

In the second verse, however, it is the law itself that seems to calm the nervousness prompted by that State intrusion. The answer to the census taker's question, "if my man was decent / if he was hard-working or if he was the partying sort," displaces of the inquiry about one's private life by touching on the law and public life: "My man is Brazilian, he's a soldier." A guarantee of a "Brazilianness" that transcends institutions is seen in the form of the music itself—referenced metonymically in the lyrics via its autochthonous instruments such as the *pandeiro, cavaquinho,* and tambourine—as well as by the cloak of the patria, the flag. Even though the idea of nation is defined outside the institutions and instruments that the State commands (the census, marriage), this exteriority does not entail an opposition to or denial of the idea of the nation, but rather a reaffirmation in contrasts. In that sense, the lyrics depict a parabola that is also samba's parabola in the process of its nationalization. As Cláudia de Matos states, coinciding on this point with Sandroni, the samba that becomes a national symbol is one in which the insistence on syncopation reveals the incursion of a black rhythm in the white musical system: "Paradoxically, it was through the affirmation of its strangeness that this samba came into the recognition of global society."[47]

The accentuation of so-called primitive traits in samba comes hand in hand with a greater sophistication marked as much by the participation of middle-class musicians as by an emphasis on the relationship between melody and harmony brought about by means of "primitive" instruments such as the *surdo,* the *cuíca,* and the tambourine. These instruments allow a stronger demarcation of the rhythm, often in direct discordance with the melodic line produced by "European" instruments. "Gente Bamba," a delightful samba by Synval Simba, highlights these contrasts. While the flute underscores the melody, the *cuíca* and the tambourine go about clearly marking the rhythm, at times in contrast with the melody. In Carmen Miranda's recording, her voice follows a melodic line that departs from the rhythm as well as from the melodic lines of the other instruments.[48]

In the tension inherent in the clash of primitive and sophisticated forms of a genre, between reclaiming a past and becoming modernized, the primitive is inevitably turned into the modern, but not in the sense that the primitive necessarily vanishes. On the contrary, this is a cultural process whereby the primitive will no longer be considered or valued as exotic but rather for finding in itself a certain affinity and consonance with the meaning of the modern for the Argentine and Brazilian cultures. From the primitivist fantasy that situates difference in the other, it passes now to a reassessment of the value of the other and to a certain effacement of difference that holds multiple complications, symbolic as well as ideological.

Thus, despite the intensification of primitivism in tango and samba as exotic-national musical forms, this attitude of holding exclusively to the perception of the primitive reproduces European exoticism, which many Argentine and Brazilian intellectuals and artists in turn tended to imitate, now turning their focus on their respective country's popular culture. Together with that constructed exoticism, samba and tango also elaborate a message of modernity, in their popular tradition of chromatism and the modernist counterpoint.[49] Yet, to understand that long and complex process of the transformation of the *primitive-savage* into the *primitive-modern,* it is crucial to examine how the primitivism of tango and samba was viewed when these musical forms had not yet taken the shape of musical genres, much less national genres.

2

THE AUTOCHTHONOUS EXOTIC

As has been repeated to the point of exhaustion, the first references to tango and samba were violently negative, and, in their early manifestations, these rhythms were even persecuted, criminalized, and repressed.[1] Recognition as musical forms and popular dances becomes more consistent around the 1880s and acquires greater definition only around the first decades of the twentieth century. References crop up unevenly in print media and literature, owing to the embryonic nature of these musical and dance forms and to cultural commentators' own lack of familiarity with them. At the end of the nineteenth century tango and samba seem to be defined based on descriptions of them as objects rather than experiences. Whereas on one hand they appear as that which is abominated— they are the language of delinquency, products of savages and troublemakers, condensations of sin—on the other hand their value as "documents" of what is autochthonous becomes irresistible for the writer who cannot leave aside those objects, swept up by the impulse to employ a national vision of the subjects now starting to be narrated. In that sense, samba and tango exert a peculiar fascination, oscillating between rejection and special attraction; in being rejected they reveal that bewitching attraction exerted by that which is repressed or prohibited.

This attitude will persist very clearly in Brazilian modernism, above all in Oswald de Andrade and Mário de Andrade, or in Gilberto Freyre, Emiliano Di Cavalcanti, and Lasar Segall, and somewhat less evidently in the Argentine avant-garde, not only in Borges but also in Güiraldes' *Raucho* and even in Girondo. The process is ambiguous and ambivalent, revealing the attempt by the Latin American artist or intellectual to emulate the European by internalizing the nation's gaze, as well as the often desperate attempt to recover something of popular culture in order to construct a national tradition.

Tango and samba fulfill a fundamental role for learned culture in that process of exoticizing one's own culture. In early references to them one perceives the ethnologizing of the nation that will be, for nineteenth-century Argentina and Brazil, a fundamental operation in the process of planting the idea of national culture. I would like to mark a hiatus between the *ethnologization of the nation* and the *construction of a national culture*, between one attitude that gazes with puzzled eyes on its own country and tends to position the subject as an eternal exile, and another, more constructive attitude that would prefer to erect pantheons and found cultural nationalities upon the supposed desert or jungle of one's national culture.[2]

Already at the beginning of the twentieth century, diverse factors have an influence on the clearer definition of tango and samba, principally the ability to record sound and thus convert music into *documents*. The appearance of the radio disseminated those songs to every corner of the two nations, clearly facilitating the diffusion of tango and samba.

From the Autochthonous to the National

O Cortiço (The Slum), by Aluísio Azevedo, is not the first novel in which a representation of Bahian samba appears.[3] If it interests me to begin there it is because in that work samba fulfills structurally important objectives in the plot and thus ceases to function simply as the typical exoticist portrait of local color. Moreover, it represents samba as the formula for a *tropical style* in which one can read that double, amphibious functionality of the autochthonous: disdain of the autochthonous for its savagery ignites a fascination about a product that can be converted into an indicator of differentiation from Europe and, hence, into a national characteristic. Tristão de Alencar Araripe Júnior, in one of the first articles written about *O Cortiço*, titled "Estilo Tropical: A Fórmula do Naturalismo Brasileiro" (Tropical Style: The Formula of Brazilian Naturalism), praised the deviation that Azevedo's novel signaled in relation to its model in French literature, Emile Zola.

The concept of tropical style created by Araripe Júnior displaces the search for similarities in genre and the importation of models of the novel. The writing itself comes to define a differentiating style, rather than a specific genre such as the novel, which, having been conceived in Europe, carries with it a certain secondariness or deflection on being transferred to new lands. Araripe Júnior's critical lucidity on this point is vast, even casting him as a formalist critic, given his concentration on writing, avant la lettre, before concern with form acquired central importance in the study of Brazilian literary construction. It calls into question, ahead of his time, practices abounding in the circles of Latin American literary and cultural criticism. In effect, *O Cortiço* seems to elaborate the notion of a typically Brazilian style based on a combination of scientific organicism born of positivism and of the Romanticist idealization of nature. This is the source of its highly erotic, even pornographic content for the moral structures of the time, because in *O Cortiço* natural beauty, that of bodies or landscape, simmers and boils with all its humors and secretions.[4]

The novel, like the collective space of the slum it is set in, clearly has a center where the fundamental transformations presented in the plot meet and converge. According to Carlos Sandroni, the greater functionality of samba in this novel is correlative to the increased presence of samba in social life in Rio de Janeiro during that same period.[5] Its figuration in the novel, however, presages its historical evolution. True to the portrait of an age that its poetic register chronicles, samba appears there as an exclusive characteristic of the Bahian descendants of Africans and mulattos.[6] Yet, samba in the novel is ultimately representative of that which is typically Brazilian, functioning as a catalyst of the mixing and transformations that will "infect" the entire lower class, regardless of its place or nation of origin or, in naturalist terms, no matter its "blood." In that movement, Azevedo's novel not only distances itself from reality by representing a future of samba rather than its current state, but also reveals the contradictions, paradoxes, and problems in the construction of a national identity for Brazil in the late nineteenth century.

O Cortiço explores the lower classes of Rio de Janeiro through the residents of the tenement slum, and the uncomfortable coexistence of the different social classes, separated by the division between the slum and the manor contiguous to it.[7] The side-by-side positioning of upper and lower classes marks a space in which groupings and identities commingle, while the slum setting merely exacerbates that proliferation of differences. This space houses mulattos, blacks, foreign immigrants, poor whites, and people of the middle class who have come under hard times and dropped in status, such as dona Isabel and her daughter. In his representation of difference Azevedo did not neglect to include a homosexual character and a scene of lesbianism among the characters of diverse social extraction and "moral dispositions" who mill about the rooms. As Araripe Júnior will signal already in 1888, "the tenement slum is the mob mentality."[8]

The novel is constructed by way of a series of social and cultural transformations, to which the characters and the spaces they inhabit are subjected.[9] João Romão, a small-scale shopkeeper, becomes a bourgeois who aspires to purchase a title of nobility; Jerônimo, an honorable and hard-working Portuguese immigrant, becomes an indolent alcoholic who abandons his daughter; the slum itself, one reads in this novel, was "aristocracized."[10]

In this depiction of differences, samba functions as a catalyst of one of these transformations. At first it is the typical, autochthonous dance of one of the characters, Rita, a mulatto woman from Bahia who lives in the slum and who initiates and directs all the sambas that are danced in the neighborhood. Here, samba begins to be seen as representative of something typically Brazilian that transcends that regional identity. The impressions of Jerônimo, the Portuguese man who has just been seduced by Rita, upon witnessing samba for the first time signal unmistakably that national flair:

> In that mulatto woman resided the great mystery, the sum of all the impressions he had felt since arriving here: she was the burning midday light, the red heat of the siestas at the plantation, the hot aroma of the clovers and the vanilla plants that had dazed him in the Brazilian jungles; she was the virginal, elusive palm tree that did not bend before any other plant; she was the poison . . . that spit a flash of that Bahian love into his blood, a note of that music made of the moans of pleasure.[11]

This description of the mulatto woman is charged with ambiguity, not only regarding the moral evaluation that is made of her and of samba, but also in relation to the place it occupies in the social space of the novel. The author's use of a free, indirect style works an intromission of the narrator into the character's consciousness, melding the character's perceptions with the narrator's rhetoric and the ideological charge it presupposes. The passage begins by linking the mulatto woman with the idealized beauty of Brazilian nature, privileged metaphor of the national that predates even romanticism in Brazil. Yet, unlike the romantic vision of nature, in this case positive images of natural beauty represented in Rita and in samba are combined with negative images such as poison and spitting that are identifiable with the sexual suggestion of samba, that "music made of the moans of pleasure." The quotation exhibits two opposing forces, one emphasizing an idyllic image of nature and of the mulatto woman and associating the idea of purity with virginity and integrity ("the virginal, elusive palm tree that did not bend before any other plant"), and another in which nature, divested of idyllic beauty, appears in the raw crudeness of its physiological processes ("she was the poison . . . that spit a flash of that Bahian love into his blood"). From a picturesque discourse the description passes, seamlessly, to a scientific one, in which the idea of the primitive associated with the mulatto woman and with samba acquires an ambiguous value. A continuity with Brazilian primitivism or romanticism is detected, the first moment of defining, and corrupting, the idealist vision of cultural nationalism.[12] Those unpleasant aftertastes expose, more than the out-of-step superimposition of a European style transferred to Brazil, the irresolvable contradiction that the ideology of primitivism (fundamentally racist and condemning of racial mixing) represented for Brazil. The persistence of a romanticist idealization of nature works like an antidote for that positivist condemnation of the possibility that Brazil would succeed in constituting itself as a nation.[13]

Rita's carnal sensuality is identified with and expressed by samba, and it is precisely after seeing her dance and owing to the movements she makes that samba will play a role in Jerônimo's transformation in the novel, from a hard-working and honorable Portuguese immigrant to one who, lost at the hands of the Bahian Rita, will be "Brazilianized," becoming a drunkard and a disloyal and lazy man.

> The Portuguese man was "made Brazilian" forever; he became lazy, friendly with extravagance and abuse, lustful and jealous; he was divested forever of the spirit for savings and for order; he lost the hope of gaining wealth and gave himself over completely to the happiness of possessing the mulatto woman and being possessed by her, by her alone and none other.[14]

The notion of Brazilian characteristics is distinctly unfavorable in these lines. Yet, the rhetoric with which that moral lowness is signaled, and the cultural contents that it operates with, are not without meaning in themselves. The negative portrayal of acquiring Brazilian traits is built on the inversion of the equally negative characteristics ascribed to the Portuguese by Brazilian culture at the end of the nineteenth century, such as greed and avarice, emotional indifference, and social ambition. These traits also define this character's counterfigure in the novel, Portuguese tenement owner João Romão, who eventually takes advantage of everyone in order to raise his own social status.

Moreover, samba seems to extend to characters who are not essentially sensual ("and even, who would have guessed! the grave and sober Alexandre"), ultimately encompassing all the slum residents. In fact, Jerônimo's fate, wrought by samba and Rita, will also befall the other diverse characters of the slum. Those who come from higher social levels or other countries and potentially offer some element of differentiation to the slum will all be converted in the end, by the art and magic of the corrupting slum, into the same downtrodden bottom-feeders that live there. The slum ends up erasing any original differences, and one of the principal equalizers is, precisely, samba. Toward the end of the novel, samba remains confined to a social class, from which the characterization of Brazil's typical *estalagem* (tenement house) will later emerge in the form of the "Cabeça de Gato," a new inn of even lower quality that emerges once the *cortiço* is all burned up). Samba and the displacements of that dance metaphor—contagion, sickness, sexual relations—seem here to characterize an entire class, passing from a Bahian *mulatta* to embrace the whole of the lower class.[15]

It is curious that samba is held up as representative of all that is Brazilian in the novel when, still at the end of the nineteenth century, it was an attribute pertaining to only a fraction of the Brazilian population. The figuration of samba in the novel functions as one more metaphor for the mix and hybridity that, through a variety of procedures, will become the most cited characteristic of Brazilian nationality. Not only does the Portuguese man adopt Brazilian traits through his cohabitation with the Bahian Rita, but she also chooses the immigrant over her Brazilian lover because "the blood of the mixed-race woman demanded its rights to purification, and Rita preferred the European as a male of superior race."[16] In that way, samba, as an agent of contagion, and despite its being presented negatively, also provides the possibility that, via *mestizaje* (in Spanish) or *mestiçagem* (in Portuguese) (racial mixing or interbreeding of European and American Indian ancestries), the differences between races will be erased. Thus, inverting the meaning of that same racial mixing, samba could also be associated with the possibility of whitening as an outcome of interbreeding, something that, according to Roberto Ventura, will be the Latin American contribution to European racist theory. According to Ventura, the penetration of European racist theories into the Brazilian cultural field at the end of the nineteenth century produced a sort of self-exoticism—similar to that postulated by Flora Süssekind in relation to the constitution of a fiction narrator in Brazilian literature—which allows Brazilian intellectuals to distance themselves from the customs of their own society via an anthropological gaze.[17] Those theories, however, will be reformulated on Brazilian soil in a critical and selective way, in accord with the political and cultural interests of the learned circles, leading to a reassessment of the value of *miscegenation* and the ideology of whitening that attenuated the scientific racism dominant at the time. Ventura states:

> The ideology of miscegenation, as a fusion of races and cultures, became a re-curring element in Brazilian literature, historiography, and essays. Based on said ideology, racial and cultural "synthesis" is seen as a specific trait, or mark of identity, that founds homogeneous and hardly differentiated conceptions of culture. In Brazil and in Latin America, a unified image of nation was defined on the basis of the incorporation of European, indigenous, African, and Asian cultural forms. Yet, the sectors representing Western civilization and the champions of the written word—and, in recent decades, the audiovisual me-dia—accepted and rejected the possible figures of identity constructed via that mix of elements. The result was not the formation of a collective conscious-ness, but rather the emergence, among the learned, of a psychosocial ambiva-lence whereby cultural identity is perceived as a problem, an ambivalence that reveals the tension between the integration of civilization and the genesis of the nation.[18]

That ambivalence and tension are apparent in samba's representation and functioning in Azevedo's novel. Here, the genesis of the nation is contrasted with samba's integration into civilization, manifested, rather, as a process that is opposed to that integration. While not unique to Azevedo nor to Brazil-ian naturalism, ambiguity is specific to the contradictions that emanate from a process of nationalization and modernization that for Latin America was always ambiguous and contradictory. Its national contents both provide the autochthonous substance that building a national culture requires and dis-tance the Latin American nations from the European model, the teleological end of a possible evolution.

The Güiraldes Case

Responding to an appeal communicated by the journal *Martín Fierro* in its fourth issue, summoning those who favored a "new sensibility," Ricardo Güiraldes an-swered in the next issue: "Yes, an Argentine sensibility and mentality exist. If this were not so, we would have no reason to be more than vacant land to be sold in lots."[19] Considering that he was writing from La Porteña, the family ranch to which he had withdrawn to write *Don Segundo Sombra*, disillusioned by the poor reception of his previous books, his statement acquires added meaning. No fate is worse to a rancher than the thought of vacant land being sold in lots; nothing more devastating for an Argentine nationalist than the patria being sold off, and, adding insult to injury, in miserable little lots. Not only does that "Argentine sensibility" exist, according to Güiraldes, but it also is the reason that defines and bestows upon the Argentine nation the right to exist.

Despite the stylistic differences that separate *Don Segundo Sombra* from Güiraldes' previous literary production, a shared literary basis in the construction of a national mythology can be discerned in *El Cencerro de Cristal* (The Crystal Cowbell) (1915).[20] An example of that mythology can be seen in "Tango," a descriptive poem in that volume about the sexual and troublemaking elements of the tango of the brothels. The man is described as *guaso* (uncouth) and the woman, a *china guaranga* (coarse peasant girl), adjectives that at that time denoted those who were not part of the patrician class.[21] They are referred to as male and female, which both animalizes the participants and positions tango and its representatives as primitive. The sexual relationship between the different genders that tango proposes is depicted as a fight, something that splits and wounds and leads even to death. In contrast to samba at the turn of the century, rather than proposing the union or homogeneity of a class tango instead offers images of fighting, severance, and blood. Violence resignifies the eroticism in the tango dance, repeated in indefatigable lyrics and visions of tango as an eroticism of the rupture and not of the suture.

The poem bears the place and date of Paris, 1911, and contains its lyrical subject within that frame. In a poem about tango, written by an Argentine, these two inscriptions are not insignificant. The tango that was all the rage in Paris at that time is a much more stylized, elegant tango than the one represented here. In the first decade of the century two types of tango can be found in Paris: that of the ballrooms and that of the music halls.[22] Güiraldes' tango is neither of these, but rather the tango of the brothel in the poor outskirts of an Argentine city. The gesture of placing a heading on the poem that situates it in Paris, therefore, when what is being described in the poem is not the Parisian tango, delineates a position for the subject that is not strictly observational, as the poem's descriptive disposition would have one suppose. Instead, it utilizes the innocuous deceit of memory, of evocation, to vocalize a position that the poetic speaker acquires in several of the poems in *El Cencerro de Cristal*. Another poem in that same volume, "Nido" (Nest), also Paris-based, features the representation of an animal typical of Argentina or South America, the condor. Here, then, its appearance marks another difference: that of a poetic speaker who stands doubly outside, from Paris and on the margins of the poem, observing a tango in which he does not participate and with which he does not feel identified.[23] The subject who recalls the Argentine bordello tango rather than the one being danced in Paris is thus remembering a zone of the patria and, in that evocative motion, is also nearing (by opposition to the tango in Paris) that tango of the poor Argentine periphery. What I am interested in noting is that the lyrical subject is also found, albeit on the margins, in this poem and in the world of tango.

A strong tension exists in the construction of that tango as representative of a class that is, however, pervaded by the conflict; in the poem, tango itself represents that conflict. A further ambiguity is present here in addition to those that have already been pointed out in Güiraldes' liminal position in the Argentine avant-garde and in this text that precedes it.[24] Tango "wants" to be confined to a class, as a characteristic exclusive to one class, yet it represents a conflict internal to that class, which only impedes its homogenization. Tango writes, here, of sexual difference.

El Cencerro de Cristal contains, starting with the title's crystal cowbell itself, a project to convert the national into art that will be precipitated in that great novel of the Argentine land, *Don Segundo Sombra*. Yet, the ambiguity remains here in that art, as for Baudelaire, can be "ugly" and should not necessarily be idealized, as by contrast the pampa will be in *Don Segundo Sombra*. The Güiraldes of *El Cencerro de Cristal* is much closer to the avant-garde than the Güiraldes of *Don Segundo Sombra*. In fact, Borges, in *El Idioma de los Argentines* (The Language of the Argentines), originally published in 1928, cites that exact poem by Güiraldes, in one of the texts that Borges will revisit two years later to write *Evaristo Carriego*. In 1938, in an episode that is fundamental for understanding both Güiraldes and Argentine culture, Borges also makes a very respectable mention of *El Cencerro de Cristal,* in which he considers it superior even to *Lunario Sentimental* (Sentimental Almanac) by Leopoldo Lugones who, after so many diatribes, in that text decided to redeem himself.[25]

In 1917 Güiraldes published *Raucho*. The novel highlights the elegant tango danced in the posh Parisian ballrooms of the upper-class bourgeoisie to which the protagonist, an Argentine landowner and excellent tango dancer, belongs. His participation in the Parisian world of tango is seen as a moral lapse, as it causes him to stop thinking about his family and homeland. Tango, like the protagonist himself, figures as the national product that has allowed itself to be made foreign in its passage through Paris, which bears with it a moral condemnation.

The Construction of a National Culture

It is possible to discern two paths in the shift from the ethnologization of the nation to the construction of a national culture, which the cultural elaborations of tango and samba elaborate over the course of the first decades of their evolution. In the case of samba, the transition consists of a specific endemic characteristic pertaining to a regional population, which is generalized as the defining trait of the popular classes; in the case of tango, the transition embodies the generalization of a conflict. Those paths can be read as problematic elaborations of two different cultures. For Brazil, its African legacy must be recovered if it is to propose a viable modernity, despite the racist doctrine that reigned during the nineteenth century and ruled out a future for a culture with strong African components. Reversing that prejudice and replacing it with others was the task of a great number of intellectuals of the era.

In Argentina, by contrast, the imperative seems to have taken a different direction. While in the elaboration of tango the immigrant population's participation is absolutely undeniable, its condition as "autochthonous" is perceived by many artists and intellectuals to be the essence of tango's role in the construction of a national identity. Simultaneously national and cosmopolitan, tango and its image in the first decades of the century accompany the vicissitudes of Argentine cultural nationalism, as well as the contradictions it inherently harbored.

Many of the tangos produced by descendants of Italians comprise a definite criollo lineage, emphasizing tango's peasant gaucho traits over its immigrant ones, such as the use of the guitar in the music and the suspension of the *bandoneón*, together with lyrics with rural references. "Betinotti" or "La Morocha" are two early examples. On the other hand, Lunfardo, the idiolect used in many tangos, reveals the ambivalence of a language that is simultaneously typical of a population and invented on the basis of borrowings from several different languages, territorializing and deterritorializing at one and the same time the national condition of *rioplatense* Spanish (Spanish spoken in the River Plate area).

In the first sambas, in contrast, there seems to be a suppression of any effort to confine the rhythm to a population of African origin, as much in the music, which scorns the typically African instruments, as in the lyrics with their clearly urban and modern content, as the first samba-maxixe indicates in its title, "Pelo Telefone" (By Phone). These other characteristics, moreover, will emerge with an unavoidable forcefulness in the sambas of the 1930s, exhibiting in their "Africanness" new mechanisms in the process of constructing a nation.

3

PRIMITIVE AVANT-GARDE ARTISTS

La pura impura mezcla. (The pure impure mix.)

Oliverio Girondo

Down with Tango and Percival.

The heaviness of English tangos, German tangos, desire, space mechanized by tuxedos that can't even express their sensibility, the plagiarism of Parisian and Italian tangos, mollusk couples, felinity and Argentinean savagery idiotically softened, morphinated, made heavy. Possessing a woman is not rubbing yourself up against her, it's penetrating her. Barbarians! A knee between the thighs? Come on, man, what it takes is two! Barbarians! Yes, let's be barbarians. Daughters of the tango and of its slow swoons, you think it's fun to look at each other's mouths and have reciprocal relations of the teeth like two hallucinating dentists?

—Got to pull it? Fill it?

You think it's funny corkscrewing each other to release the spasm in your partner without the two of you ever getting there together? Or staring at the tip of your shoes like two hypnotized shoemakers? [. . .] Tristan and Isolde slow their spasm down to excite King Marc [. . .] a miniature of sexual anxieties, lollypop of desire, lust in the open air, delirium tremens, hands and feet of a drunken man; mini-coitus of a moviemaker, a masturbated waltz. Ugh! Daughters graduated with diplomacy of the skin. Long live the savagery of a brusque possession, the hold of a muscular exalted and fortifying dance! Tango and tango world of sailboats, explode with tenderness and lunar imbecility. Tango, tango, the world of tango to the point of vomiting. Tango, slow and patient funeral of dead sex. It's, of course, about religion, morals and prudishness; these three words have no meaning for us. But it is in the name of health, strength, willpower, virility that we boo tango and its pastime weaknesses.[1]

E. T. Marinetti

. . . we cannot ignore the fact that the primitive aspect of all new art, from folklore to the Blauer Reiter's interest in Bavarian peasant painting, had a reactionary potential from the outset.

Theodor Adorno

Around the 1920s it is possible to find in the Argentine and Brazilian cultures a strong symbolic condensation of the primitive and the modern. The historical conditions of that condensation can be read in some of the more canonical cultural forms in both cultures, products of the respective national avant-garde movements. Yet, a basic contradiction arises upon proposing, as a national symbol, a form that had been considered primitive and savage at the peak of violent, selective modernization. In that contradiction the Latin American avant-garde is revealed as a function of cosmopolitanism; it is the desire for modernity, speed, and an absence of boundaries that is also manifest in primitivist nationalism. The condensation of the primitive and the modern is fundamental, not only for the Latin American avant-garde, but also for the nationalization of tango and samba.

The bibliography on the Latin American avant-garde abounds with nationalism and cosmopolitanism, in an insistence on self-critique that stands in contrast to the scarcity of equivalent critique by the European avant-garde. The importance that primitivism—which is, in a certain sense, an inverse cosmopolitanism—held for the European avant-garde, however, can be compared with the Latin American avant-garde's cosmopolitanism/nationalism dialectic. I am interested in this contrast in order to mark how the term *cosmopolitanism* can come to be constituted as a colonial term that would signal the relationship between a subject or a nation and a determined and specific outside: the outside that is Europe, the West, or "nonprimitive" cultures. In avant-garde terms, Latin Americans are seen as cosmopolitan when they refer to Europe, but Europeans are seen as primitivists, not cosmopolitan, when referring to Latin America or Africa.[2]

To counter its dependency on Europe, it was necessary in Latin America to effect a differentiation with respect to Europe. The tendency to both imitate Europe (adopting that avant-garde) and to mark a difference (instituting one's own, national avant-garde) coincided with and explained nationalism in Latin America. That rationale is commonly called on to explain Oswald de Andrade's "*antropofagia*" (cannibalism) as well as the nationalist penchant of the *Martin Fierro* group, from Borges' *criollismo* to Girondo's peasant cosmopolitanism.[3]

In those years also, tango and samba, in the process of nationalization, seem obliged to pass through Europe. Tango, it is said, triumphed first in Paris, and samba was incorporated into the compositions and poems of Europeans such as Blaise Cendrars and Darius Milhaud. Acceptance of these forms on the Parisian music scene is seen in much of the bibliography as a precondition for acceptance in their own contexts of origin.[4] However, new research has demonstrated that the process entails greater complexities.

In *Tango and the Political Economy of Passion*, Marta Savigliano extensively analyzes tango's long Parisian voyage as "one episode in the long history of the colonial manufacture of the exotic,"[5] in which tango factors among *les dances brunnes* (brown dances) such as the African American cakewalk, the Brazilian maxixe, and the apache. Although for Savigliano the European acceptance of tango is fundamental for its later acceptance in Argentina, she recognizes the role of its local development in that acceptance.[6]

A common curve can be discerned in the trajectories of the nationalization of tango and samba and the primitivism of Argentine and Brazilian avant-garde: the dependency on Europe explains the cosmopolitan zeal as much as it does the acceptance of a product of local popular culture and the latter's conversion into a symbol of national identity only after its acceptance as exotic in Europe. Even the anticolonialist discourse of those national modernisms has been read as an outgrowth of European colonialism.[7]

Reading both processes simultaneously can throw light on other zones of Argentine and Brazilian culture in the 1920s and 1930s. In the condensation of the primitive and modern that some avant-garde practices formulate around tango and samba, one can read a coincidence rather than a contradiction between the cosmopolitanism and nationalism defined simultaneously by a specific inscription, both Latin American and alternative, of a modernization process of artistic languages as well as of the Argentine and Brazilian cultures.

Peter Osborne has pointed out the need to think of modernism, in this general sense of the cultural modernization of artistic languages, as a concept whose abstract logic acquires particular contents according to its concretization in a particular historical field. In *The Politics of Time*, Osborne approached modernism as an abstract, philosophical category as opposed to a movement occurring in a given historical period. While that book is interesting as a reflection on modernism, even more relevant for our present parameters is the twist a later work will give to those considerations, *Philosophy in Cultural Theory*. There, Osborne studies modernism as a paradigmatic concept in terms of a Western cultural concept that is generalized on a global level through a highly conflictive and disputed process that oscillates between the imperialism of an obliteration of cultural differences and the production of counterhegemonic interpretations and alternatives. According to Osborne, there are two semantic contents for the term *modernism*: as a historical and, to a certain degree, sociological phenomenon, and as a temporal form that cuts across different forms of historical life. The questions Osborne poses concern how this logic is produced and plays out under different but always related social and historical conditions, and what kind of relationships it forges with that which falls tenuously under the title "national culture."

Osborne's study seeks to come free of the restrictions of a typological empirical concept of modernism in literature and art, which is almost always the one put forth in sociological studies in this area: modernism as an epochal style. For him, modernism as a translational term can only be standardized at the level of a pure temporal form. He seeks then to reposition the historical material of modernism fundamentally as a temporal and cultural form and thereby instill a meaning more suited to its historical logic. I quote:

> If modernism has the universality of a philosophical concept, then—a concept constructed at the level of a certain phenomenologically *absolute* (albeit historically conditioned) universality—it nonetheless derives its concrete meaning from the distributive unity of its specific instances, as a particular constellation of fields of negation, at any particular time. Hence its potentially contradictory manifestations in, for example, both radically nationalistic and radically antinationalistic, cosmopolitan forms, in different historical and national contexts, or according to different political projects within the same historical and national context. This is dependent upon whether its field of negation is constituted internally or externally to the idea of "national culture."[8]

In that sense, there cannot be a necessary and unique relationship between national culture and modernism as a cultural form. The only distinctive aspect of modernism as a cultural form per se, before its specification, is that the modes of identification it designates involve a sense of future rupture from the present as an always partly destructive transition toward a new temporary order.

Thus, beyond the fact that the avant-garde in Latin America would have been an echo of European manifestations, the peculiar forms it adopted are also tied to other exclusively Latin American conflicts. Some manifestations of the avant-garde movements and modernisms in Argentina and Brazil articulate a response to typically Latin American conflicts surrounding the question of a national identity for which Europe, inasmuch as it is universal, functions as the always traumatic horizon.[9]

The analysis made by the Argentine and Brazilian avant-garde of tango and samba can remove the imperialism implicit in a generalized avant-garde that, being a European notion, could even disarticulate the modernization of artistic languages for Latin America.

Primitivism in the Avant-Garde

It is possible to draw comparisons on the nationalization processes of tango and samba based on representations of these musical and dance forms in avant-garde texts. In both processes we can note that cosmopolitanism is not opposed to nationalism in the specific forms that this apparent contradiction acquired for Latin American cultures, but instead that they constitute two sides of the same coin. For the avant-garde, tango and samba are amphibious products representing both the local, national primitive and the sophisticated and modern quality of the European primitive concept, which is so important in a certain European avant-garde current that it will serve as the model, often implicit, for reassessing the value of the primitive in Latin America.

While in the European avant-garde primitivism operates in a discursive field at a distance from tradition and from what is national, in Latin America the primitive acquired other connotations. In fact, in Brazilian modernism and in some forms of Argentina's *Martin Fierro* avant-garde, primitivism is fundamental in the construction of Latin American modernities. What is there in primitivism that brings it into association with modernity? Why do some Latin American avant-garde movements appeal to this concept in order to devise modern forms of art?

With the amphibious figuration of the concept of the primitive, the Latin American avant-garde separates from the European. The primitive/other equation does not work dichotomously in Brazil or Argentina, but rather doubly: whereas the appeal to the primitive in Europe can imply a break with national tradition, in Latin America the primitive *is* the national.[10] Thus, the appeal to the primitive in Latin America is at once cosmopolitan and nationalist, a status that simultaneously breaks with tradition and recuperates a past.

Analyzing the paradox set forth by primitivism in Latin America can be a way of investigating the consequences that the oxymoron of cosmopolitanism/nationalism has for a theory of the avant-garde and modernity in Latin America. To do so, one would first have to dismantle the idea of cosmopolitanism and nationalism as mutually exclusive terms. Nationalism outside of Europe, Partha Chatterjee points out, "was historically fused with the colonial issue," and the combination of cosmopolitanism and nationalism is one of the historical forms in which that fusion was manifested.[11] To propose that primitivism was the same for Europe as it was for America (Leiris, Bataille, and others) is to ignore the ambiguous structure of the primitive in Latin America and the consequences that its place on the margins has for the avant-garde.[12]

Is it possible to think, on the other hand, of a displacement of that primitive fantasy, from the gaze that is prepared to read the other (Orientalist, if one wishes) to the gaze of the Latin Americans? Antonio Candido in *Literatura e Cultura de 1900 a 1945* (Literature and Culture from 1900 to 1945) points out: "However, in Brazil primitive cultures blend into everyday life or they are still vivid reminiscences of a recent past. The terrible defiant audacities of a Picasso, a Brancusi, a Max Jacob, a Tristan Tzara were, at bottom, more coherent with our cultural legacy than with theirs."[13] This new "*congenialidade*" (congeniality), to use Haroldo de Campos' expression, of primitivism with Latin American cultures explains certain changes in the meaning and function of the figure of the primitive.[14] Nonetheless, it also proposes an apparent contradiction in the association between modernity and primitivism that the aesthetic avant-garde movements of Brazil and Argentina elaborated during the 1920s. What Candido proposes seems to explain that the Latin American avant-garde was nationalist in order to copy Europe, but it does not explain why that nationalism evolved into a strong primitivism, nor the characteristics that this primitivism adopted in the Brazilian or Argentine avant-garde.

I would like to examine two texts in relation to these problems: *Evaristo Carriego* by Borges and "Carnaval Carioca" by Mário de Andrade (included in

Clã do Jabotí [Clan of the Turtle]).[15] The dismantling of the primitive fantasy that these texts carry out in their figuration of tango and samba resituates some issues for a historicizing of certain texts of the Argentine and Brazilian avant-garde.

The problem of the primitive—its representation, its functions, and its way of articulating cultural differences—presents the Latin American avant-garde with a problem it had already debated: the questioning of the rhetoric of rupture.[16] Whereas in Europe the appeal to the primitive figures as a rupture with European tradition and therefore as a vector of newness, in Latin America it entails an immersion in the national past.

The cannibal of Oswald de Andrade or the *"herói sem nenhum caráter"* (hero with no character) of Mário de Andrade (within Brazilian modernism) or the gaucho (Argentine peasant or cowboy) and *compadrito* (urban braggart) of Borges (within the *Martin Fierro* group) involve a certain immersion in the national past, disruptive though that may be. Although concern for these "primitives" does not necessarily indicate a desire to recuperate that national past, it nonetheless does prompt certain reservations regarding the notion of the avant-garde as a break from national tradition.

While emphasis has been given to the rupture that the notion of the primitive in Oswald de Andrade and in Mário de Andrade would entail with respect to Romanticist Indianism, warnings against the risks of proceeding with a purely Dadaist reading of Brazilian modernism had already been sounded by Silviano Santiago.[17] By concentrating on the gestures of rupture, that Dadaist reading ignores the strong relationship with the past that marked the Argentine and Brazilian avant-garde movements, a trait that has been largely overshadowed by these movements' mimetic relationship with the European avant-garde and European modernity. Or, when acknowledged, it has been read as the mark of tepid avant-garde thinking in which this immersion into the national past is read as the mark of a weaker break, which would in turn be indication of an avant-garde emerging in a context or cultural field that is less prepared for gestures of rupture.

One of the more recent and inspiring formulations of this problem proposes that these issues be deliberated via other parameters. According to Adrián Gorelik, in reference to what he calls a certain "classicism" of the Argentine and Brazilian architectural avant-garde:

> At issue, in this case, is not moderation, or at least it is not only that, but rather
> a response of the avant-garde to a specific problem in American moderniza-

tion: classicism is what the avant-garde recurs to in the face of the need to produce an essence of the national culture. It is the same necessity that the different attempts to construct a national identity have manifested in each country,
at least since the end of the nineteenth century. What has changed, however, is
the gaze on the sources from which that identity would be extracted and with
which it would be legitimized: the avant-garde discovers that the American
territory is the environment where the most archaic of things settles and stays
and yet, because of that, it is also the place where newness can emerge purely,
and that hidden in that constructive potential lies that much yearned for "cultural specificity."[18]

I believe it is necessary to reconsider that relationship of the Argentine and
Brazilian avant-garde movements with a certain national past, viewing it as
a new type of rupture and devising concepts that would allow for a better
understanding of the specific dialectic of these Latin American avant-garde
movements. To return to what Peter Osborne set forth, if we understand
modernism to be the cultural affirmation of a temporal logic of negation
(newness, what is new), the meaning of any negation will be determined by
the delimitation of the cultural field within and on which it acts. In the Brazilian and Argentine cultural field, where reference to Europe was the convention, replacing that orientation with a reference to a discarded national
past till then preferably forgotten paves the way for an even more scandalous
rupture than any imitation of European modernity. In the words of Peter
Osborne:

> Whatever "national culture" may be, there can be no conceptually necessary
> relationship between it and modernism as a cultural form, specifiable in ad-
> vance. There are only historically specific conjunctural relations, constructed
> by the (politically defined) terms of identification of particular fields of nega-
> tion. In particular, one can make no legitimate inferences from the founding
> conjunction of specific canonic modernisms with particular national projects
> to the possibility or impossibility of other forms. Indeed, the "national" charac-
> ter of specific modernisms is often national in a dialectical sense only, as deter-
> minate negations of received national-cultural forms: internally oppositional
> cosmopolitan projections, only later put to hegemonizing nationalistic use.[19]

It is true that this connection with a national past was erased at times, even by
the modernists themselves. Mário de Andrade, for example, nullifies the dedi-
cation to José de Alencar—the great Romanticist Indianist—from *the* Brazil-

ian avant-garde novel which is *Macunaíma*. Though this has been read as a great gesture of openness toward the more Parisian propositions of Oswald de Andrade, this purely cosmetic and political effacement in no way accomplishes an erasure of the work with the past that permeates the entire fabric of *Macunaíma* and which is, moreover, one of the strategies whereby *Macunaíma* produces its own modernity.[20]

Borges too seeks proximity with the past in his figuration of tango. For Borges, tango is a continuation of the gaucho or Argentine peasant tradition in contrast to Lugones, who sees tango as slanderous, "that reptile from the brothel," considering it foreign and alien, yet who, on converting tango into a figure of his own poetics, establishes connections in it—complex ones, to be sure, but connections nonetheless—to a national past. If Lugones constructs a national past in *El Payador* (The Folksinger/Minstrel), his national past and his recuperation of popular peasant traditions, in itself a dismissal of tango, comprise a way of looking at the past as if it were universal. He salvages, or rather constructs on top of the national past, a universal past that can be constituted as a national past because of its similarity to a universal tradition. For Borges, the past is separated clearly from an idea of tradition, in order to superimpose upon it the idea of a living history. In a footnote in *Evaristo Carriego*, he points out: "I affirm—without fastidious fear or my imaginative love of paradox—that only new countries have a past; that is, an autobiographical sense of that past, a living history. If time is succession, then we must admit that where there is greater density of events, more time flows, and that it flows abundantly in this inconsequent part of the world."[21]

In some texts of the avant-garde that favored tango and samba, it is possible to trace a spatialization of the notion of the primitive, no longer as an inhabitant of the patria's past but rather of its present, but figuring there as an inheritor of that past. A successive, uninterrupted line would be constituted, then, in clear opposition to the notion of a break with the national that those same products represent for other intellectuals.

On the other hand, acceptance or rejection of tango and samba splits the field inside the avant-garde, distributing internal differences that seem to design other networks for thinking about the Brazilian and Argentine cultures in their internal differentiation movements and in their heterogeneities. In the comparison between these models it becomes evident just how agonic the process of imagining the nation is, and in the different positions of that struggle culture can be traced as difference and as disagreement.

Evaristo Carriego:
Image of Tango, Fragment of the Nation

Many of Borges' texts interconnect with tango,[22] but the most extensive or most systematically argued is his "History of Tango" included in the revised edition of *Evaristo Carriego*. Considering Carriego and tango together strikes us today as almost inevitable, and in fact, many of the later texts on tango have taken up that relationship between Carriego and tango as one of tango's many primitive scenes. Yet, the chapter by this title did not appear in the book's original version.[23] Comparison of the 1930 and 1955 editions poses a series of questions that address not only the aesthetic mutations in Borges' work but also problems entangled in the definition of the national for some Latin American modernisms.

The later edition is not so much a correction of the original as it is a supplement to it; a few new chapters are added and certain fragments remain uncorrected. Together with their repetition in the new interpolation, this prompts a certain uncanny sensation of something previously experienced and familiar now returning in an unfamiliar way, introducing a repetition that is at the same time a displacement. In this way, certain of Carriego's verses on tango are duplicated,[24] and references to historians or polemicists on tango are repeated.[25] In "History of Tango" from 1955 we find a reiteration and intensification of the propositions about tango's genealogy that were already present in the 1930 edition. *Evaristo Carriego* presents three propositions for identifying the history of tango, which appear in identical form in both editions.

The first proposition involves the multiplicity of tangos. For Borges, tangos are many and varied, even contradictory; no one tango is legitimate while others are bastard offspring. Rather, all the diverse tangos are valid, though not all are valued by him in the same way. On the origin of tango, Borges, referring to different historians, states the following: "I do not find it difficult in the least to declare that I subscribe to all their conclusions, and any others as well."[26] Borges' typical irony here both demonstrates its polemical function and offers a circuitous indication of his own construction of tango as one of the forms in which avant-garde and nationalist aesthetics are manifested simultaneously.

The second proposition is nothing more than a corollary to the first, reiterating tango's birth in the brothel, a space of heterogeneity and mixing.

Lastly, the construction of a linear genealogy is proposed in which the cult of courage positions tango and the *compadrito* as successors of the gaucho and the gauchesque (peasant) tradition. Let us look at his formulation:

> We would have, then, men of the poorest kind of life, gauchos and men from the shorelines of the River Plate and the Paraná, creating, without their knowing it, a religion, with its mythology and its martyrs, the hard and blind religion of courage, of being ready to kill and to die. That religion is as old as the world, but it would have to be rediscovered and lived, in these republics, by shepherds, slaughtermen, cattle drovers, fugitives, and ruffians. Its music would be in the styles, in the milongas and the first tangos.[27]

Heterogeneity, then, and tango's linear *criollista* genealogy turn out to be operations that were already present in 1930 and that, through repetition and insistence, become intensified in 1955. It is clear that for Borges the gaucho and the *compadrito* serve to mark an identity that is not connected to the state. His nationalism is more spiritual than material; it is a cultural nationalism that confronts even the nationalism of the state and signals one of the possible positions in the struggle to imagine the nation that constituted Argentine culture in the 1920s and 1930s.[28]

In a text published in the magazine *Nosotros*, Borges stated in this regard:

> Contrary to the solemn chauvinism of fascists and imperialists, I have never incurred that sort of intellectual blunder. I feel more *porteño* [from Buenos Aires] than Argentine, and more from the neighborhood of Palermo than any other neighborhood. And even that small patria, which was Evaristo Carriego's too, is becoming part of the center and one must seek it out as far away as Villa Alvear! I am inept at patriotic exaltations and Lugones' kind of declarations: I am bored by visual comparisons and will always prefer listening to the tango "Loca!" (Crazy!) to hearing the National Anthem.[29]

The contrast between "Loca!" and the national anthem strikes one as an outburst with a clearly avant-garde function: it is a scandalous, irreverent affront to national honor as represented by its most respected symbol. Yet, national honor is not denied but rather reorganized on the basis of two very evident operations: the fragmentation of the nation, including even a tendency toward infinite fragmentation ("I feel more *porteño* than Argentine, and more from the neighborhood of Palermo than from any other neighborhood"), and the response to tradition, both national and literary and here represented by Lugones' central placement in the intellectual field of that period. These operations are sustained by the choice of a particular past, opposite to and unknown by that other "national tradition."

In that discursive context, postulating a continuity between the *compadrito* and the gaucho strikes one as more avant-garde—read: revolutionary, rebellious, disruptive—than proposing an absolute break from the past. The linearity makes it possible to connect a type of tango to a particular past and, on doing so, to reject other tangos that do not coincide with that or other pasts. In a more reactionary sense, the linearity also denies the importance of immigration in the formation of tango, imagining its origin in a past that would have been previous to that immigration. In the 1930 edition of *Evaristo Carriego*, the figure of Carriego contains a mixture of the *criollista* tango, the tango of courage, and the tango of the *milonguita*. For this reason, as national hero, he is simultaneously praised and criticized.[30]

Postulating a linearity between tango and the gauchesque, moreover, accomplishes a much more disruptive function than could be effected by any rupture. Linearity entails as its guiding theme a displacement from space to time or temporality—read: the gauchesque defined by the countryside, tango by the poor urban outskirts—thereby bringing a mechanism of the most revolutionary sort into play: displacing the gaucho and the *compadrito* from their conventional frameworks and removing them from a possible topographical appropriation by the nation. The nation is not a space but rather is the past; and the past is a construction, the cult of courage and of the primitive function seen in the first edition of *Evaristo Carriego* as an appeal to a different, barbaric tradition.

If copying Europe was a common gesture in Argentina at that time, repeating it would have signified continuing rather than breaking from convention. By contrast, the return to a national past, neither forgetting it nor pretending to abolish it, was a more disruptive gesture in relation to convention and, though perhaps perceived as the action of a watered-down avant-garde, it is in fact more radically avant-garde in relation to Argentine cultural space.

The construction of a *criollista* genealogy for tango fulfills in Borges the important function of mitigating the influence of immigration, so present in tango, and perpetuating instead the interpretation of tango as the corruption of a true and original tango. In that move, it is clear that Borgesian primitivism carries out a retrograde function here: rejecting the present and valuing the past. From an ideological point of view, we encounter in Borges the not-uncommon idea of an avant-garde with reactionary biases.

The most significant difference between the 1930 and 1955 editions of

Evaristo Carriego is that the added chapter "History of Tango" brings the *criollista* text closer to the universalist texts in *Discusión* (Argument) or *El Jardín de los Senderos que se Bifurcan* (The Garden of Forking Paths), in which reference to what is criollo and what is *porteño* is analogous to universal references to Western culture. On that basis tango can be seen as similar "to the music of Greek and Roman rhapsodists."[31] In the transition from the early to the later edition of *Evaristo Carriego,* the universal references of 1955 undo any and all theories of the national; given the assimilation of all that is European, the national cannot be the mark of a specific nation. What defines the nation turns out, in the end, to be an aspiration that is universally shared.

Yet, if the national is the primitive represented by the gaucho and the *compadrito*, with a writerly pirouette Borges' text places these figures in that terrain that is one's own and yet is confused with that of the other (one must think of the constant repetition of this gesture, in "Historia del Guerrero y la Cautiva" [History of the Warrior and the Captive Woman], for example).

This sentiment was expressed in a text written in the first edition (1923) of *Fervor de Buenos Aires*, which Borges withheld from publication in his complete works.

> **"Música Patria"** (Homeland Music) by **Jorge Luis Borges**
> Moorish complaint
> bordering darkly on both eternities
> of the giant sky and the tawny sands,
> carried with dread of heroic scimitars
> to the limpid Andalucian fields
> ripping like a bonfire through the undergrowth of time,
> slipping through the centuries
> igniting *vihuelas* in flames of bright song
> until the miracle of the exploit of the Indies
> when the Castilians
> plunderers of worlds
> went robbing lands at random westwardly.
> Disarranged by the pampa plain
> shuffled from Creole guitar to Creole guitar
> intermingling with the sorrow
> of villainized Quechua people
> wrenched apart in the insolence of the port,
> made once again the pillory of roguish lives

and the shrine to evil women,

it has been able to descend with such virtue into our soul

that if of an evening a window

gives it with sonorous generosity to the street

the passerby

feels as if a hand has touched his heart.[32]

In "Música Patria" a possible lineage of tango is reconstructed that moves from a "Moorish complaint" to "a pillory of roguish lives" in a continuity that unites European roots with an indigenous past. However, while this poem accentuates the marks of a *criollismo* that could be interpreted as exclusionary, for its emphasis on identity and pronounced picturesque inclination, in comparing the two editions of *Evaristo Carriego* the trajectory of universalism in that first avant-garde *criollismo* in Borges becomes more evident. This is especially true if one compares the tone, so divested of *criollismo* terms, in "History of Tango" in 1955 with the text that prefigured it in 1928, "The Origins of Tango," which appeared in *El Idioma de los Argentinos* (The Language of the Argentines). While the two accounts of tango coincide on some points, especially in tango's contentious origins, in "History of Tango" tango no longer appears as representing a national characteristic of a specific people, as was the case in "The Origins of Tango," but appears instead as representing a general sentiment: "the conviction that a hand-to-hand fight can be a party." In that text, on a single page, there are quotations from Jordanes, Homer, Quevedo, Hugo, Ariosto, and Schopenhauer, among others, to demonstrate the universality of that thinking, with this conclusion: "the ancient tango, like music, usually transmits in a direct way that bellicose joy whose verbal expression was exercised, in remote epochs, by Germanic and Greek rhapsodists."[33]

Carnival and Differences

We must be done with that prideful individualism that would make us into gods and not men. Today I am very humble. My greatest desire is to be a man among men. To melt into the rest. To merge.

Mário de Andrade, letter to Manuel Bandeira, August 5, 1923

Mário de Andrade was traveling to Rio de Janeiro and had promised he would visit Manuel Bandeira. That encounter never took place; de Andrade was captivated by the carioca carnival and forgot about the visit.[34] From that experience of being waylaid or mislaid, a poem is born, "Carnaval Carioca" (Carnival of Rio de Janeiro), which will itself become the space of the encounter with Bandeira. In the version published in 1927, in *Clā do Jabotí* (Clan of the Turtle), de Andrade incorporates a series of corrections and interpolations that were suggested by Bandeira in a letter from 1923.[35]

The first of the corrections that Bandeira suggests makes for the appearance of the lyrical "I" of the subject in a poem that up to that point had been structured like a descriptive piece, with a first strophe that was pure landscape with no first-person speaker. This is Bandeira's suggestion to insert part of the letter in which de Andrade narrates his experience of the carioca carnival and signals his subjectivity as separate from the object he is describing. The lines that follow—

> At first I became angry.
> So much vulgarity!
> Such ranting!
> My misty São Paulo coldness.[36]

—are the ones with which Mário de Andrade will construct an entire stanza, beginning with the almost exact repetition of those lines:

> My São Paulo coldness
> Internal policing
> Fears of exception . . .[37]

With these corrections, the final version of the poem ambivalently combines description and subjectivity; the poem is a narrative of the carnival in Rio de Janeiro, a festivity that is both external and alien to the subject ("My São Paulo coldness," begins the second stanza), and it is also the self-expression (at times almost confessional) of the subject. There is an oscillation in the poem between the description of a collective festivity and the impact of this experience on an individual subject; a continuous swinging back-and-forth between external description—objective and even mimetic—and confessional enunciation or the lyrical first-person speaker's recounting of his subjective experience at the carnival. The boundaries between one kind of enunciation and the other seem difficult to discern. Subject and object are not provided as separate and static entities; indeed, our focus is drawn to the subject's transformation caused by the experience he is describing. The poem is the narrative of an experience that, being collective, is integrated by the self.

The distance between the self and the experience is, at the beginning of the poem, a distance of foreignness: the self is not only a self but is a different self, one defined by "my erudite prejudices." It is possible to say that the self is devised as a poet-enthnographer.[38] That self that appears at the beginning as different and dissimilar stands apart from everything that is identified, in the carnival, with the primitive: "excessive mobs of blacks," sensual sambas of females "in heat," "shameless." Yet, the carnival here is not just experience, it also—in a personalized form (now capitalized)—becomes the interlocutor of the lyrical speaker. Through the transformation and the effacement of boundaries, that lyrical speaker shifts into an identification with and even a confused fusion with others; he who has participated in the carnival experience ceases to be an other, but at the same time he ceases to be himself. He transforms from "I" to "he" ("the poet"), representing a deindividualized poet, with only the poet's essence intact. The self's move into identification with the experience of carnival seems to separate the speaker from a fixed identity. It is interesting to note not only a transformation of the self of the poet in the poem but also, and above all, a transformation of the task that this self as "I" supposes for itself. In verse ninety-three and subsequent verses, there is a dismissal of the vision of the poet as he who unravels the poetry of things, who dives into the outside world, into the real, in order to find and unravel the poetry there. While that vision of poetry comes near to Bandeira's compositional method, it nonetheless does not crystallize in this poem, which seems more to narrate the failure of that "I."[39]

Of the three stages that Roberto Schwarz points out in Mário de Andrade's itinerary, this poem would seem to fit in with the second stage pertaining to an "anti-individualist moment," the stage in which "individual lyricism goes so far as to disappear even, in order to give way to a collective source of emotion, folklore."[40] However, I believe it is clear that this poem also narrates the constitution of a subject whose individual lyricism does not disappear but rather is enriched by that collective source of emotion, in this case carnival.

To "Carnaval Carioca" one could apply what João Luis Lafetá saw in *Pauliceia Desvairada* (Hallucinated City) in regard to São Paulo: a double movement in which the gaze upon the city, in this case Rio, registers both the external face of that city and the impressions it leaves inside the lyrical subject, showing that double visage in the poem. "Modern life maddens the poet," says Lafetá, "and he transfers his madness to modern life."[41] Lafetá's formulation insists nonetheless on something that it seems to me does not occur in this case: the splitting and separation of poet and city, or poet and experience, that in "Carnaval Carioca" become fused or confused.

In the economy the text instates, samba is represented as the symbol of the agglutination that defines carnival and the poem. It would be no exaggeration to postulate the figuration of a metonymy in which the carioca carnival is represented by samba and maxixe. The poem includes, in several stanzas, descriptions of carnival and of samba. In one of them we can read:

> Under the Hotel Avenida in 1923
> in Brazil's most thriving civilization
> the blacks doing the samba in rhythm.
> So sublime, so Africa!
> The youngest polished female effluvium undulations slow slowly
> with rings sparking gold Glauco rays in the hairy powdery light.
> Only the belly haunches dissolving in sways of waves in heat.
> She ends blessing herself religious just like in any other ritual.
> And the bass drum laughing in big pinches
> syncope of bedeviled grace.[42]

As they approach their climax, the verses grow longer, dropping syntactical connectors, producing a syncopated structure that simulates samba's chords. In the line "Sambas bumbos guizos serpentinas serpentinas" (Sambas bass drums bells serpentine serpentines), note the alliterative alternation of the nasal sounds, and of the occlusive velar and palatal consonants, that mimic the *tchiquimbum tchiquimbum* sound of the percussion in samba and that, moreover, are phonemes that are closely associated with Brazilian Portuguese.

> And the dense multitude agglomerates agglutinates masticates the merriment
>   with relish
> desired suffocations delirious sardines swoons
> serpentine serpentines colors lights sounds
> and sounds![43]

It is possible to read in these verses the functional initiation of the harmonic polyphonism that Mário de Andrade himself had expounded in theory as his modernist technique:

> Well: if instead of only using horizontal melodious verbs [. . .] we make it so
> that the words follow one after the other without there being an immediate

connection between them, then these words, due to the fact itself of not being pursuant to each other in the intellectual or grammatical sense, become superimposed in our sensations, forming no longer melodies, but harmonies.[44]

The poetry becomes polyphonic precisely when it describes samba and maxixe, and these in turn become a metaphor of the social mixing that carnival makes possible and of the aesthetic that directs how the poem is constructed. As if Mário de Andrade had found in carnival and in samba the condensation of his poetic aesthetic.

Primitivism functions in Mário de Andrade as a synthesis of that which merges together, in the experience of carnival; the most disparate of heterogeneities that do not cease to be heterogeneities, even during that momentary union. De Andrade's theory of harmonism, which we see put into practice in those verses describing samba and maxixe, could explain that persistence of difference in the union: the words, divested of their syntactical connectors, produce not melody but "harmony, arpeggiated chords."[45]

Yet, while the primitive appears in the introduction to the poem as another coding, the poem produces the incorporation of all of that into the self, whereby the conjunction of opposites assembled by the dichotomous formulation of the primitive is cut off from the outset. The closing stanza is unequivocal: carnival has turned into "a barulhada matinal de Guanabara" (the morning noise in Guanabara) in which the outside world is the poet's lullaby that puts him to sleep, "sem necessidade de sonhar" (with no need to dream). The outside world has fulfilled the need for dreaming; the dream, that which is most intimate to the poet, is the outside world; it is carnival.[46]

Raúl Antelo discovered a text written by Mário de Andrade in the margins next to a reference to Ortega y Gasset on the primitive. This commentary clarifies the construction of the primitive in "Carnaval Carioca":

One likes the primitive because of what is primitive about it and not because of what is not primitive about us. What we like about the primitive is that it is synthesis, it is realism, it is deformation, it is symbol. In the art of the primitive there is an abandonment of the particularities and a systematic revivification of essential values, religion, beauty, politics, society, truth, goodness, love, etc., etc.[47]

Primitivism, therefore, is not in this case a term of opposition against the other, but rather a term of synthesis.

The Uses of Primitivism

The apparent contradiction between cosmopolitanism and nationalism also can be seen in texts of the Argentine and Brazilian avant-garde, in which the national primitive figures as a form of self-differentiation from the European avant-garde. On situating that concern in the Latin American context, and on construing that context as the space typical of and proper to the primitive, Borges' and Mário de Andrade's texts were able to differentiate themselves from the European avant-garde by converting an alien tradition into one that was specific and their own, redefining in that attempt the gestures that would define a zone of the Latin American avant-garde. Linearity, the search for traditions of one's own, immersion in a past that was seen as present though not anachronic; these were ways of proposing, at the margins, a modernity that intended to be different from European modernity, which, as Oswald de Andrade stated in the *Manifesto Antropófago* (Cannibalist Manifesto), "without us would not even have its poor declaration of the rights of man."[48]

With these discourses, Borges and Mário de Andrade also revealed the structure of national discourse, an expression of cultural differences that, even if there have been those who have wanted to see it as sutured and stitched together, does nothing but repeat, in each of its inflections, the impossibility of that very suture. These texts cannot be inscribed in a nationalist tradition that exposes the agonic play revealed in those discourses. Both were able to choose, in the face of the political nationalism of other formulations, a cultural nationalism in which those differences are even more forceful. As Mário de Andrade states in "O Poeta Come Amendoim" (The Poet Eats Peanuts), the first poem of *Clã do Jaboti*):

> Brazil beloved not because it is my patria
> patria is the random chance of migrations and of breaking our bread where God
>   sees fit . . .
> Brazil that I love because it is the rhythm of my adventuresome arm,
> The pleasure of my rests,
> The swinging back-and-forth of my love poems and dances.
> Brazil that is me because it is my most humorous expression,
> Because it is my slow, soothing sentiment
> Because it is how I earn my keep, how I eat and sleep.[49]

The figuration of primitivism in both Borges' and Andrade's texts makes reference to the national as a means of finding difference in it. Those primitive structures, however, are also points of contact with the rest, with the universal, because they are useful for conceiving of the relationship between specificity and what stands apart from specificity. The construction of Argentine and Brazilian particularism, in both of the texts analyzed here, is sustained on a double strategy, universalist and particularist, that would seem to be one of the characteristics of peripheral cultures conceived as continuous and nonconformist struggles whose relationship with Europe and the discourse of the Enlightenment is always ambiguous.[50]

Cosmopolitanism and nationalism were not, then, two moments that happened to coincide chronologically by chance, but rather one single moment that, straddling both present and future, allowed for the Argentine and Brazilian avant-garde to write about nation without abandoning their concern for heterogeneity and difference. In those discourses, tango and samba move on to become mirroring objects of the avant-garde aesthetics that these artists went about progressively constructing. And in that same movement, the primitive became a vector of modernity.

The Painting of National Icons

Certain visual iconographies of tango and samba produced during the decades of the 1920s and 1930s show a very clear condensation of the primitive and the modern. Artists clearly associated with the Argentine and Brazilian avant-garde dedicated themselves in various works to the construction of a visual iconography of tango and of samba that can also be read as a narrative of artistic modernization in Argentina and Brazil. Some of the most important paintings in this project are "Samba" by Emiliano Di Cavalcanti; "Bailarines" (Dancers), "Mi Arlequín" (My Harlequin), and "La Canción del Pueblo" (The Song of the People) by Emilio Pettoruti; and a series of drawings by poetess Cecília Meireles that were exhibited in the Pró-Arte gallery in Rio de Janeiro in 1933.[51] These drawings are reprinted today in *Batuque, Samba e Macumba: Estudos de Gesto e Ritmo, 1926–1934* (Batuque, Samba and Macumba: Studies on Gesture and Rhythm, 1926–1934), which includes several texts on batuque and samba.[52]

Di Cavalcanti painted "Samba" in 1925 after a sojourn in Europe. Páulo Reis considered Di Cavalcanti's return to Brazil to have been one of the conditions for his break with the language of the avant-garde, but what is certain is that "Samba" can also be inscribed in the *rappel a l'ordre* (return to order) that the European avant-garde was suffering during those same years.[53]

The neoclassical composition of the painting places the women in the center, almost like two Madonnas, and undoes, via the dynamic of the gazes, the exacerbated sensuality that was ascribed to samba at that time. Although originally the women were nude in the painting, Di Cavalcanti decided later to dress them in order to achieve a certain unity based on color.[54] That strategy, which recurs through use of the same palette in different places on the canvas, produces a homogeneity in the painting while avoiding any shrillness in the colors, contributing in turn to a subduing of the sexual contents associated with samba.[55] In "Samba," thanks to these strategies, that sensuality is very understated and its sexual nuances quite reduced. While the women who are dancing look at the viewer, the men look at the women, but not with a gaze of evident desire. The man on the left is not even looking at the dancers and hardly seems to be listening to the music, as though samba were not music to dance to sensually, but rather to perceive intellectually.

The representation of samba in Di Cavalcanti's painting articulates a complex language. For Picasso, with whose neoclassical period this painting shares some similarities, neoclassicism was a way of reproducing avant-garde self-referentiality in terms of content. According to Rosalind Krauss, Picasso thus rejects the representation of a reality to opt instead for the reference to painting itself, through the repetition of other historic pictorial techniques. In sum, it is a way that Picasso would have devised in order to make references to the history of painting.[56]

It would be possible to make a similar interpretation of "Samba." In this case, the aforementioned style must be associated with the naturalism of Almeida Júnior, as has been pointed out by Tadeu Chiarelli. But this citation must be understood not only in the appeal to a representative style but also as a way of referring to the representation of popular traditions in the realm of painting, which entailed one of the greatest debates of the end of the nineteenth century between academicism and the younger generation represented at the time by Almeida Júnior.[57] In Di Cavalcanti's case, this is a reading of a Brazilian pictorial tradition of popular sectors, which is nonetheless recuperated as a fundamental episode of confrontation against academic language, thus creating a "precursor," in the Borgesian sense, of his own gesture of avant-garde rupture.

Yet, that citation of Di Cavalcanti's painting reveals perceptions of samba at the time of its execution. It takes distance from the common and traditional representation of samba that is contemporaneous to Di Cavalcanti, and also elaborates a distance from the realist representation itself, accentuating this distancing by way of the caricature-like quality—not realist, but rather *deforming* of reality—in his figurative language.

Di Cavalcanti's style has been understood as a conservative modernism, given that he would not have been able to "adhere to the European avant-garde's more radical delineations."[58] Nonetheless, I believe it is possible to read in Di Cavalcanti the gesture toward creating a modern Brazilian tradition, via reupdating the language of Almeida Júnior as a discourse of opposition to emulating Europe that, in Almeida Júnior's day and age, represented the language of the Academy and that, in Di Cavalcanti's age, was condensed in a direct imitation of the historical European avant-garde movements that were contemporaneous to him. In this painting, in contrast, Di Cavalcanti finds in samba the *national* modernity so sought after by Brazilian modernists.

The abandonment of the language of the European avant-garde can be read, then, as a strategy of double legitimization and transformation. On the one hand, on representing, in neoclassical canons, samba and the popular sectors that produce it, "Samba" legitimizes, as an object of art, a popular product that had been rejected until then. Even if on doing this he effaces samba's more obscene sides, he also restructures European avant-garde language into a more revulsive form than what would have been the effect of a more abstract interpretation. The comparison between the figurativism of "Samba" and the realism of Almeida Júnior allows one to see the scope of "deformation" in Di Cavalcanti's figurativism. Its appeal to national elements is offered without the naturalist or academic language with which those sectors had been represented previously. One can also see that gesture of greater revulsion in the choice of the national social in detriment to the national landscape, so characteristic, for example, in some paintings by Tarsila do Amaral. Di Cavalcanti, as Mário de Andrade observed, "without abiding by any nationalist thesis, is always the most exact painter of national things. He does not confuse Brazil with its landscape; instead of Sugarloaf Mountain he gives us sambas, instead of palm trees, mulatto women, blacks and carnivals."[59]

Emilio Pettoruti's trajectory is somewhat different, but shows another operation of condensing of the national and the modern. Pettoruti painted several works on the world of tango in the 1920s and 1930s, such as "Bailarines" (Dancers), "La Canción del Pueblo" (The Song of the People), and "Mi Arlequín" (My Harlequin). While the national reference persists in the titles, the paintings themselves take distance from representation and thereby efface any kind of local color or typicality.

"Bailarines" (1918) uses cubism, *the* modern language of the era, to depict the national dance, while "Mi Arlequín" (1927) represents a tango singer with the modern figure of the harlequin. In both cases the national symbol seems fragmented and condensed into a specific characteristic: in "Mi Arlequín" it is the *bandoneón*—although here it is represented as an accordion, indicated by its keys—that, with the folds of its bellows, reproduces cubism's multiplication of planes; in "Bailarines" it is the famous *"corte y quebrada"* choreography (tango's cut-and-break dance step that involves a dramatic hesitation followed by a twist or swing of the hips) that identifies the dancers as dancers of tango by making use of cubism's angles. In this way, Pettoruti's

FIGURE 3. "Bailarines" [Dancers] by Emilio Pettoruti, 1918, 77 cm x 55 cm, oil on canvas. Collection of the Emilio A. Caraffa Provincial Museum of Fine Arts, Córdoba, Argentina. Garramuño, *Modernidades Primitivas*, p. 138.

paintings on the national symbol take distance from picturesque and *costumbrista* (mannerist) representation, combining two apparently contradictory elements: the modern language of cubism and of the European avant-garde and European modernity; and the insistence on representing, with that language, a national and primitive form. Thus, the national or primitive symbol appears as a figuration of the modern technique with which it is constructed.

Also interesting in these paintings by Pettoruti is the question of color, generally excluded from the more paradigmatic cubist paintings such as those by Braque and Picasso, to name the most classical examples, because of their concentration on form. In the case of these paintings by Pettoruti,

FIGURE 4. "La Canción del Pueblo" [The Song of the People] by Emilio Pettoruti, 1927, 73.5 cm x 64.7 cm, oil on wood. Malba-Costantini Collection, Buenos Aires. All rights reserved. Pettoruti Foundation, www.pettoruti.com. Garramuño, *Modernidades Primitivas*, p. 138.

however, color is fundamental and also imitates the collage technique that will reincorporate color in the European avant-garde, principally on the basis of tapestry paper. The use of this technique appears limited to tango's cut-and-break dance step, which is not only tango's most identifying trait among other *dances brunnes* but is also the most polemical, as it makes reference to a sexuality considered indecent and primitive.

The journal *Martin Fierro* published a few of Pettoruti's paintings, among them "Bailarines" (on the cover) and "La Canción Popular" (The Popular Song) in its issue 10–11 of October 1924, recognizing in Pettoruti "one of the criollo avant-garde" in a text signed by Xul Solar. Indeed, the work on the primitive,

FIGURE 5. "Mi Arlequín" [My Harlequin] by Emilio Pettoruti, 1927, 113 cm x 73.5 cm. Private collection, Buenos Aires. All rights reserved. Pettoruti Foundation, www .pettoruti.com. Garramuño, *Modernidades Primitivas*, p. 139.

FIGURE 6 (a and b).
"Bahianas" [Bahian Women],
by Cecília Meireles, 1934. From
Batuque, Samba e Macumba
(Rio de Janeiro: Martins, Fonte
Editora, 2003). Garramuño,
Modernidades Primitivas, p. 141.

especially that of Borges and Girondo, presents a similar condensation of the primitive and the modern that seems to be one of the marks of this Argentine avant-garde.

The path that Cecília Meireles pursues to modernize the national icon is somewhat different. Her "feminine" drawings depict black women in traditional attire and exhibit a supremely sophisticated movement that calls to mind drawings of fashion figures, particularly the fashion figures for tango clothes that emerged during the 1920s in Europe and expanded to the rest of the world. Her portrayal of Bahian women in traditional clothing evinces a premonitory figurine, anticipating the Bahian fashion that will follow Carmen Miranda's success in the 1940s and expressing the all too common use of this costume in musical revues in the 1920s and 1930s.[60]

The black and white drawing "Roda de Samba" (Samba Circle) of women carnival participants seems to minimize the sexual nuances that had represented samba until then. Its caption reads: "In the carnival of Rio de Janeiro, undeniably wanton and vulgar, as everywhere in the expansion of persons who are habitually civilized, the carnival of the blacks retains still a unique aspect of respect, elegance, and we may even say a surprising artistic distinction."[61]

FIGURE 7. "Roda de Samba" [Samba Circle] by Cecília Meireles, 1934. From *Batuque, Samba e Macumba* (Rio de Janeiro: Martins Fonte Editora, 2003). Garramuño, *Modernidades Primitivas*, p. 143.

Thus the primitive becomes modern and fashionable. These works that construct national icons seem to resolve the tension between those autochthonous products looked on (by the ethnologizing gaze of the nation) as exotic and at odds with the civilizing spirit presupposed by the entry into modernity. In the new modern meaning acquired by these "primitive" cultural products lies their entry into national culture.

The Ambivalent Legacies of Modernity

The condensation of the modern and the primitive devised by the Argentine and the Brazilian avant-garde makes evident the pronounced overlapping or interweaving of modernization and nationalization in Latin American cultures, to the point that both impulses together defined some Latin American modernities like two sides of the same coin.

What did it mean, for Latin American countries, to be modern? If we take the names of the most important avant-garde movements in Brazil and Argentina, *Martín Fierro* and *Antropofagia* (Cannibalism), we can perceive in both the simultaneous appeal to the national and primitive symbol that they themselves were constructing for their nations.

It is clear that the problem of the primitive in Argentine and Brazilian culture is connected to the dynamic of modernization. According to its implementation in Latin American culture, the primitive in the 1920s is an amphibious signifier. It refers at the same time to the modern and sophisticated expression of the European avant-garde, the creator of this "problematic," and to the national past, where this primitive aspect is "discovered." The changes in the Latin American meaning of the primitive are not merely a function of imitating the European avant-garde, as James Clifford has suggested. In fact, the primitive figure is manifested in products not associated with the avant-garde, such as novels about tango and samba that crop up principally in the 1920s and 1930s. Those changes condense strategies of nationalization used as much by the avant-garde as by other movements that were more critical of modernization and less euphoric about European modernity. In its changing meanings, the idea of the primitive can be explained more on the basis of a reference to Europe, keeping in mind the historical condition of Latin America in relation to the process of modernization. For Latin America, being national is equivalent to being modern, and being modern, in turn, is synonymous with being national. Tango and samba, and the idea of the primitive that they came to condense, create some of the scenarios where the ambivalent legacies of modernity for Latin American cultures can be seen.

Tango and samba became national symbols in the 1920s and 1930s precisely because they present the best example of this condensation of modernization and nationalization. Yet, other factors accelerated the process, such as the exoticization of these rhythms that the Parisian music scene prompted (to the horror of several representatives of the elite), the uses of tango and samba during the avant-garde period, or their instrumentalization in the construction of a national cinema. Any contradictions in the narrative of the modernization of Argentine and Brazilian cultures were in the end negotiated via the culturally constructed meaning of the primitive surrounding tango and samba, which allowed the Brazilian and Argentine cultures to put themselves forth as sites of an alternative modernity.

In a chronicle titled "Carnaval na Ilha do Governador" (Carnival on Ilha do Governador Island), Rachel de Queiroz notes that already-recognized similarity between samba and the avant-garde:

> Near the restaurant and club Praia da Freguesia, the false aristocrats show their disdain for the black people's carnival, as they sit in their pajamas in their carriage seats, with their children dressed up like Indians, whining all around them. In that moment a raggedy group passes by with tambourine, three *cuícas* and the bagpipes playing a solo: they were singing the year's most beautiful *chorinho*:
>
> Here comes the moon, rising in the sky. . . .
> —And what do I care?
>
> A man with a goatee cupped a hand behind his ear, heard the tune and became agitated:
>
> A futurist verse! Gentlemen, even in samba there are futurist verses![62]

The coincidence between samba and modernity was, just as Rachel de Queiroz perceived it, perhaps something more than merely a strategy of the Brazilian avant-garde to construct the nation.

PART II

MODERNITIES

1

THE EXPORTATION VOYAGE AND THE
AVANT-GARDE AS COMMODITY

Travel has been a fundamental mechanism in the construction of Latin American culture. The voyages made by Europeans such as Darwin, Humboldt, Spix and Martius, Debret, or Levi-Strauss to Argentina or Brazil have been important for the construction of a national tradition, as has been convincingly shown by Flora Süssekind for the case of Brazil and by Adolfo Prieto for Argentina. Argentine and Brazilian artists and intellectuals had to run the same course, in the opposite direction but with the same objective; from Sarmiento's trips in the nineteenth century, or Güiraldes' and Girondo's, to those made by Oswald de Andrade or Tarsila do Amaral, the sojourn abroad corresponds to a preamble that was often vital to the constitution of Argentine and Brazilian artistic and literary languages.[1]

Tango and samba performers also traveled, and their journeys coincided chronologically with the sojourns of Argentine and Brazilian avant-garde artists. The first trip made by Argentines of the tango world seems to have been that of the Gobbi couple and Villoldo, in 1907, contracted by the Gath & Chaves company to make recordings in France. Even before this, some copies of the sheet music for "La Morocha" and "El Choclo" seem to have been distributed in diverse European port cities by cadets of the Frigate Sarmiento.[2] The first journey for samba would have been in combination with maxixe and choro; the band Os Oito Batutas traveled to Paris to play at the Duque Café in 1922, and that trip was financed by Arnaldo Guinle, the millionaire from Rio de Janeiro who would also finance Heitor Villa-Lobos' first trip. There are indications, however, that the Duque Café had already showcased performances of choro and maxixe dances before the Batutas' journey.[3]

The journeys made to Paris in relation to tango and samba invert the postulate of cultural voyages; the musical travelers no longer made the voyage to learn or to absorb knowledge that would be more advanced in Europe, but rather fundamentally to export their music, now deemed a national product like any other raw exportable material, cultural rather than natural. Apprised of the passion for exotic dances, primarily in Europe but also in the USA, tango and samba travelers found in the journey the possibility of an adventure in which a bohemian attitude was one with a distinctly commercial tenet. No longer a journey of apprenticeship for learning or researching, these voyages were impelled by economic need and shaped by the market. Early voyages undertaken by artists and intellectuals had been largely sponsored by personal family fortunes or by patrons, as well as by grants from the governments of inviting countries. At times, entrepreneurs contracted samba and tango musicians to travel abroad, establishing with them a clearly commercial relationship.[4] Notably, around the same time, the voyages of other artists were similarly financed by entrepreneurs and gallery owners with commercial motives.

The transition from the voyage of apprenticeship and learning to the exportation voyage works as a vector of transformation. The apprenticeship voyage supposes a vision of culture as adornment, a quality that can be acquired but that is presumably excluded from all commercial transactions. Here, culture comprises utility goods whose exchange value is masked, and its counterpart is a consumer of foreign culture who will later import it to his country of origin, reworked into other cultural objects such as Darwin's theory of species, Humboldt's work on nature in the new world, or Oswald de Andrade's *Poesia Pau Brasil*. According to Candido Portinari: "I go to Europe to study the greats. [...] I prefer to return from Europe without huge amounts of luggage (paintings), appearing to the unknowing eye to not have done anything at all, but bearing instead a profound quantity of observations and explorations."[5] Upon returning to Brazil, Portinari's immersion in studies is reworked into a painting style that fuses the many European pictorial schools.[6]

The exportation voyage, in contrast, replaces family-based or State sponsorship with the market. Now it is the market that governs and directs commercial tours, length of stay, and even the form of behavior that the travelers should conform to.[7] Musicians earned both money and fame on these trips; many who were unknowns when they left their own countries arrived home not only with capital but also with another, quite important, kind of exchange goods: the prestige of having triumphed in Europe.

Many Latin American artists found themselves immersed in the avant-garde journey of seeking out new worlds in order to incorporate them into their art and translate them into a peripheral culture. In fact, the journey fulfills one of the possible forms of avant-garde convulsion, embodying the metaphor of displacement while also reducing the metaphor to its formal closed function. A notion of culture is presupposed that is closer to that of the nineteenth century, whose outdatedness the avant-garde itself exposes and even exacerbates, branding it with particular characteristics. The exportation voyage is in fact the consummation of the avant-garde journey and of one of its mentors, Oswald de Andrade. In the *Manifesto da Poesia Pau Brasil* de Andrade had urged for "Poesia de Exportação,"[8] and it would arrive at the hands and bodies of those who produced the sounds: the Batutas. Although the voyage of apprenticeship or learning and that of exportation present the two poles of maximum opposition for the concept of the journey, the training of the artist abroad reached such a consumerist disposition, at times, that culture began to seem like an item among exchange goods and no longer exclusively an instance of utility goods.

Tarsila do Amaral's and Oswald de Andrade's journeys exhibit several signs of this transformation; not only are they seen as visibly anxious to acquire all that is related with European modernity (Poiret fashion designs, tableware sets, furniture, and diverse and not exclusively artistic objects), but also, even in the case of Tarsila, the very learning of new techniques in modern painting seems to run counter to the guiding idea behind the journey of apprenticeship and learning. In a letter to her family, Tarsila recounts the following:

> Today I began lessons with Léger. I spent last Saturday in his atelier and took some of my latest and most modern works. He found me to be very advanced and liked some of the pieces very much. I returned home very enthused. I am going to see if I can take some classes as well with Gleizes, a most advanced artist. [. . .] With all these lessons I will become conscious of my art. Of what the instructors say, I only listen to what is useful for me. After these classes, I will not continue with instructors.[9]

That displacement suggests a parallel conversion from the studious individual who has gone abroad to learn, to the bohemian who squanders his or her fortune in Europe (like Raucho in the novel of the same name by Güiraldes) and who crosses paths, in a number of scenarios, with the tango and samba bohemians themselves. In that sense not only do the Argentine and the Brazilian avant-garde coincide circumstantially with the bohemian set, but also a specular resemblance is constructed in relation to that other bohemia, in which the elite and the producers of popular culture mixed together and collaborated in the production of sambas, poems, tangos, and novels.[10] Oswald de Andrade perceived this transformation of the place of culture and art from the vantage point of his bitter lucidity in the prologue to *Serafim Ponte Grande*: "The revolutionary situation of this South American mental manure is presented in this way: the opposite of the bourgeois was not the proletarian, it was the bohemian!"[11]

The fact that it would be the same millionaire, Arnaldo Guinle, to finance the trip to Paris for an orchestra that played choros, maxixes, and sambas as for the most sophisticated modernist of erudite Brazilian music, Heitor Villa-Lobos, is no mere coincidence. In a letter to Oswald de Andrade and Tarsila do Amaral, written in Paris in 1927, Villa-Lobos mentions this coincidence. Not by chance it is a letter colored with the mercantile vicissitudes of his concerts:

I do the rounds of the cabarets, still without Jazz, but in a powerful samba bass drum full of catiras and mindinhos from Bahia.

Here you have, dear friends, in a confused synthesis, without barter-idylls nor high praise, what my imagination of a foreign country has come to.

You cannot imagine the care one must go to to distinguish our true music from Jazz, since both are a result of black African drunkenness, and the foreign auditorium only recognizes as original that which has obtained greater publicity. Nonetheless, much before the first fox-trot made its appearance, already more than three centuries ago in Brazil (from Minas to Bahia) this same rhythm has been sung and danced among the people. I judge this fact to be due to simple racial affinity . . .

Well, enough . . .

Enthused by writing to two batuta friends I was heading straight into heavy-handed erudition . . . Fortunately I have realized just in time.

Let's get to practical matters. Together with this one there are two further programming plans for my concerts here that have already been totally organized through the initiative of the Max Eschig house, O., who will take on half the expenses; for the other half I have already asked for assistance from friends, some of whom have responded agreeably.

I chose eight of my friends (who are precisely those whom I have dedicated the greater part of the pieces that will be performed) in order to not be a burden to one or two of you who'd like to sponsor me. Consequently, each of them must commit to 2,500 pesos because the total of the part I am to cover comes to 20 contos, to justify the total of all expenses for these two monstrous concerts. [. . .]

You both will have the opportunity to hear *Pájaro Carpintero Brasil* (Woodpecker Brazil), with the one hundred voices of true professional artists frightening the Parisian audience with those savage inflections with which you already are familiar. I thought of you two for a joint portion, if by chance you consider I might deserve such sacrifice.[12]

Nor is this any exception or the gesture of one eccentric millionaire; Dona Olívia Guedes Penteado as well, solidly positioned in the history of Brazilian modernism as *the* sponsor of the movement, was the mediation for samba, choro, and maxixe played, by none other than Os Batutas, at the Brazilian embassy of Paris.[13] Villa-Lobos, also in Paris, was fully aware of that position and of the change this voyage of an avant-garde artist signified with respect to the previous kind of artist's sojourn abroad, as can be read in an interview: "I did not come here to learn; I came to show what I have already learned."[14] The voyage of apprenticeship ends, and the exportation voyage begins.

Güiraldes also frequented the same cabarets where the tango musicians were performing tangos, and judging by certain anecdotes one might speculate that the crossing of paths was fundamental in the creation of an idea of the national novel that Güiraldes would later carry out in *Don Segundo Sombra*. Francisco Canaro recounts in his *Memorias* that one night he played his tango "Sentimiento Gaucho" in a Parisian cabaret. Güiraldes was in the audience, and, when the tango ended, he approached Canaro and asked him for the title of the tango he'd just heard. In the face of Canaro's reply, Güiraldes answered: "It'd have to be gaucho to be that good."[15] Moreover, Pettoruti recounts in *Un Pintor ante el Espejo* (A Painter before the Mirror) that his painting *Bailarines* (Dancers) was inspired by one night out on the town in Florence when he saw his friend Xul Solar dance an Argentine tango. In those contrasting motions and clashing perspectives Pettoruti found a form for representing the fluid movement apparent in *Bailarines*.[16]

The confluences of the journey of tango and samba and the one realized by the figures of the Argentine and Brazilian avant-garde are not limited to contextual meeting points in a certain space. Rather, their contingent confluence was made possible by a fundamental transformation of the place and function of culture that in turn became relevant for the constitution of a modern and national language. If the musicians were valued for their exotic and autochthonous condition, so too would the avant-garde artists begin to perceive in Europe a simultaneous demand for national specification in their art. The fact that this demand and this quest take place during those early decades of the twentieth century, and are made manifest as much in practices of popular culture as in high or erudite culture, can be explained on the basis of a transformation of culture in the 1920s that covers and encompasses both voyages and both cultural manifestations. The strong commodification of culture during those years would have dramatic consequences for artistic languages as well as for the construction of a national identity.

The avant-garde voyage and the musical one present obvious differences. If the avant-garde artists seemed able to elide a dependency on the market for the realization of their journeys, inasmuch as those travels were ultimately financed by their own family fortunes or by funds of the State or of sponsors who invested in their artistic formation, also true is that the commercial character of the avant-garde voyage seeps in through other, far from insignificant gaps. In any case, a constant pressure persisted, whether it was accepted or rejected, to produce relatively immediate results from putting that investment to use. Pettoruti runs the risk of losing his grant and hence sends his patron paintings to demonstrate his progress; Candido Portinari returns from abroad without paintings and must defend himself on the point of that "nonproductivity"; Tarsila do Amaral's letters show numerous signs of that same anxiety.

Culture as Commodity

While tango and samba begin to function as commodities, as cultural products in the incentivized exchange of goods that took place during the golden years of the 1920s, the notion of the avant-garde also shares many of these same characteristics.

As Sven-Olov Wallenstein points out:

> It has often been remarked that the development of modern art runs parallel to the quick expansion of the commodity world during the 19th century. This is confirmed, rather than contradicted, by the violent resistance that many early modernists exhibited to industrial capital and its annexing of the life-

world. As the commodity more and more comes to define a new status of the art object and give it an increasing mobility, the resistance to this development grows as well. The very idea of aesthetic autonomy, of the work as a self-enclosed and self-referential reality, rooted in Kant's philosophy but perfected only in the late nineteenth century, may be seen as a complex reaction. It is only by internalizing, in a paradoxical way, the commodity form, by becoming an absolute fetish, that the work may escape humiliation.[17]

Perhaps Benjamin was one of the first to perceive the phantasmagoric quality of the market in those avant-garde gestures. In "False Criticism," he indicated: "All writers want to prove one thing only: that they know perfectly the latest fashion."[18] He makes note in *The Arcades Project* of an interesting critical path whereby that work can be read as a kind of spread-open map: "The influence of commercial affairs on Lautréamont and Rimbaud should be looked into!"[19]

The complications of that transformation of the place of culture can be read in one of the most defining traits of avant-garde art: artistic autonomy. On the one hand, autonomy is a function of the strong institutionalization of art apparent toward the end of the nineteenth century and of which the avant-garde, as seen in Peter Bürger, is conceived of as a historically logical consequence; regarding the development of the artistic language, autonomy appears as a consequence and a rejection in relation to the commodification of art, which the institutionalization of art also presumes and enables. It is worthwhile to quote an extensive extract of Jon Roberts analyzing the problem of autonomy in Adorno's theory of aesthetics:

> What distinguishes Adorno's theory of autonomy from the early Romantics, the neo-conservative New Criticism of the 1950s, and Greenbergian modernists, is that art is seen simultaneously as socially determined and autonomous. Or rather, the autonomy of the art object is something which is produced out of the social relations which constitute the institution of art itself. It is not something which is produced immanently out of the object and therefore transmittable as a particular "style" or "look." This means that autonomy is the practical and theoretical outcome of the contradiction between the artwork's exchange value and use-value. Because of the perpetual threat of the loss of the artwork's use-value, art is continually propelled by its own conditions of alienation to find aesthetic strategies which might resist or obviate this process of critical and aesthetic dissolution—the history of the "new" in modernism derives from the resistance of art to its exchange value. But, at the

same time, under capitalism art derives its social identity and value from this process. Thus authentic modern art acquires identity and value in a double movement of negation and self-negation: art achieves visibility through positioning itself in relation to the prevailing norms, interests and protocols of the market and intellectual academy. But once the work achieves institutional and market visibility, the artist is forced to resist the work's own subsumption under a new set of norms if he or she values the thing that defined the work's initial moment of production: its critical difference or aesthetic "otherness." For once the value of the new work is institutionally established, the work finds itself part of a new set of prevailing norms and protocols. The exchange value of the artwork, therefore, operates as a kind of fiction: artists seek to transform the normative values of the market and the critical academy in their own image, but in the interests of escaping from these values and self-image. That is, the fiction of autonomy has to be dismantled by the artist if the pursuit of autonomy is to be able to continue to prosecute art's failure to realise its freedom from social dependency. Art's autonomy is necessarily dependent, on the alienated conditions of its realization, because it is through art's connection to the 'unresolved antagonisms' of reality that the social content of autonomy is generated. Commodification, then, locks art into an impossible logic: art can only renew itself through undermining or disrupting those qualities that bring it into being. Yet, if this logic is impossible, for Adorno it is necessary and inescapable under current relations of production, because, paradoxically, it is this logic that sustains the possibility of art's (and human) freedom.[20]

Thinking autonomy, therefore, entails conceiving of two different meanings of the same idea. Going back to Roberts, "autonomy is the name given to the process of formal and cognitive self-criticism which art must undergo in order to constitute the conditions of its very possibility and emergence."[21]

On the other hand, autonomy is the result of a historical process that transcends the formal conditions of its manifestation. The specification varies for the Brazilian and the Argentine cases. If one thinks in terms of artistic field, their "uneven" modernization, to use Julio Ramos' term, prevents them from completing their autonomization. Neither is it possible to speak of a strongly constituted art market in Brazil or in Argentina until at least the 1930s or 1940s, nor is that formal autonomy, in terms of artistic languages, radically completed in the modernism of the 1920s.[22] A greater attachment to representativity, to mimesis, would indicate a lesser autonomy in Latin American modernist forms, in which national fields come to be interrupted by those "areas outside the field" that were made manifest in the avant-garde and the tango and samba voyages, with Europeans traveling to American lands, the pronounced development in communications, and the huge efforts toward artistic updatedness that the national Latin American avant-garde movements evinced. In those voyages—in that "outside" where the construction of a national culture is defined—diverse actors such as tango and samba performers, poets, and musicians coincide and cross paths.

Yet, it is possible to speak of a pronounced commodification of art even before the constitution of an art market with all its rules, not only regarding what the artists negotiated and invested—if not in capital power then in symbolic power, as Bourdieu conceives of it—but also because many of those works were also thought to function within the market of European art as new objects, precisely because of their national autochthonous character. In that sense, it is not only necessary to incorporate the avant-garde voyages as founding moments in that definition (Paulo Renato Gueriós shows how the musical definition of Heitor Villa-Lobos' language changes with his sojourn in Paris[23]), but also to identify in the transformations of those languages' forms the operations whereby these trajectories leave their imprint on the form itself. These forms are thus explained not only via their national contexts but also via the displacements they themselves register and provoke.

The Outside in the Form

The passion of Tarsila do Amaral and Oswald de Andrade for the latest fashions was registered in their letters as well as in a famous photograph: dressed in a design by Poiret, the most sought after and *en vogue* designer of 1920s Paris, Tarsila do Amaral went to the opening of her first solo exhibition in that city, in 1926.[24]

The continuity between the dress fabricated by the fashion designer who was considered a great artist and the painting by Tarsila in this photograph speaks for itself. Not only do the geometrical lines that grid the landscape of the painting repeat the dress's checkered pattern, but also the curves of the trees can be seen in the dress's bows on the sleeves and in the folds and gathers of the skirt. Curve and grid could very well be thought of as Brazilian characteristics of a modernism that, resisting abstraction, still does not renounce the geometricization and the rationalization of space that international modernism preached.

Oswald de Andrade dedicated a poem to Tarsila do Amaral, which he included in *Poesia Pau Brasil*, "Atelier":

Little peasant dressed by Poiret
São Paulo's laziness resides in your eyes
That saw not Paris nor Picadilly,
Nor the clamoring of the men
in Seville
as you passed between the rings

Locomotives and autochthonous animals
Geometricize the neat atmospheres
Congonhas pales beneath the pallium
Of the Minas processions.

The green in the blue claxon
cut
under the red powder.

Skyscrapers
forums
viaducts
a whiff of coffee
framed
in silence.[25]

The poem is constructed on the basis of an almost paratactical coexistence of modern signs (generally associated with one form or another of technology: cars, viaducts, locomotives, skyscrapers) and national autochthonous signs (generally associated with nature, the landscape, or what in those same years would come to be defined as the epitome of national patrimony, the architecture: animals, green, Congonhas, Minas, coffee). These signs, although they should be thought of as originating in opposite symbolic spaces, appear combined by a poetic structure that makes effort to combine both elements without marking a disjunction between them, but rather producing an almost complementary coexistence. In the first two lines of the second stanza,

Locomotives *and* autochthonous animals
Geometricize the neat atmospheres (emphasis mine)

the conjunction is realized not only by the particle *and* that combines technology and nature, but also in the syntactical function of both elements, actively producing a geometry in which the grid appears in both the modern product represented by the locomotive and in the natural landscape. The typically Tarsilesque translation of Léger's operations in painting are expressed in her geometricization—no longer just of the city or technology, as in Léger, but also of the natural landscape—and in her combination of rounded curving lines that frequently interrupt the grid's organizing plan.[26] This operation becomes exasperated in the following stanza, where the *klaxon*—a technological product that was so significant to modernity that its name was taken for the title of the first Brazilian avant-garde magazine[27]—describes the color that frames the landscape ("the green in the blue claxon"; "the red powder"), or the quality of the smell of coffee (a typical Brazilian commodity that is also intimately related to the history of Brazilian modernism)[28] frames an entire stanza built on parataxis involving the most modern symbols imaginable.

The poem can be thought of as a development of what the first verse proposes; "Little peasant dressed by Poiret" would be a contradiction if one imagines in abstract terms a peasant dressed in the latest fashion, but not if those two signifiers are thought of in historical terms with what corresponded to those abstractions in that moment, as Paul Poiret remained for all time as the fashion designer who imported from the so-called primitive cultures not only elements of their autochthonous attire but also lines, designs, and fabrics; the confluence of the purest bastion of an exotic nationality and the most refined modernity is revealed, thus, with all its luminous edges.

More than descriptions of a few paintings by Tarsila of the *"Pau Brasil Exótico"* phase[29]—among them, precisely "Morro da Favela" (Slum Hill), the painting in front of which Tarsila appears wearing a Poiret design (and perhaps Oswald had that same photograph before his eyes as he composed the poem)—the stanzas, in avoiding all directionality in the descriptions and proposing instead a pure linguistic visuality, use the collage technique—so richly employed by Oswald de Andrade in this book of poems as well as in his two more avant-garde novels, *Memórias Sentimentais de João Miramar* (João Miramar's Sentimental Memoirs) and *Serafim Ponte Grande*. In the text, fragments of the image of Tarsila and of various paintings by her, paratactically combined, dismantle all direct referentiality, making the poem an intersection site for those indexes that the different fragments are transformed into.[30]

The collage has been one of the mechanisms devised by the avant-garde to obliterate the boundaries between art and life. Yet, it can also be thought of as one of the forms in which commodities—the piece of glass from a bottle, the fragment of wood—enter into art to emblematize how much the fetishistic character of commodities coincides with that of avant-garde art. As Marjorie Perloff has indicated, a dual function must be recognized in the collage: each element refers to an outside reality at the same time as, in compositional terms, its impulse is to undermine the very referentiality it seems to affirm.[31]

FIGURE 8. Tarsila do Amaral in front of her painting "Morro da Favela" [Slum Hill], in the opening for her first individual exhibition in Paris, 1927. In Aracy Amaral, *Tarsila: Sua Obra e Seu Tempo* [Tarsila: Her Ouevre and Her Era] (São Paulo: Editora 34 & EDUSP, 2003). Garramuño, *Modernidades Primitivas*, p. 166.

Beyond the importance given in modernism and the avant-garde to form and self-referentiality, perhaps a way of conspiring for the world to enter or overflow into art can be envisioned. Collage translates into form, and freezes in form, the threat of the commodification of art, regardless of whether a national or international market even exists. Argentine and Brazilian avant-garde art, though it may not be able to survive in a market of its own and though its aesthetic options are limited, those limitations are suspended by the intervention of various and constant areas "outside the field." The journeys of the avant-garde are the most perfect of metaphors for this.

"Self-Portrait" (Manteau Rouge), by Tarsila do Amaral, brings these energies into confluence on the surface of this most famous of her portraits, in

FIGURE 9. "Self-Portrait" (Manteau Rouge) by Tarsila do Amaral, 1923. Fine Arts Museum, Rio de Janeiro. Garramuño, *Modernidades Primitivas*, p. 173.

which she appears wearing the Manteau Rouge she had purchased from Paul Poiret.[32] The palette is reduced to a minimum quantity of primary colors—red, blue, and also black and white—used almost flatly, without nuances, without volume, and suspending any and all naturalist plans; the same shade of red for the lips is repeated for the cape and is used to reinforce the shadow on the left eyelid and on the right side of the neck. That object of desire that is the Poiret cape is transferred by way of these procedures to the surface of the painting, transferring the fetishization of commodities to the fetishization of form. From the edges to the center of the painting, from the commodity (the Poiret design) to the form, the trajectory seems to be that of the conspiracy to convert form itself into commodity.

In many of these forms, if one renounces the gaze that confines them in their functioning to the painting itself, a differentiated functioning of culture emerges. These formal innovations impart meaning to the transformation that precedes them and transforms the place of culture—high, erudite, or popular—in those years of intense modernity,[33] in which the crisis of liberalism and European modernity allows Latin America to be thought of as the possible place for a different path of modernity. This transformation of culture explains, in conceptual terms, the avant-garde's fascination with tango and samba as well as other manifestations of popular culture. Something in the accepted mercantile character of popular culture is looked on by modern art with fascination and at times a certain envy; at issue is a new way of functioning of culture as a space striated by the outside, which popular culture was the first to find a way to exhibit successfully, both formally and commercially. That striated character of culture in the 1920s would also be manifested, in the case of Latin American modernisms, in the nationalism-made fetish that reproduces those phantasmagoria of that "very queer thing," in Marx's words, that is the commodity.[34]

In *Modern Art in the Common Culture*, Thomas Crow highlights the relationship between modern art and mass culture. Beyond the use of popular culture as a means to displace accepted conventions, Crow proposes that the modernist negation proceeds from a productive confusion within the normal hierarchy of cultural prestige and legitimacy. The avant-garde finds an intermediate position between the high and low zones of commodity culture, operating as a necessary mediation between superior and inferior and functioning as a kind of "research and development" arm of the culture industry. In the case of Latin American cultures, certain popular symbols appealed to many of the avant-garde movements, which contributed to the fetishization of the nation.

The Nation and the Fetish

In Brazil, the narrative begins with Oswald de Andrade's famous phrase from his conference: "I discovered Brazil from La Place Clichy" and has its perfect complement in another phrase from one of Tarsila do Amaral's letters to her family from Brazil: "Don't think that this Brazilian tendency in art is not looked well upon here. On the contrary. What is desirable here is that each person bring his own country's contribution. Thus is explained the success of Russian dances, Japanese engravings, and black music. Paris is sick of Parisian art."[35] That nationalism of the avant-garde—to which could be added that "urban *criollismo* of the avant-garde" in Borges' formulation—found in the avant-garde journey its primordial impulse. One would have to add to it, nonetheless, the patently modern content of that national quest, not only because it came motivated by the most conspicuous moderns of "advanced" Europe, but also because of the pronounced affinity between modernity and nationalism. Tom Nairn states in "The Modern Janus":

> Nationalism was the effort by one "backward" culture and people after an-other to appropriate the powers and benefits of modernity for their own use. Having been redefined as backward, they aspired to move forward. However, this motion occurred partly against the tide coursing over them from the central domains of industry and urbanisation. The pressure wave was mainly imperial (arrogant, egocentric, homogenising, and armed to the teeth) as well as gift-bearing. In order to appropriate the gifts without enduring the imperial wrappings, overborne populations had to assert "their own terms"—that is, political and cultural independence. This implied that, in most cases, the terms had to be "discovered" via scrutiny and vindication of their own past history. There seemed no way for nationalities to become nations without such new retrospect. Hence, modernising ambition and novel cults of a particular past and tradition notoriously co-exist within most varieties of nationalism: the backward- and forward-looking faces of any discrete population or area struggling for tolerable survival and prosperity.[36]

The Latin American avant-garde's nationalism was fundamental for the con-struction of a cultural modernity in Argentina and Brazil, as fundamental as it was to accentuate national traits in tango and samba in order to achieve recognition as modern musical forms. Many tango and samba lyrics emphasized nationalism even without the excesses of *samba exaltação* (laudatory samba) or "patriotic" tangos. Two songs in particular allow us to enter into the vicissitudes of the exportation voyage: "Disseram que Eu Voltei Americanizada" (They Said I Came Back Americanized) sung by Carmen Miranda, and "Anclao en París" (Stuck in Paris) sung by Carlos Gardel. Paradoxically, both become, over time, parodic icons of a national identity. Moreover, each of the songs has its own history of mix-ups and clashing requests. "Anclao en París," with music by Guillermo Barbieri, was composed by Enrique Cadícamo in 1931 in Barcelona, recalling Montmartre and the life of Argentine musicians in Paris. Gardel recorded it in Paris in 1931. Cadícamo recounts the following in his memoirs:

> My imagination flew back to Montmartre, where I remembered having seen some young fellow Argentines making anchor there and getting their start in the cruel task of "running that gauntlet" and to whom I was always able to toss a few Francs to help them get by on. That could be the theme for those tango lyrics. I asked the waiter for a large coffee and a cognac, lit a "black market" Aristón and got to writing a few verses that I continued ruminating on and that in a single shot, in less than an hour I had and titled "Anclao en París."[37]

The song, nevertheless, does not speak of others, but rather announces in the first person:

> Thrown about by the life of an errant bohemian
> I am, Buenos Aires, anchored in Paris.
> Drowning in troubles, chased by pressure,
> I evoke you, from this distant land.
> I watch the snow falling softly
> from my window, over the boulevard:
> the reddish lights, with a dying tone,
> they look like pupils of a strange stare.
>
> Distant Buenos Aires, how lovely you must be!
> It's already ten years since you saw me shore off . . .
> Here, in this Montmartre, sentimental faubourg,
> I feel memory stab me with its dagger.

How much your Corrientes Street must have changed! . . .
Suipacha, Esmeralda, those poor outskirts of your own! . . .
Someone told me you are in bloom
And that a set of streets crisscrosses around you . . .
You can't know how much I want to see you!
Here I am, stranded, no money and no faith . . .
Who knows if one night death might not imprison me
And, good-bye Buenos Aires, I'll never see you again![38]

"Disseram que Eu Voltei Americanizada" was composed at Carmen Miranda's request by Vicente Paiva and Luiz Peixoto, on their first trip back to Brazil after a long stay in the United States. At the Da Urca casino, Carmen Miranda sang "South American Way," among other songs, and was cooly received by the upper-middle-class audience that frequented the casino. According to the numerous accounts that exist regarding this episode, she left the stage in tears and that same night asked her composer to write her a song with which to respond to that audience. The following night she debuted the new song on the same stage:

They said I came back all Americanized
loaded with money
that I'm very rich
that I can't stand the sound of the tambourine anymore
and that hearing a *cuíca* gives me the chills
and they said that, with my hands,
I'm worried
and run around and about
that I know a certain *zum zum*
that I no longer have salsa, or rhythm or anything
and of my trinkets none is left.

But, tell me, why such poison?
can I become Americanized?
me, who was born with samba and who live in the open air
the whole night long with the old batucada
In the *malandro* circles that are my favorite
And I always say *te amo* and never *I love you*
As long as Brazil exists,
When it comes time to eat,
I'm for the shrimp stew with *chuchu*![39]

In one song after another, the journey figures as a space that cannot erase the memory nor the identity of the traveler, sustained in certain characteristics that are only autochthonous because they are associated clearly with the world of tango and samba: Corrientes Street, the "shrimp stew with *chuchu*," the poor outskirts. These songs propose that the journey does not erase national identity but rather seems, through nostalgia, to highlight its traits.

2

EXERCISES OF CONTAINMENT AND LOSS

É tempo de partido;
tempo de homens partidos.
(Now is the time of partisanship
the time of men enduring partition.)

Carlos Drummond de Andrade

Some novels published during the 1920s and 1930s in Brazil and Argentina that deal with the world of samba and tango illustrate a tension that also can be perceived in many of the lyrics of these song forms. A vacillation between *costumbrismo* (mannerism) and *fragmentarismo* (fragmentarism) can be seen in the mannerist representation of typical characteristics of the national—and the relevant scenarios, characters, moralities, sentimentalities, and intrigues from the world of tango or samba—and a certain impossibility of narrating that national identity that would crystallize in those cultural forms. Given the mannerist impulse of these worlds, permeated by a violent transformation wrought by the loss of certain traditional values, tango and samba act simultaneously as repertoires of national typicality or autochthony and as modern forms wherein one perceives the hint of implacable corruption of national culture.

Milonguitas (Loose Women) and Malandros (Malefactors): Modernity and National Identity

The female fulfills a fundamental role in that articulation, at the same time innocent victim of the corruption brought about by men who harass women and end up seducing them, and as the perpetrator of corruption throughout the fabric of society. In this way, tango and samba are put forth in novels as evidence of the criminal record of a modernization that is corrupting of "pure" national characteristics. The modernization that is "photographed" (I will return to the documentary character of these stories further on) in those national worlds of tango and samba supposes the corruption of a national identity while also exhibiting the national and characteristic version—autochthonous, mannerist—of that modernization. At issue is a modernity with clear characteristics that are one's own and that also belong to the nation, autochthonous and at the same time modern. This is a national modernity.

The intrigue that unifies these novels parallels the stories narrated in tango and samba lyrics, which these novels seem to overwrite; they are stories of social mobility and social transformation, seen through a critical lens, even when that criticism is cloaked in irony, which is especially the case in samba lyrics.

Recalling Araripe Júnior and his notion of "tropical style" to refer to Azevedo,[1] it would be fitting to speak of a "hot realism" in these novels (and the recurrence of sexual scenes in them has to do precisely with that heat). The dispassionate state of the "scientific" narrator who seeks to know reality, or of the conscious distance imposed by the Flaubertian narrator, is less at stake than is a realism overflowing with the very stuff of which the story is made. Tango and samba lyrics infect literature with their melodramaticism in a kind of discursive contagion; literature interprets those lyrics, develops them narratively, but ultimately remains trapped in their net, unable to take distance from them or to leave them. The novels end up seduced by the tango and samba they intend to criticize, and this leads to the undoubtedly ambivalent—which is not the same as saying ambiguous—representation of these forms. Being equally critical as the lyrics themselves, the novels, in their social denunciation, cannot stop functioning as ascertainment of a transformed reality. The dislocation of realism exhibited by the novels should be read as a cultural fact. More than a defect or an inability of the authors, the dislocation of realism demonstrates reality exceeding the form. Form is, thus, in Foucault's use of the term, the best document of cultural context.

In the offbeat functioning of a mannerist realism, countered by a fragmentarism that undermined coherence in the realist novel, one can read the tension between modernity and nation distilled in the novels, tangos, and sambas of the era. If the attempt to represent the nation can no longer lead to narrative cohesion, this is because the modern character of that identity and its national typicality or autochthony are equally important, and both seem to enter into a tension that is only resolved by the formal irresolution itself that the novels exhibit. Moreover, this modernity entails the need to construct an identity on the basis of disparate fragments, often unrelated and pervaded by difference. It has thus been treated as a sort of aborted realism, and perhaps precisely in that elimination lies its triumph: inasmuch as the novels seek to document a national reality, the appeal to these strategies responds to a mannerist narrative impulse; inasmuch as the cultural space in which that realism must be evoked appears pervaded by difference, their mannerist strategies are ultimately interrupted by a fragmentarism that cannot be sutured and incorporated in the construction of a single and united, coherent national identity. If tango and samba are conceived of in some discourses as symbols of a national identity, that identity is inevitably contested, principally from other spaces external to the influence of the cities of Buenos Aires and Rio de Janeiro, where tango and samba were born. These musical forms were thought of exclusively as a city phenomenon, and their supposed representivity of outlying areas was often strongly questioned.

I am interested in examining some novels that are paradigmatic of this disparity and its relationship to some tango and samba lyrics: the novels by Manuel Gálvez about lower-class areas of Buenos Aires, *Nacha Regules* (1919) and *Historia de Arrabal* (A History of the Periphery) (1922), and their relationship with the *milonguita* tradition in tango lyrics, and *A Estrela Sobe* (The Star Is Rising) (1937) by Marques Rebelo, which recovers the descriptive vision of the samba neighborhoods of Rio de Janeiro and their world as razed by modernization, a theme that also appears in various samba lyrics. With that narrative gesture of passing through the city's different neighborhoods, *A Estrela Sobe* recovers not only the tradition of the urban novel that had been practiced in Rio de Janeiro since the nineteenth century (from Almeida to João do Rio), but also that of the great writer of modernization in Rio de Janeiro, Machado de Assis.

The novels find in the city a mixture of modernity and national autochthony that the narratives succeed at articulating through the unique combination of national inventory and narrative irresolution. As collection, summary, and list, the novels operate via accumulation and redundancy—of "exemplary" stories, of "typical" characters, of paradigmatic situations—that do not seem to transform into the articulation of a convincing plot, as in the case of *A Estrela Sobe*, whose story does not so much end as it is interrupted, or the case of *Nacha Regules* and *Historia de Arrabal*, the endings of which are determined by random chance and coincidence, which dismantles any realist proposal to articulate a meaning that would have been progressively constructed over the course of the narrative and that the ending would only have had to make explicit.[2] Narrative unity is supplanted by a movement of redundancy, a repetition of situations and stories that, on abolishing narrative time, replace the horizontality of a plot with the verticality of the list and the inventory.

Hence, the plotline is reduced to the recounting of a movement, a contingent and random displacement. Almost all the narrative situations that transform the story in the novels, that shift the direction of the plotline and, in doing so, construct it, work by converting random chance and contingency into episode. The story is focused on a feminine protagonist's movement across the city, a character who, on penetrating into the world of tango and samba (often at the behest of a male *malandro,* or malefactor, who corrupts the female protagonists), ends up being constructed in the narrative as a "lost woman." More than novels of formation (bildungsroman), these are novels of *de*formation or, to use a term more in accord with the concerns of the age, of *degeneration.* These novels present fact as event and are less concerned about the chain of events in a plot whose meaning would be constructed diachronically.[3]

Realism's typical third-person narrator often insists on some distance, fundamental for the construction of a more or less credible notion of objectivity, with respect to the world he is narrating. Such that, in the case of *A Estrela Sobe,* the narrator carves a space for his voice in the margin, in the notes at the bottom of the page, or even within parentheses. That formal device is evidence of a narrative decision revealed in the absence of plot: the impossibility or the negation on the part of the narrator to intercede as articulator.

The figuration of tango and samba in these novels is ambivalent. Both appear in different social spaces—they are habitually enjoyed in these novels by not only the lower classes, but also the middle and upper classes—and have their "moral" value ascribed to them via their fluctuating figuration in those divergent spaces. In *Nacha Regules,* for example, tango is clearly the music of the cabaret, a convening space for different social classes, and for that reason it was at times valued negatively as a violent musical form that promoted vice, and at other times as a libertarian musical form with a special sensitivity. In *Historia de Arrabal*, tango is what Linda dances with "el Chino," the degenerate malefactor, as well as with Daniel Forti, the righteous anarchist. In *A Estrela Sobe*, samba is the music of the radio; it reaches all houses and all social classes, and it can be heard not only in private spaces but also flooding into the public space of restaurants and cafés.[4]

In all these cases we are dealing with urban novels that map out the city, describing a constant movement across the topography of Buenos Aires or Rio de Janeiro. The outskirts, the marginal areas and boundaries, are their privileged places. When they describe the center of the city, it is hesitantly, as if the protagonists had arrived there on the run from the places that actually corresponded to them. Indeed, the protagonists do escape from their "natural" place: their homes in the poor outlying areas. The setting of these novels is eminently public; on telling the story of a "public" woman, they replace the private space of the house with the public space of the café, cabaret, brothel, or factory, or for certain private spaces that have something of the public about them, such as the *garçonnière* or *bulín* (well-furnished, classy bachelor apartments used for "encounters"). Yet, beyond the public scenarios of open-air squares, trolleys, movie theaters, radio stations, cafés, bars, taverns, tenement houses, bordellos, and hospitals, the novels weave an urban trajectory by way of those diverse public points in the city. From Belgrano to Barracas, or from Bairro da Saúde to Lapa, the novels not only describe the movement of their protagonists around and about the urban topography, but they also progressively narrate the possibility of that movement and the city as the space of mobility. Hence we have the constant figuration of means of transportation—an abundance of trolleys, omnibuses, local buses, cars, taxis, and trains—signifiers of mobility that are also associated with technological modernity. This mobility, however, is neither easy nor free; neither in material terms of the money that is lost and gained, the fortune that is squandered or dreamed of, nor in moral terms of the virtue that is lost, the ideology that is transformed, the values that are discarded.

Milonguitas of the Poor Outskirts

As in a sort of musical modulation, *Nacha Regules* is recognized as a story about the world of tango that draws on various tango lyrics in circulation during the years the novel was being written. Especially in the chapters in which the documentary impulse is intensified, in which the narrative becomes less a novel about the protagonist Nacha and resembles more of a social chronicle, the insertion of tango lyrics illustrates a documentary pressure that sustains itself on redundancy. In the chapters that describe in condensed fashion some of Nacha's friends, the women's stories are recognized as having been narrated, during those years, by tangos such as "Flor de Fango" (Flower of the Mud) or "Francesita" (Little French Girl); the story of the *milonguita*, the young woman who, betrayed by her handsome gentleman suitor, leaves her neighborhood—or her country, as in the case of the French girl—to "lose herself in the life" of the tango. Nacha's story melodramatically exaggerates, if such a thing is possible, the tango lyrics themselves, wherein resides its often greatest documentarism. The story of Julieta in *Nacha Regules*, for example, introduces an issue that was not uncommon in the lives of the prostitutes in the world of tango, yet never surfaces in tango lyrics: abortion—although tangos did narrate other equally illegal zones such as drugs and delinquency.[5]

The tangos about the *milonguita* also speak of spaces in continual transformation and of women on the threshold of perdition. Though not explicitly, that tradition is already presumed in what is often considered the first tango song, "Mi Noche Triste" (My Sad Night) (1917). Pascual Contursi, who wrote that tango, that same year also composed "Flor de Fango," whose lyrics initiate the tradition of the *milonguita* explicitly. One of the countless disputes about the origins of tango inevitably concerns the identity of the first tango song, and even if "Mi Noche Triste" usually wins the debates, the polemic is interesting precisely because it proposes the birth of the tango song as simultaneous to that of the tango about the *milonguita*. The principal rival of "Mi Noche Triste" for that first-place spot is none other than "Milonguita" by Samuel Linning and Enrique Delfino, recorded in 1920. While "Mi Noche Triste" appeared by chance when Contursi's verses were added to preexisting music by Castriotta that had originally borne the title "Lita," "Milonguita," on the other hand, arose intentionally as a tango song, with words and music produced together. The second rival is none other than "Flor de Fango," which some believe was recorded by Gardel even before "Mi Noche Triste," though it did not come out for sale until two years later.[6]

If "Flor de Fango" functions as a denunciation of the morality of the world of tango on recounting the catastrophic result of that behavior, it nonetheless neither silences nor conceals that other morality. What is more, this tango,

structured like a hypothetical dialogue that blocks out the voice of the woman
being addressed, indicates another possible story or perspective, the responses
of which are pointed out in the dialogue form's own marks:

> Girl, I just recognized you a while ago
> sorry if I let the word out on you
> that I was there when you were born . . .
> Your cradle was a tenement
> lit by kerosene lamps.[7]

That answer is in the detailed description the tango makes of that other morality:

> In your fourteenth April
> you gave yourself over to the parties,
> a tango's delights . . .
> you went in for jewels,
> fashionable dresses
> and champagne bashes.
>
> Later you were the little girlfriend
> of a ridiculous old druggist,
> and the son of a police commissioner
> took all the money off you . . .
> Your decline began,
> you hocked the jewels
> rented a little room
> in a boarding house.
>
> You became a tawdry singer,
> went through strange times
> and got cheated on so often
> you ended up without a heart.[8]

A different morality and a transgression that are, clearly, condemned because
of their failure:

> Your life was like an iris . . .
> of all the distress and torment
> a single weight was too much for you . . .
> you didn't have a single comfort in the world

you never had your own mother's love.
You were a lovely girl child of the mud
and a tango's delights
dragged you from your room
those friends deceived you
and even they lost you
night after night partying.

Girl, I just recognized you a while ago
sorry if I let the word out on you
that I was there when you were born . . .
Your cradle was a tenement
lit by kerosene lamps.
In your fourteenth April
you gave yourself over to the parties,
a tango's delights . . .
you went in for jewels,
fashionable dresses
and champagne bashes.[9]

The circularity of this tango, both in the story and in formal terms, can close
off the discourse but not divest it of that other morality. The final chorus repeats the first verse but is not used, as so many choruses in tango are, to
cut the music. The reasons for that other morality will appear in the tango
whose lyrical subject is the woman, as in "La Mina del Ford" (The Girl and
the Ford), from 1924, also written by Pascual Contursi in collaboration with
Enrique P. Maroni and recorded by Gardel that same year.[10] As an articulation of a supposed feminine desire, the three symmetrical verses begin with
the syntagma "I want":

I want a rented room
that has balconies,
very long curtains
made of crepe silk . . .
Watch the fat cats
passing by in droves,
to see if any bum
says to me: How you doing! . . .

I want a rented room
with a polished floor,
that has a little rug
to walk on.
Leather armchairs
everything *embossed*
and a cheeky parrot
that knows how to sing . . .

I want a bed
that has a spread . . .
and I want a heater
to get warm . . .
and for the butler to come in
running in a hurry
to say: Ma'am!
Watch out! The Ford is here . . . [11]

Feminine desire? The title, "La Mina del Ford," proposes a double interpretation. If one refers in third person to that "*mina*" (term in argot for "young
woman") who would be the lyrical subject of the tango itself, then the title necessarily introduces another person, showing, in the irony with which that supposed feminine desire is articulated, an interference in the lyrics of this tango.
Indeed, when sung by a man, as it often was, the lyrics must insert the mascu-
line voice into the recitation, as done in the version that Gardel sang in 1924:

[That's why the dame, bored
with enduring the life I provided her,
grabbed the trunk one night
and went off singing this way:]

I want a rented room
that has balconies,
very long curtains
made of crepe silk . . .
watch the rich cats
passing by in droves,
to see if any bum
says to me: How you doing! . . .

I want a rented room
with a polished floor,
that has a little rug
to walk on.
Leather armchairs
everything *embossed*
and a cheeky parrot
That knows how to sing . . .

[Well what do you say about this *milonga*'s pretensions?
A parrot, embossed armchairs, a Ford . . .
And I can't even hit one winner, penniless, can't even get back from the tracks
And at the end she still comes to me with this:]

I want a bed
that has a spread . . .
and I want a heater
to get warm . . .
and for the butler to come in
running in a hurry
to say: Ma'am!
Watch out! The Ford is here . . .

[Cheers, Garibaldi,
let some other fellow put up with this corpse
what I am, I go][12]

Yet, the tradition of the *milonguita*, while conceivably summed up as the denunciation of social mobility, also has success stories. "Muñeca Brava" (Tough
Doll) makes this explicit:

Hey lady who speaks in French
now you laugh at my backwards way of talking
but someday you'll come back disillusioned and with no faith
and then I'll be the one saying to you
hey, tough doll, how you doing.

Hey lady who speaks in French
and throwing money around with both hands
dining with well-chilled champagne

and in tango your dreams will entangle
you are a sweetcake of very curly lashes
tough doll fetching top dollar
you are from the Trianon de Vill
what a vampire plaything you are
you have a banker who treats you to little pleasures
And twenty Aprils are fleet-footed
and your coin purse is bursting to skip from north to south
they all rat you out, tough doll
because you run circles around fools without a lie
for me you're always the one who didn't know
how to hold on to a piece of youthful love
from me who always dreamed of your affection
and back in the neighborhood I loved you as a kid
but why bother, with empty pockets, bringing up those things
since you doll have already changed your heart.[13]

The tradition of tangos about lost *milonguitas* includes tangos that, like this one, tell of success in that social mobility, although success is seen from a condemning position regarding the crossing of boundaries.

Gálvez' novels depict the poor through separate and opposite geographical spaces, among which there is no uniformity, nor any easy connections or communications.[14] The distance between those spaces is marked in the text by the narrative gap between events and by the immense difficulty the characters have in passing from one space to another. Characters from opposite spaces must overcome numerous restrictions to be able to meet with one another. They must intentionally seek each other out in the populous urban geography they inhabit, where the only figures they meet by chance are those who belong to the same social space by natural right or by design, as seen in Monsalvat's encounter with the wealthy women who do charity work in the tenement house, or with Dr. Torres in the street, or on the way to the café where a ladies' orchestra is performing.

Those disconnected spaces cannot even be narrated with the same language. On passing into the world of prostitution, in the case of *Nacha Regules*, or of prostitution and delinquency, in the case of *Historia de Arrabal*, even the language changes with the incorporation of words in Lunfardo slang or other popular ways of speaking, be that the broken Spanish of the Italian immigrants, the French accent of those of that origin, or the lower-class intonation full of grammatical errors.

In tango, the paths sketched out are usually two-way, and guilt falls not to the *bacán* (wealthy gentleman) but to the *mina* (young woman) herself, accused of being pretentious and overambitious and whose very ambition is what drives her to perdition. Contrasted with the feminine victimization in Gálvez' novels—a characterization that corresponds perfectly with the irrationalism of their antiheroines—a calculating ambition imbues the women of tango.

In *Nacha Regules*, the world of the prostitutes—which is confused, almost, with that of any woman of the lower class or who has come down in economic status—is seen as "the catacombs of the subterranean world,"[15] antiheroines and entering it has a high price: "But those hellish circles were not for the first-comer to traverse with impunity. Montsalvat had to bear mockery, humiliation, insult. In some of those houses his money was taken; in one he was robbed. More than once he was not allowed entry, and they shut the door on him throwing invectives and foul language at his back."[16] The encounter takes place only once the novel has, symbolically, erased the differences: the house where Monsalvat finds Nacha "was an old family home, democratized into small rentals; the room, on the highest floor and overlooking the street, was occupied immediately by Monsalvat. Thus, when he appeared in his lady friend's room, he was already a resident of the house."[17]

Those spaces, so rigidly airtight and opposed to each other, are nonetheless constantly traversed; the story consists precisely in establishing that crossing from one space to the other and in making that passage insistently. The movement is constant, both among the characters and in the storyline itself, which seems foolishly indecisive and unable to settle on the development of a narrative situation. Instead, it insists nervously on putting forward new ones, which often are nothing more than the same situations repeated to the point of exhaustion: Monsalvat and Nacha find each other only fleetingly; Nacha is "regenerated" only to "fall into vice" again on a back-and-forth journey that repeats at least four times; Monsalvat "is strong in his love of goodness, but he doubts"; Nacha flees the house run by Pampa Arnedo, the *cafishio* (pimp) who corrupted her, only to desire "irrationally" to return to him.

That same nervousness in the storyline is repeated in *Historia de Arrabal*, where Linda, the "antiheroine heroine," is a simple and good girl who is, however, transformed into a prostitute and a bloodthirsty murderess with circuitous ways who makes sustained though inconstant attempts to flee. In situations and spaces, in their characters and plots, the tango novels are novels of movement, of the constant crossing of boundaries and limits, of repeated transgressions; hence the "irruption" scenes in which the idea of penetration is an assiduous concept and, while not explicitly related to sexual penetration, it functions clearly to metaphorize a type of relationship between the genders. A scene with Eugenia, Monsalvat's sister, illustrates this:

> Arnedo took her hand at the same time as he *drilled his gaze into her* and ordered:
> "Stay!"
> "They might come. . . ."
> "I don't care. I have seen you and it has driven me mad," he exclaimed, with simulated rapture.[18]

Or in *Historia de Arrabal*, "el Chino" pursues Linda with his gaze:

> The malefactor had drilled his gaze into Linda's eyes and looked as if he wanted to *penetrate her*. For a moment she resisted that dominating, dark, brutal gaze *that beat on her feminine eyes like a physical thing, that penetrated her face like two knives*, that had something incomprehensible she could not define, something fatal, something horribly perturbing.[19]

The Chronicle of the Symbol

A Estrela Sobe tells the story of Leniza, about a woman but principally a *type* of woman that was extremely important in the 1930s, as much for being a novelty as for being so typically Brazilian: the female samba singer.[20] The story of the protagonist is interrupted, however, because of a certain oscillation in the text between the chronicle—the realist recording of spaces, types of persons, and neighborhoods—and the narrative story that is never strongly articulated. Raúl Antelo had already observed "the composite character" of Marques Rebelo's creation and how much that character conspired against the articulation of a narration. According to Antelo, "the form that suits the relationship between writer and reality is that of fixing what cannot be apprehended: snapshots. With narration impossible—time was abolished—social life is described."[21]

For this reason the novel is as much about the city of Rio de Janeiro, un-disputed protagonist of many of Marques Rebelo's texts, as about the female samba singer.[22] Inasmuch as it is a portrait of Rio's neighborhoods, the novel corresponds to an entire tradition of self-referential sambas that speak about life in the city. The *malandro* or rogue character is another typical subject of samba lyrics. Moreover, the lyrics describe a world undergoing transformation also apparent in the process of modernization of samba, as seen in the adopting of a different rhythmic pattern, which Carlos Sandroni called "Estácio's paradigm." This categorization corresponds quite precisely with that of the samba-samba, by Luiz Tatit, as "the one that elevates the virtues of the genre itself."[23] While the lyrics speak of a world on the brink of disappearance that is identified with the abandonment of *"a malandragem"* (the roguish life), the music accentuates the syncopes and the references to instruments of African origin that define the more modern samba.[24]

Samba lyrics figure fundamentally in Marques Rebelo's chronicles, many of which are merely elaborations of those lyrics.[25] In the novel, however, the opposite seems to be true: the numerous samba titles it mentions do not exist and instead seem to be predicted by Leniza's story. When, for example, Leniza discovers that she will not be paid for singing sambas on the radio and sees her dream of triumph and fame destroyed, at that moment she hears on the radio, by coincidence, a samba titled "Foi um Sonho e Nada Mais" (It Was Only a Dream).[26] The novel, in fact, is only in a very marginal way about the world of samba; rather, it is a text in which the *movement* of samba functions as cartographic inspiration.

More map than novel, the plot of *A Estrela Sobe* is built on the protagonist's trajectory and movement through the neighborhoods of Rio de Janeiro while treating her story secondarily. Leniza is portrayed as a lost woman in a double sense of the word, first for having sexual relations with several men and even a woman with the sole objective of raising her social status. This social mobility is accompanied by a gradual fragmentation of the narrative that follows her progressive isolation with respect to her original world—her family, the boarding house—but also with respect to any other new world that would replace that original one. She ends, finally, literally lost in the multitude: "She walks like a blind woman through the crowd. It is the multitude that carries her, that drags her, like an irresistible current that leaves her, without a destiny, on every street corner."[27]

While in the beginning of the novel the omniscient narrator accompanies Leniza as she wanders in the city and in her fantasies, after she has a nearly fatal abortion the narrator disappears almost completely. The novel then adopts the structure of a highly impersonal diary—the dates of the events are incorporated as a kind of punctuation and break in the text—the narrative point of view of which is no longer clearly identifiable. The disappearance of the narrator produces a textual displacement whereby situations crucial to the development of the narrative are only insinuated. Toward the ending, after Leniza has been abandoned even by her own mother, the narrator returns to his function as the provider of meaning and sense, but only to confess that he has lost the protagonist: *"Here I end Leniza's story. I have not abandoned her, but, as a novelist, I lost her. I still, nevertheless, find myself thinking about that poor soul as weak and miserable as mine. I tremble: what will become of her, in the inevitable balance of life, if a light from heaven does not descend to illuminate the other side of her vanities?"*[28]

This narrator who abandons the protagonist, this novel lacking an ending and almost truncated by the disappearance of its main character, exposes a narrator's role that is present in several moments of the novel and makes the novel itself an instance of chronic fragmentarism. This is a narrator who chooses to hide his voice between parentheses or in footnotes, which contribute plot information withheld from the story itself as well as his own subjective observations and judgments about the narrative situations. The proliferation of ellipses marking the absence of continuity between one scene and the next in many cases makes explicit a narrative strategy that prefers the displacement of the narrator over "mystification," as in this quotation: "Doing his best, the author is deeply sorry for his weakness about such a strong fragment as this and most of the fragments that follow. In compensation, he refrained from using mystifying resources that would cater to naive readers."[29] The predominance of brief phrases connected paratactically defines the story as much as the city and its neighborhoods. Both zones combine to construct an image of modernity in which subject and city are confused, a figure in which the subject is lost in the city and the multitude.

When the waiter arrived with their order, she was on her way out. Mario Alves left two thousand reis on the table and followed her. They were lost in the multitude. It was very late at night. Neon sign spots were glowing. The trams, packed; the buses, full. Blaring of claxons, stampeding, bells, screeching of brakes, steel blinds falling closed with a crash like machine guns. There is a mob and the vociferating of pedestrians, the sensational shouting of newspaper venders, a hot stench of gasoline. They walk, as quickly as they can, through the human wave. They don't speak. They see a corner. The stoplight is

illuminated with a blood-red eye. Leniza felt her legs weaken and topple. She
felt something passing over her eyes, a cloud filled with brightly lit points.[30]

Like the arbitrary pattern in a mosaic comprised of encounters and divergences, on the basis of that parataxis the novel constructs a figure of modernity in Rio de Janeiro that, without ceasing to manifest its accentuated
autochthonous quality, does not, however, spend time on the construction of
a national identity.

Modern and National

In these novels, the simultaneous figuration of tango and samba as national
and modern forms produces a condensation that elides formal, symbolic unity
in the narrative structure. The formal irresolution of these novels, in their oscillation between chronicle and attempted narration of a story—the ending
and resolution of which, nevertheless, either remains open-ended or finalizes
hastily in random chance and contingency—seems to harbor a dialogue that
these novels share with tango and samba. At issue here is a figure of the nation
that, on setting itself forth as modern, cannot be constructed as a compact,
cohesive, unique, and general whole. The meanings of that combination of the
national and the modern—of that combination of novel and chronicle—appear
as liminal products that negotiate their meanings in dissimilar spaces without attempting, or achieving, a homogenization of both spaces. If samba and
tango can figure as much in an elegant salon as over a radio broadcast in a dark
boardinghouse, or be heard as much in brothels or *garçonnieres* as in national
theaters and luxurious cafés, the listening is, in each case, a particular and differentiated mode, a function of each specific contextual situation in which nation figures as vector of modernity in the tension between documentary and
realism.

Hence, tango and samba figure as forms of the national that those narratives attempt to represent, and at the same time they appear also as signifiers
of the modernization that Argentine and Brazilian societies were undergoing
during that period. Yet, the novels do not seem to be able to bring the narrative cycle to a close and reestablish social cohesion and unity. Even when reference is made to those "national symbols," they seem able to represent only
the cracks, conflicts, and differences that comprise nation.

On mapping the city, these novels insist on not ever showing a homogeneous space, nor do they attempt to condense the nation. In this sense, the

novels present an interesting paradox. They seek to register in an almost documentary fashion the typical customs and situations of a period and of a city. But on taking up the worlds of tango and samba as paradigmatic forms of the nation, all of them ultimately break with one of nineteenth-century realism's more preemptory conditions: the articulation of meaning and the idea of totality, or, to use the words of Bersani, "the containment of fragmentation."[31] Instead of representing the national symbol, these novels show the city's heterogeneity and signal, through different mechanisms, the fragmentation of experience and of narration. Thus, the novels undermine the realist and representational narrative that puts itself forth as a chronicle of the national symbol. In one way or another, all of them break with certain realist prerequisites upon which, however, they are assumed to have been constructed.

PRIMITIVE CINEMA AND MODERNITY

In *L'Eve Future* (Tomorrow's Eve) by Villiers de l'Isle Adam, written two years before Thomas Edison began his research on animated photography, the protagonist describes a new invention that makes the following possible:

> the transparent vision, miraculously caught in color photography, wore a spangled costume as she danced a popular Mexican dance. Her movements were as lively as those of life itself, thanks to the procedures of successive photographs, which can record on its microscopic glasses six minutes of action to be projected on the screen with a powerful lampascope. [...] Suddenly a voice, rather flat and stiff, a hard, dull voice, was heard; the dancer was singing the *alza* and the *olé* of her fandango.[1]

André Bazin saw in that novel the myth that guided the invention of cinema and dominated all the techniques for the reproduction of reality during the nineteenth century, from photography to the phonograph: "an integral realism, a recreation of the world in its own image, an image unburdened by the freedom of interpretation of the artist or the irreversibility of time."[2]

Even prior to the invention of the technology required for that utopia of *L'Eve Future*, in almost all the arts during the second half of the nineteenth century, and in conjunction with that realist impulse, "the conversion of the anonymous into an object of art" functioned as the precondition for the development of the mechanical arts. According to Jacques Rancière, one would have to turn the proposed formula around:

In order for the mechanical arts to be able to confer visibility on the masses, or rather on anonymous individuals, they first need to be recognized as arts. That is to say that they first need to be put into practice and recognized as something other than techniques of reproduction or transmission. It is thus the same principle that confers visibility on absolutely anyone and allows for photography and film to become arts. We can even reverse the formula: it is because the anonymous became the subject matter of art that the act of recording such a subject matter can be an art. [. . .] On the one hand, the technological revolution comes after the aesthetic revolution. On the other hand, however, the aesthetic revolution is first of all the honour acquired by the commonplace, which is pictorial and literary before being photographic or cinematic.[3]

That increase in value of the anonymous entails, in addition, another characteristic that was central in the history of cinema and that is also present in the invention of that character by Villiers de l'Isle Adam: the increase in value of the popular and the conversion of the popular into an aesthetic object. In fact, in cinema's first stuttered articulations, the appeal to the popular is central. The circus, the mime, and the popular theater supplied the first films not only with characters and performers, actors and directors, impresarios and costume designers, but also—and very fundamentally—with narrative structures and forms of organization for cinematographic discourse; hence the preeminence of certain popular genres such as the melodrama, the farce, or the "romance."[4] That relationship appears in *L'Eve Future* encoded in the Mexican dance.[5]

But in the utopia of *L'Eve Future* there is something more. The subject of the filming described in the novel is nothing more and nothing less than a woman dancing, using the new invention that seeks precisely to capture the combination of movement and sound that had eluded the non–mechanical arts. Perhaps a Mexican dance was chosen because there is in cinema a voyeuristic desire for which exoticism is central. In the quotation from Villiers de l'Isle Adam, exoticism is both central and exaggerated, with the *olé* and the fandango functioning as justification for the invention. Together with the almost scientific description of the technology, plagued with technical terms, the sensual amazement is prompted by the sheen of the spangled dress, the dancer's transparent skin, and her exotic *olé*.

That combination of exoticism, voyeurism, modernity, and popular culture present in cinema's first moments formed a set of preconditions that was widely exploited for the development of national cinematography in Argentina and Brazil. The first Argentine and Brazilian films, even before sound movies, appealed to the worlds of tango and samba. Silent films counted on the presence of musicians to play in the salons where the films were projected, thus providing one of the paths for professionalization of bohemian tango and samba musicians who until that time were only able to play, in Argentina, in *peringundines* (low-class dance venues) or, in Brazil, in the *terreiros* (yards) of the homes of their Bahian relatives. Many of the audience members went to those shows less for the films than for the music that was played in the movie halls and which the middle-class audience members, especially women, could not experience in its other, more typical contexts that were, per the suppositions of the day, of plainly dubious moral character.

Those first tango and samba films, clearly episodic, take place in a kind of flat, empty space that enables the artists' performance to be exhibited and captured. The lax narrative structure of the musical theater revue, in Brazil, and the *sainete* (one-act farce, comedy sketch), in Argentina, which these early films feed off of, facilitates a certain arrest of the narrative in the pure visuality and sonority of the artist's performance, whereby the cinema is in those films more "visuality" and less "grammar."[6] Yet, also on show is the exposition, or exhibition, of technology itself, the great modern invention of cinema, that enables the observation and capture of those performances. Hence, the camera's point of view usually reproduces the camera obscura of the Renaissance perspective; the experimentation with a new "language" does not matter as much, in these moments, as the exploitation of an invention. Thus, those first films are semidocumentaries in that they maintain a kind of documentary impulse that is strongly articulated in the use of the front-camera angle and the *pintoresquista* (picturesque-style) description.

A news piece constituted the very first Argentine film, "Dr. Campos Salles' Visit to Argentina," filmed by Eugenio Py on October 25, 1900, as the Brazilian president disembarked and embraced the Argentine president Julio Argentino Roca. The first Brazilian film was "O Maxixe" (The Maxixe), made in 1897 by Víctor Maio. In those beginnings, not only is the presence of tango and samba substantive, but it also allows the filmmakers to lend a specific, national content to the visual dimension of that early cinema. In the case of Brazilian cinema, this visuality draws notably on the carnival and on the cinematographic adaptation of national novels such as *A Viuvinha* (The Little Widow), by José de Alencar.

In the case of Argentine cinema, in addition to the world of tango one observes a strong inspiration taken from episodes of Argentine history—as in Gallo's early films such as *El Fusilamiento de Dorrego* (The Execution of Dorrego), *La Revolución de Mayo* (The May Revolution), or *Güemes y Sus Gauchos* (Guemes and His Gaucho Cowboys). *Nobleza Gaucha* (Peasant Nobility) (1915), with a screenplay by José González Castillo and music by Francisco Canaro (two tango artists), exemplifies this tendency in its combination of both possibilities.[7] Paramount in this new medium is for cinema to make a reality visible, and in tango and samba Argentine and Brazilian cinema find both their originality and their raison d'être, as well as the possibilities for the construction of a national cinematography.[8]

The great development of national cinematographies arises with the feature-length sound films of singers and dancers from the worlds of tango and of samba, who inaugurate a specific genre for each country through which the respective incipient cinematographic traditions will progressively expand and evolve. With the advent of sound films, and before the development of subtitling and dubbing processes, the momentary displacement of Hollywood due to the language gap was taken advantage of in Latin American countries to galvanize a national industry that found in tango in Argentina, in the rancheras in Mexico, and in samba in Brazil the right bait to attract a Latin American audience. Moreover, tango was the product that foreign industries, especially Hollywood, later appropriated in order to conquer a Spanish-speaking audience.[9]

Tango in Argentina gave rise to the development of a specific cinematographic genre, the tango film or "tango opera," as Domingo Di Núbila called it.[10] On the other side of the border, samba and popular Brazilian music would lead to the construction of a genre that would also have a prolonged existence in the Brazilian tradition, the carnival film, which included the participation of one of the greatest names in the Brazilian cinematographic avant-garde, Humberto Mauro, with *Alô, Alô Carnaval*. This tradition would be one of the antecedents of the typically Brazilian genre, the *chanchadas*, which, even if it has its national origin in the carnival films, its constitution as a genre goes hand in hand with the Hollywood musical.[11]

The persistent relationship between the beginnings of a national cinematography in Argentina and Brazil and the materials of tango and samba is, on the one hand, an episode of that more general fascination that cinema has with popular culture. Yet, among the numerous examples of Argentine and Brazilian popular culture, the fact that the cinema of those countries has privileged tango and samba also has to do with those musical forms having been made into autochthonous national products. That visual and voyeuristic, documentary-oriented impulse in early cinema finds its raison d'être in what is specific. Hence, tango and samba, already autochthonous, are especially interesting to that early cinema.

In many cases, that relationship between tango and samba and cinema seems obvious: the producers of the recording industry themselves sought in cinema a medium for converting their singers into top roles in a future national star system. Especially two producers of the United States recording industry in Rio de Janeiro, Wallace Downey of Columbia and Leslie Evans of RCA Victor, attempted to convert their singers into movie stars by delving into the cinematographic industry. Downey opened a movie production firm and produced a series of films, first through Columbia itself and later in association with Cinédia studios, which were directed by Adhemar Gonzaga, impelling simultaneously the growth of filmmaking and of Brazilian popular music.[12] In the case of Argentina, similarly, entrepreneurs connected to the radio industry initiated one of the most productive cinematographic studios of the period, Lumiton, where the first films related to tango were produced.[13]

Yet, the relationship between popular music and cinema transcends that specific connection, principally if one analyzes the meaning those films attribute to that relationship. Humberto Mauro—along with Adhemar Gonzaga, who had no ties to the recording industry and who dreamed of a type of large-studio cinema—ended up, in contrast to that initial project, going outdoors to film carnival. Humberto Mauro seems to have been quite conscious of the need for, and the limitations of, a specifically national cinema, for which carnival would supply the material. In an article, he observed: "Filmmaking in Brazil will have to emerge from our Brazilian context, with all its qualities and defects . . . If North American cinema has already gotten us used to the luxury and the variety of its productions, it has still not robbed us of our natural enthusiasm for the faithful representation of everything that we are or wish to be."[14] The similarities between this position evinced by Humberto Mauro and Glauber Rocha's "Estética da Fome" speak to the success of an early solution that Brazilian filmmaking found for its peripheral situation, as much in the relationship of Cinema Novo as with the *chanchadas* (so evident, for example, in the case of *Macunaíma* by Joaquim Pedro de Andrade) and the documentary-oriented camera of the cinematographic newsreels. Even if the impossibility of developing that first industrial dream has its consequence in the early days of Brazilian cinematography, on the basis of that lack there arises a whole idea of national filmmaking, which will be important in the history of Brazilian cinema.[15]

Tango and samba were, thus, resources that cinema called on in response to the specifically Latin American challenge of developing a cinematographic industry in a context in which the incipient state of industrialization and film distribution impeded the development of a great film industry.

The Autochthonous as Emblem of Modernity

In contraposition to the pure visuality in the making of those films, already in the first Argentine and Brazilian feature-length films the strange atmosphere of modernity (introduced by the novelty of modern cinema's technological procedures) is combined almost always with a national, autochthonous content held in relation to the tango and samba stories narrated in these first films.

Tango!—the first Argentine feature-length sound film, made by Luis Moglia Barth in 1933—begins with images that combine technological modernity with the autochthonous neighborhood in a unique way.[16] Among the film's first shots, which function as a backdrop for the opening credits, an image appears that became, over time and with tireless repetition, one of Buenos Aires' most typical representations. In a full shot, framed by a view of the river and port of Buenos Aires, the large Riachuelo bridge functions as a double signifier by highlighting modernity in an industrial and technological context and by introducing an image of the Boca neighborhood that will remain in the future as the epitome of the autochthonous. The film will tell its story through the characters of the poor city outskirts, on a round-trip voyage between that neighborhood and Paris. Built out of iron just two years before the premier of this feature-length film, the Riachuelo bridge looms as Azucena Maizani sings a tango, and it also appears in the poster for *Riachuelo*, another film by Moglia Barth that features tangos.

The arrangement of the figures in the *Riachuelo* poster is significant and repeats a structure also seen in the *Tango!* poster. Moreover, the *Riachuelo* poster employs a picturesque-style colorfulness that contrasts the autochthonous characters with the frenetic port traffic—at least four ships are depicted in intense movement—indicative of the heightened commercial transit that modernization entails. In the black-and-white *Tango!* poster, modernization is projected in the profusion of skyscrapers framed and crisscrossed with the portraits of tango stars. That combination of modernity and popular culture articulates, in some tango and samba films, a narrative mechanism through which the popular is made into an emblem of modernity.

The first two feature-length films with Carlos Gardel (1890–1935) showed a progressive association of tango with an urban and modern identity. *Luces de Buenos Aires* (Lights of Buenos Aires) (1931) is structured on the opposing nature of country and city, in a double structure that allows it to negotiate the myriad meanings of tango represented in the film as well as urban modernity itself.[17] This feature-length film includes one of the typical characteristics of the melodramatic form, which the Hollywood musical borrowed from other genres, a binary structure of opposites between vice and virtue that presumes the confrontation of clearly identifiable antagonists and the ultimate expulsion of one of them.[18] That binarism is spatially distributed between two spheres and identities: the countryside, realm of innocence and purity, and the city, site of vice and depravation. To each of these spaces there corresponds

FIGURE 10. Film publicity poster for *Riachuelo*, 1934. Image from Claudio España, *Elena Goity, Ricardo Manetti, Cine Argentino: Industria y Clasicismo, 1933–1956* (Fondo Nacional de las Artes, 2000). Garramuño, *Modernidades Primitivas*, p. 217.

in the film a specific type of music: tango, representing the city and amorality, and peasant songs, associated with the morality and fidelity inscribed in the landscape of the *pampas* (central Argentine plains). While this is the initial adjudication of values that the film opens with, over the course of the narrative it is possible to observe a significant displacement whereby the film will have each of those binary poles progressively incorporate elements of its other.

Luces de Buenos Aires tells the story of a young peasant girl (Sofía Bozán) who is contracted by a businessman from the capital to sing in Buenos Aires. She abandons, in that change of place, her fiancé, who is none other than the ranch owner, played by Gardel. With a focus on this relationship, the film progressively weaves a plot of betrayals, ascents, and moral descents that are articulated in connection with tango. The journey to the city signifies the abandonment of her peasant roots, the economic ascent of the *chinita* (peasant girl) who now receives dresses and jewelry as gifts, as well as her moral descent. Her willful distancing from her roots goes hand in hand with her indifference toward her fiancé and a new adherence to illegitimate sexual relations.

Not only do tango songs and dances figure in that narrative, but also the story itself is a typical tango tale of a *milonguita* (loose or fallen woman), with the exception here of a happy ending owing precisely to the intervention of the countryside and its representatives. Toward the end, two fieldhands from the ranch who have gone to look for the *milonguita* find her singing on the stage of a Buenos Aires theater. They lasso her from the theater's box seats and end up forcing her to return to the country and integrate back into life in her habitat and with her fiancé, her original "owner." With this ending, the film would seem to respect the melodrama's operation of expelling one of the poles of the original binarism. However, the film's diegetic plot is interrupted by a series of performances by Gardel, with the resulting effect on the narrative of twisting, or at least lending complexity to, that story of "the triumph of good."

As a gaucho character, in those performances Gardel naturally sings peasant songs, and with that choice the film taps into several zones of the culture of the period. Gardel was already identified as a singer of tangos at the time of the film's premiere, yet his association with peasant music was not considered strange because he began his artistic career precisely with that kind of music. Moreover, his repertoire continued to include peasant songs even up to his last performances.[19] Nonetheless, one of Gardel's performances cannot be ascribed to that stage identity, and actually contradicts it. What Gardel sings toward the end of the movie is unmistakenly a tango. Even if the film links tango with the city, a connection that will definitively triumph in the history of tango, this association is in fact negotiated by the film.[20]

This association of tango with the city and the question of national identity as urban or rural forms the conflictive backdrop of this feature-length film. On the one hand, it seems clear that, in a mannerist gesture, the film allocates peasant songs to the country and tango to the city. The peasant identity is personified by Gardel, who sings the same song ("El Rosal" [The Rosebush]) three times. The city, in contrast, is represented by tango; a tango is what the disloyal *chinita* (peasant girl) sings in the downtown theater, and a tango dance party is the setting for one of the film's most dramatic moments: the scene of the *chinita*'s "perdition" in the context of a *casita* (little house) or *garçonnière* (bachelor's rented room).[21] It is precisely in a small house and to the tune of a tango that the moral descent of this character takes place: drunk, dazzled by the money and luxury, she loses her dress (literally ending up in nothing more than a slip) and delivers herself up to her new patron, the musical entrepreneur of spurious interests.

Curiously, though, tango also appears in a performance carried out by the ranch owner himself, Gardel, who after witnessing the betrayal of his former fiancée makes his way to a *peringundín* (low-class dance venue) in the port to drown his sorrows in alcohol. There, with the tango "Tomo y Obligo" (I Drink and I Oblige), he condemns a woman's betrayal. That denunciation is articulated in a tango in which Gardel's performance both enunciates and embodies gaucho morality and which makes references to the rural landscape in its lyrics ("*Si los pastos conversaran / esta pampa le diría*" [If the grass could talk / these pampa plains would tell him]).

While the film's plot poses country and city as opposites, the figure of Gardel, singing peasant songs as well as a tango, leads to a mediation between both spaces. Tango's amorality, associated with the city, is displaced in Gardel's performance with the female figure, cleansing tango of that amorality in a certain sense, since tango itself, the tango sung by Gardel, is the one that denounces and condemns such amorality. "Tomo y Obligo" condemns the amorality of the young woman and, on denouncing her, is itself "cleaned up."

From the tango dance to the tango song, *Luces de Buenos Aires* recounts the transformation of the initial meanings of country and city. Together with that transformation of the peasant song and what it represents, the film progressively lays down a pattern for a shift in tango; from symbol and perpetrator of amorality, the tango is converted into its accuser. It is no coincidence, in this sense, that the scene in which Gardel sings "Tomo y Obligo" in the common city dance hall would repeat and copy a previous scene in the country tavern, when Gardel sings "El Rosal." With this repetition, the film puts peasant songs and tango on the same level and, with them, country and city. Even if the movie ends with the return of the *chinita* to the countryside and the story seems to be that of the triumph of virtue, the countryside has been contaminated by tango's "indecency" and tango, in turn, has been cleansed by the "purity" of the singer, embodied by Gardel, both *tanguero* (tango character) and gaucho. Thus the film proposes toward the end a different image of tango and the city than the one it had started with.

Besides the country–city opposition and the peasant song–tango opposition, the film is also negotiating a fundamental contradiction about tango that surfaced during that period: between the tango that was sung and the *criollismo* that attempted to reclaim a criollo origin for tango. This is also the operation carried out by Borges, suggesting that his avant-garde urban *criollismo*, as Beatriz Sarlo puts it,[22] more than an individual operation, is a possible result of a cultural transformation at work at the heart of the modernizing nationalization of Argentine culture.

Melodía de Arrabal (Melody of the Periphery) (1932), Gardel's second film, tells the story of the ascent of a singer from working in a marginal, lower-class bar to performing in a downtown city theater. From the margin or shore to the center, in that displacement the transformation of tango is also recounted. However, by way of a series of formal tactics, the film chooses to narrate that process of transformation as the revelation of something that was hidden at the beginning; tango's modern identity would be, according to this tale, something that tango had concealed in its primitive origins.

From the beginning, Gardel's character in this film has a double identity: he is both Ramírez, a gambling deceitful *compadrito* (braggart), and Mr. Torres, the son of a wealthy landowner. Moreover, this urban character has a double, embodied perhaps by Gardel as the good *compadrito* and by Rancales as the bad *compadrito*, an accomplice to Ramírez from whom the latter "takes distance." I am interested in emphasizing that difference is set up within the same space/class; it is in the downtown bar and in the world of the poor urban outskirts that Ramírez objects to and opposes Rancales. Each represents a different side of tango, and the two places act as allies in a bond that, even within that same space, will give rise to a conflict. The law's representative becomes an accomplice of the crime. The scene in the bar ends precisely with Ramírez confronting Rancales in order to defend someone from outside the world of tango, a police inspector who is looking for Rancales. Ramírez/Torres will find himself involved in a murder despite his better intentions, slaying the bad *compadrito* and, symbolically, the bad side of tango. When the inspector looking for the murderer discovers that Torres is the same *compadrito* who at one point saved his life, he will forgive him and keep under wraps the secret of Torres' crime.

As regards the plot, the story that is constructed seems to address the social ascent and acceptance of tango, encoded in the story of Ramírez (Gardel), a singer working low-class venues on the outskirts of town but who by the end of the film achieves his triumph in a downtown theater. Yet, other meanings appear that are complementary to this tale of the social triumph of tango and its singer. When, in the final scenes of the film, the character played by Gardel sings "Melodía de Arrabal" in the downtown theater, he reiterates the performance he had already given in the marginal, low-class bar, when the police inspector observed him singing that same song. This second performance, in the theater in the center of the city, is framed by various shots of the inspector, in a sophisticated shot-countershot tactic. While Gardel performs his image of the malefactor here, the film ties in scenes from his earlier performance of this same tango in the marginal bar, thus illustrating the inspector's recollection and recognition of what he had seen earlier. In the staging of this final scene, the inspector's association of Ramírez with the low-class bar singer works as proof of his crime; the cameras first show us a shot of Ramírez singing in the theater, followed by a shot of the inspector observing him with a pensive look, and finally by a shot of Ramírez singing in the bar, a scene that had occurred in full at the beginning of the film. Thus, the shots of Ramírez in the low-class bar function as memory and as the association the inspector makes between Ramírez and Rancales, recognizing him as *compadrito* and, once linked with Rancales' malevolent world, as Rancales' murderer. The association also identifies Ramírez as the one who saved his life, for which reason the inspector decides to hide his secret. The tango and the singer's identity appear as innocent parties simultaneously to being revealed as responsible for a crime. The image of Gardel thus encompasses the criminality adjudicated to tango and its world, together with the "noble" sentiments that make Ramírez acceptable for the inspector, the representative of the law.

While in the first performance of "Melodía de Arrabal" Gardel is associated with the world of tango and with Rancales, the second performance, framed by the gazes of the upper-class audience in a downtown theater, displaces him toward legitimacy and the law, the opposite of the illegality that surrounded Ramírez in the world of the marginal bar. Yet, both are present in the final scene, literally, in that this sequence of the film is constructed with fragments of the first performance and places both identities of Gardel's character side by side, in order to convey that they are one and the same man.

In both *Luces de Buenos Aires* and *Melodía de Arrabal*, the celebration of modernity takes diverse paths, from the figuration of technology and an aesthetic of the machine centered on the capacity to represent movement and sound (numerous manifestations of technological modernity appear, such as phonographs and cars in motion), to a strong syntactical articulation of images centered on the shot-countershot interplay, abandoning in this way the centered perspective produced by the fixed camera of the documentary. More than documents, cinema now makes possible the representation of tango itself using a modern syntax as a way of condensing, in the very materiality of cinematographic language, the autochthonous modernity of a nation metonymized in tango. Tango, an urban product of modern culture, finds in cinema the best medium for the exhibition of its modern traits.

"Bananas Is My Business"

The construction of the image of Carmen Miranda (1909–1955), reproduced and caricaturized by her Hollywood films, in fact began with Brazilian cinema. From 1933, with her participation in *A Voz do Carnaval* (The Voice of Carnival), until *Banana da Terra* (Banana from the Land), made in 1939, Carmen Miranda participated in numerous episodic films produced to publicize the music of carnival, usually with a quite loose narrative structure centered on the world of shows and musical revues.

Banana da Terra takes place on Bananalandia, a fictitious island in the Pacific. The queen of Bananalandia attempts to sell the island's overproduction of bananas in Brazil, something she ultimately achieves via radio and newspaper advertisements. For the first time, Miranda uses the typical attire of women from Bahia, which the Hollywood movies later immortalized, to sing *O Que É Que a Baiana Tem?* (What Does the Bahian Woman Have?), by Doryval Caymmi. Caymmi's samba speaks of the adornments of Miranda's garb, which has a clearly literal, visual justification in the plot, with the end result of portraying Miranda as a promotional product herself.

In *Down Argentine Way* (1940), the first film Miranda made in the United States, her performances of Brazilian music appear in a diegetic plot in which the dance episodes figure alongside an image of modernity. Directed by Irving Cummings, this film together with *The Gang's All Here* displays the negotiation of cultural differences that would separate the United States from its South American neighbors, proposing that those differences ultimately amount to nothing. The story, also melodramatic with a happy end, recounts the negotiation of differences that obstruct the fulfillment of the love relationship between a young North American woman and an Argentine man, whose fathers are at first characterized as enemies. On discovering the mistake in that characterization, their love can be consummated—along with the alliance between North America and Argentina—functioning, via an assortment of tactics, as the representative of a collective South American identity.[23]

The credits indicate that Carmen Miranda appears as "herself," and indeed her film persona represents the singer and her performance is limited to the artistic exhibitions attended by the film's protagonists. In the first scene, dressed as a Bahian woman, Miranda sings "South American Way," an Americanized samba that also serves as a backdrop for the presentation of images of Buenos Aires.[24] The song can be said to be Americanized not only because some of its lyrics are in English, but also because its softened rhythm brings it closer to rumba than to samba, strictly speaking. The song tells of the peculiarity of a Latin American way of being—that "South American Way"—that stands out precisely because of its specificity. Yet, the images of Buenos Aires appearing in conjunction with that music portray a city that is more similar than peculiar. These are images of the "European-ness" of Buenos Aires: the national Congress building, the central post office, the principal square at Plaza de Mayo, for example, while in and around Plaza de Mayo the Casa Rosada (presidential palace) is not seen and the Cabildo (historical seat of government) is only barely visible at the edge of the shot's frame. Instead, only the more European buildings along the thoroughfare of Diagonal Norte can be seen. While the song refers, in Portuguese, to the autochthonous Brazilian market where the *tabuleiro* sells *vatapá*, the images show a city absent of autochthony conveyed in the song. Images of the city are juxtaposed with the song's chorus, an English translation of Miranda's Portuguese version. The schizophrenia is tangible: while the song claims to name the "South American" difference in its lyrics, the music and the images efface, conceal, and attempt to minimize that difference.

In that production of a Latin American stereotype, the association that the film makes between modernity and Brazilian popular music works to promote an alternative modernity that generates a strong rejection in the audience and a hindrance to that good-neighbor policy that the film might be presumed to prompt.

Nation and Differences

In the early and plainly episodic films, cinema seemed to show itself to be a kind of mechanical eye limited to capturing the autochthonous and national characteristics introduced by tango and samba. In time, the development of national cinematographic genres, in clear dialogue with films produced outside the national borders, went about setting guidelines about the structuring of a discourse through which that autochthony appeared associated with—indeed, converted into—an example of "modernity." Taking Benjamin's cue, it could be said that the development of national cinematographies updates the optical unconscious of those early shots.[25]

Even if the association with cinema is considered one of the stages in the nationalization of tango and samba, although it was not always understood as such, tango and samba also served to nationalize cinema, in a back-and-forth dynamic in which one can read the conflictive meanings that the process of nationalization entails in a Latin American culture. In these cases, nationalization was understood as a search for a specific and particular identity grounded in the meanings of the typical autochthonous that tango and samba could set in motion. Yet, the cinematographic syntax able to have these national characteristics shown as both specific and modern produces a kind of detypification of the autochthonous as typical.

A decidedly ambiguous operation is at work: on the one hand, those musical forms find a way of particularizing the stories they tell; on the other hand, the tango films as well as the early *chanchadas* reproduce and imitate a genre already quite developed by then in Hollywood's musical films, at that time clearly associated with the "North American" nationality.

Although these films with Gardel and Miranda, which fulfilled a key role in the perception of tango and samba as national symbols, were produced and filmed outside their respective countries, and despite their link to the Hollywood musical, they also form part of a system with patently national cinematographic genres, and they continue traditions that are likewise clearly national, such as the *sainete* (one-act farce or comedy sketch), for tango, and the carnival film in the case of samba. In that aporia of Argentine and Brazilian modernity that must show itself to be national in order to set itself forth as modern, the construction of a national identity is subject to the intervention of discourses and actions arising in the most diverse spaces and areas. There, in that special juncture in temporal and discursive space, modernity and nation were two vectors of opposite impulses that nevertheless defined themselves only in the attacks and exchanges that constituted them. "The nation," Renato Ortiz points out, "is realized historically by way of modernity. [. . .] Modernity, at the same time as it is embodied in the nation, brings with it the seeds of its own negation. National identity thus finds itself in disagreement with the very movement that engenders it."[26]

If these films found in tango and samba the raw material with which to express the nation, tango and samba also, on being captured by cinema, found their national condition in a dynamic of negotiations and conflicts that unfolds in those films as well as in other places.

Coda. *Notas de Tango*, by Rafael Filipelli

Two scenes stand out from *Notas de Tango* (Tango Notes), a film made in the year 2000: in the first, director Rafeal Filipelli dialogues with Federico Monjeau, a music critic and professor of musical aesthetics at the University of Buenos Aires. The event of a cinema director preparing to make a movie about tango tells us this is a self-referential film, and based on the kind of research that is conducted, a history of tango appears to be its intent. It begins with a fragment of the book by Adrián Gorelik, *La Grilla y el Parque* (The Grid and the Park), about the city of Buenos Aires, its neighborhoods, and tango. Copies of *El Alma que Canta* (The Soul that Sings) are underlined and reviewed, and the actor/singer protagonist carries out diverse interviews with tango singers and tango musicians. In utilizing these features of the documentary and in documenting the very film it is attempting to construct, the work sits on the fence between the fictional and documentary genres.

The tactile camera settles on a typical but nonpicturesque Buenos Aires that exposes apartment buildings, railroad tracks, electricity cables, and wrought-iron elevators, which together construct a city that, like tango, is more backdrop than protagonist of the film, appearing in small informative fragments as the precondition for the film and for the subject matter (tango) in the film. But this project is not about tango or Buenos Aires in the picturesque mode. The oscillation in the narrative, the interweaving of stories, the multiple cameras, and the interruption of any narrative impulse provide the first evidence of the film's indecision between documentary and fiction. The first scene begins with Monjeau talking about the color of tango. One can hear Filipelli asking questions, but he cannot be seen, and for a few minutes the film adopts the more traditional format of the documentary. At one point the camera focuses on Filipelli, who makes the ambiguous statement: "The problem is the materials. The materials are impossible." Tango's materials, or the film's? Yet, the film inserts a "true" story in which the characters' names coincide with the actors' names. Filipelli represents himself; his friends and the children of his friends appear in several scenes, and they are interrupted by the fictional story of a love between Pablo and Elsa.

All the tango clichés are present in the movie: friendship (Filipelli is filmed in conversation with Monjeau, his musician friend, and many friends and collaborators of the journal *Punto de Vista* (Point of View) appear in scenes, in the credits, or in marginal images), failure (for people of the world of tango), the lie or falsity (the "other" in the world of tango), the minor love story that is never resolved, and so on. The film recounts these topics with a certain produced austerity, precisely by way of those operations of an antipicturesque mode.

In the second scene, which appears in the final segments of the film, the person being interviewed is Gerardo Gandini, the musician. As he plays a few chords of "La Milonga del Ángel" (Angel's Milonga) by Astor Piazzolla, he concludes: "In tango, the chords are never resolved. Just like the problems: in tango, the woman never comes back." Nor is the film itself resolved, straddling the fence between documentary and fiction. In that respect, it is in the end an excellent heir to tango; the solution to the impossibility of those materials for the construction of a film about tango is found, precisely, in that indecision.

APPENDIX

Primitive Savages

La valorización del café fue una operación imperialista. La poesía Pau-Brasil también. Todo ello tenía que caer con las trompetas de la crisis. (The increase in the value of coffee was an imperialist operation. So was Poesía Pau-Brasil. All of that had to go when the trumpets of crisis sounded.)

Oswald de Andrade

From the insistent metaphor of cannibalism, passing through the *herói sem nenhum caráter* (hero with no character) that will be Macunaíma and on to the images of primitive sexualities in Gilberto Freyre's *Casa Grande e Senzala* (The Masters and the Slaves),[1] the persistence of some primitivist schemes in the early decades of the twentieth century seems to mark the unfolding of modernity in Brazilian literature. A canonical reading of this problematic relates the primitive in Brazil to its importance to the European avant-garde. These few Brazilian examples demonstrate that the primitive scheme transcends the limits of the avant-garde in Brazil, as evidenced in Romantic Indianism and in the "birth" itself of Brazilian literature, with *Carta* (Letter) by Pero Vaz Caminha.

In Europe too the problematic of primitivism transcends the avant-garde. It is not necessary to depart much from the auratic circle of French surrealism to find a certain passion for the primitive, as much in Keyserling as in those very bourgeois individuals who, supposedly affronted by the appearance of primitives in art, nonetheless applauded jazz, tango, Josephine Baker, or Os Oito Batutas in the smaller cabarets of the nineteenth-century capital, as Walter Benjamin labeled Paris. That persistence of primitivism is one of the most convincing historical facts for questioning the idea of primitivism in the European avant-garde as an affront to bourgeois taste; the bourgeoisie, perhaps more than others, also habitually enjoyed certain primitivisms. Yet, the genealogy of European primitivism extends from the first decades of the twentieth century, according to Hannah Arendt, back to the eighteenth century.[2]

A genealogy of Brazilian primitivism would be unwieldy in the context of this book. To narrow the scope we can think of the primitivist scheme as it appears, as a figure of Brazilian modernity, in some Brazilian texts from the early decades of the twentieth century. Starting with "O Tatuturema" (The Jungle's Hell)—a section of *O Guesa* (The Errant One) by Joaquim de Sousândrade, who would be called "the cannibal of Romanticism"[3]—one can speak of a radical shift in the figurations of the primitive in Brazil. If in Alencar and Gonçalves Dias, nineteenth-century writers of what is known as "Romantic Indianism," the issue revolves around a reconstruction of the Indian in his habitat—obviously fictitious and also charged with ideology—what emerges at the turn of the century is the errant or displaced primitive, the idea of a primitive who is "out of place."[4]

While the Indianism of the nineteenth century presumed a reconstruction of a mythical past, the twentieth-century primitive, in contrast, entailed a future-oriented tension, a utopia. At times, it is clearly a matter of a construction toward the future: "A nossa Independência ainda não foi proclamada" (We have not yet declared our independence), Oswald de Andrade said in his *Manifesto Antropófago*.[5] In other instances, as in Gilberto Freyre or Olavo Bilac, the primitive functions as a figure of the past, and in that displacement it establishes a certain image of dislocation: the jungle and the school; Macunaíma, emperor of the jungle of the modern city of São Paulo; the slaves from the *senzala* (slave quarters) in the master's house on the sugar plantation.

As emblem of heterogeneity, as manifestation of the nonplace of the primitive, that figuration is also not exclusive to the avant-garde. In 1906, Olavo

Bilac—the epitome of the Parnassianism that will be spurned by the modernists—is horrified at the spectacle of that dislocation:

> One these last Sundays, I saw pass by along the Central Avenue a wagon jam-
> packed with people going to the Penha procession: and on that splendid *boule-
> vard*, on the paved asphalt, over against the rich façade of tall buildings, over
> against the carriages and automobiles that were parading by, the encounter
> with that old vehicle containing those drunken devotees vociferating, gave me
> the impression of a monstrous anachronism: it was the resurrection of barba-
> rism, it was a savage age come back, like a savage soul that was returning from
> the other world, coming to perturb and shame life in the civilized age . . . If the
> unbridled orgy were confined to Penha's outskirts, that would be one thing.
> But not, after the festivity has finished, the multitude would spill like a victori-
> ous torrent toward the center of the city.[6]

Evaluated in a clearly negative way in the case of Bilac, that utopian figure of
the out-of-place or anachronic primitive persists in other texts as well, though
that shift may be evaluated positively. It is the shift, the dislocation, however,
whether positive or negative, that seems to mark not only a figure of Brazilian
modernity but also, above all, a whole scheme of production for that modernity in Brazilian territory. In the quotation from Bilac, the notion of a dislocation is clear: it is the "wagon . . . on that splendid *boulevard*," where not
only the wagon is dislocated on the boulevard, but also the signifier boulevard
itself appears in lettering that specially emphasizes it as originating in another
space, another language, via the use of italics.[7]

Vidas Secas (Barren Lives), *Casa Grande e Senzala* (The Masters and the
Slaves), *Manifesto Antropófago* (Cannibalist Manifesto), *Macunaíma*, the primitivist art of Tarsila do Amaral and Di Cavalcanti or Portinari, samba, the
chorinhos, the Oito Batutas dressed in tuxedos and playing the flute in Paris:
all are examples of a primitivist passion and markers of a Brazilian culture in
the midst of modernization.[8] They are themselves figures of Brazilian modernity. Why, then, is the primitive so insistently associated with the processes
of modernization in these texts from the beginning of the twentieth century,
and what makes for this irruption of the primitive in the very midst of Brazil's
modernization process?

One would have to question Brazil's supposed sympathy with primitive
cultures as the only explanation for why its modernist culture would embrace

primitivism. The primitivist scheme functions in these texts—many of them clearly questioning of literature as mimetic of reality—not so much as a way of representing a Brazilian identity but as a way of articulating the ambivalences that an "out of place" modernity would represent for Brazil.[9]

The primitivist tension of the European avant-garde movements, principally surrealism, and its connection to modernity was explained as one of the strategies used by the European avant-garde to break with tradition, appealing, by way of primitivism, to a certain "outside" of that tradition. Thus, primitivism was perceived as a jump backwards in time, to the past of civilization. A strategy of distancing, of the break or the collision, the appeal to the primitive was read—perhaps with excess simplicity—within a modernist paradigm whose ambiguous edges have already been sufficiently put into question.[10]

In the case of Brazil, the direct association with European primitivism supposes the prioritization of a comparative interpretation plotted on the syntagmatic axis that ignores the numerous incidences of the problem of primitivism in Brazil's culture along the diachronic axis. The primitivist scheme then becomes the mark of an avant-garde identity that adopted its national character as a distinguishing feature, as well as the figure of the primitive, one of the strategies for constructing this national character of Brazilian modernity. In any case, what the reading of primitivism in the Brazilian avant-garde derives from those European avant-garde movements, even when difference is insisted upon in Brazilian expressions (see Benedito Nunes or Haroldo de Campos), is a delimitation of the problematic to avant-garde expressions, although it is clear that the process in Brazil, given the diverse historical primitivisms, supposes a broader expression. Texts that are clearly modernizing texts, but not inscribable in an avant-garde aesthetic, appeal also to the figure of the primitive in these first decades of the twentieth century, whereby the operability of primitivism cannot be limited to a gesture of rupture from tradition or one of aggressiveness toward the bourgeois audience. On the other hand, in its delimitation to the avant-garde conceived as a break from tradition, the problematic of primitivism loses its sharper edges, since it is precisely its figuration as an ambivalent image of modernity that appears if one investigates it as a broad metaphor that traverses the diverse "-isms" in the early decades of the twentieth century.

A canonical reading of Brazilian modernism recognizes the concern about the national as a specific mark of this avant-garde as regards the European avant-garde. Such readings would suggest this concern about national identity is an originality of the Brazilian—and Latin American—avant-garde, and one of its most specific traits.[11] It is within that presumed nationalism that one explains the function of primitivism in the avant-garde movements. In its association with the avant-garde, primitivism functioned as a kind of bridge between copying the European avant-garde and discovering Brazil.

That reading is based on the supposed congeniality between the primitivist scheme of the European avant-garde and the Brazilian tradition; the presence of "primitive" races at the core of Brazilian society would explain the productivity of that scheme in Brazilian literature, as seen in the works of Candido and Haroldo de Campos, for example. Despite clear differences, both tend to regard modernity as the appropriation that the peripheral culture makes of a European product—in this case, primitivism. Here what is proposed is above all concordance (this is the word Candido uses) between Brazilian and European primitivisms, just as there is a presumed concordance between Europe's avant-garde and Brazil's.[12] The reading is grounded in the causal nexus of influence and explains primitivism as a mimetic embodiment of the national. The proposal of primitivism's congeniality with Brazilian culture serves also another purpose that is far from negligible: it cloaks the imperialism for which European primitivism is nothing but a metonymy.[13]

According to my reading of the primitivist texts of the first decades of the twentieth century, the concern about national identity has led to a non-reading—in those figurations of the primitive in Brazil and, I would add, in Latin America—of other kinds of functions fulfilled by those primitivist regimens, which establish a certain confrontation with modernity along with images of modernity. Nationalism in the Brazilian avant-garde entails a concern for the construction of a national identity as well as a simultaneous strategy for the construction of a national modernity that, because it is national, is presumed to be different and therefore also alternative. The nationalism of this avant-garde should not be read as anything other than one of the vectors of the modern state-of-being in Brazil.

Aesthetics and Politics

Canonical texts of the heroic period of Brazilian modernism, the *Manifesto da Poesia Pau-Brasil* (Pau Brazil Manifesto) (1924), the *Manifesto Antropófago* (Cannibalist Manifesto) (1928), and *Macunaíma* (1928), are organized around a primitivist scheme. As much in the manifestos of Oswald de Andrade as in the novel by Mário de Andrade, primitivism appears as a very clear mark of modernity. In the manifestos, above all, this trait functions as a negative way of establishing what is new and modern by way of the multiple "contras" that structure them. On the other hand, specifically in the case of Oswald de Andrade, primitivism instates a rudimentary aspect in the writing of manifestos—which can be associated with his "poemas *criança*" (*child* poems)—functioning as a way of tearing up the learned tradition, composed by a "fabric of alienations and preconceived notions."[14]

That primitivism, with aesthetic consequences, can without a doubt be read as an abstract logic of the modern. In fact, in the *Manifesto da Poesia Pau-Brasil* a conception and a functionality of the primitive operate very similarly to European avant-garde models. However, if we read the indisputable historical references that construct both manifestos, the primitivist regimen acquires—especially in the *Manifesto Antropófago* due to its reference to emblems of Brazilian history—consequences of its own complementarity to the aesthetic consequences.

The greater presence of the past in *Manifesto Antropófago* fulfills a double and to a certain point paradoxical function. On the one hand, it implies a movement contrary to the sharp rejection of the past evinced by a certain type of European avant-garde and that, for some theorists of the European avant-garde, even specifies the difference between the avant-garde and modernism in its Anglo-Saxon sense.[15] It is clear that in the *Manifesto Antropófago*, even though this is not a conservative revision of the past, certain lines of continuity with a national past are established, ones that would be unthinkable in certain zones of the European avant-garde. The very ending of the manifesto, "*Ano 374 da deglutição do Bispo Sardinha*" (Year 374 of the deglutition of Bishop Sardinha), marks it in an uninterrupted continuity with a Brazilian past. It would be incorrect to suppose, however, that that greater presence of the past in the Brazilian and Latin American avant-garde movements entailed a lesser revulsivity in the avant-garde as compared with the European avant-garde. In a cultural field in which the reference to European models was common currency to the detriment of the national past, Brazilian modernism breaks with the national tradition to refer to Europe precisely by referring to a national past that had not been constructed as "tradition."[16]

In this last manifesto, the appeal to primitivism constructs an image of Brazilian culture as a primitive culture that was demolished by colonization and modernization. This operation is structured on the basis of an ambivalent relationship with respect to the past, one that rejects a "civilized" past in favor of another, primitive, past considered to be desirable for building the future. On the second page of *Manifesto Antropófago* is found a reference that discloses, in the appeal to a historical event, how the primitivist scheme supersedes aesthetics. The historical reference in this case is to Father Vieira, the writer of the Portuguese and Brazilian tradition who in 1649 attempted to organize a company to exploit sugar, and drew on his already famous rhetorical weapons in order to convince the king. The manifesto states: "Against Father Vieira. Author of our first public loan, to earn his commission. The illiterate king said to him: put that on paper without much versifying. The loan was made. Brazilian sugar was taxed. Vieira left the money in Portugal and brought us verses.[17]

If in this historical reference Vieira represents the influence of rhetoric at the service of catechism and the colonization of the country, it is clear then that the manifesto's primitivist proposition to cleanse language of rhetoric is very directly tied with a nationalist, anticolonialist, and economic proposition. Beyond its aesthetic consequences, the primitivist scheme entailed, already in Oswald de Andrade, a political strategy of the dislocation of borders and cultural relations.

That presumption leads to a strong criticism, not only of the national past, but also of Europe, since the primitive functions as an alternative in the face of a modernity that is seen as insufficient. It is impossible to avoid reading in the final phrase of *Manifesto Antropófago* this attempt to subvert borders and create an alternative modernity: "We call for the Caraíba Revolution. Bigger than the French Revolution. The unification of all efficacious rebellions in the direction of man. Without us, Europe would not have even its poor declaration of the rights of man."[18] In that sense, the clearly aesthetic primitivism of *Pau-Brasil* and *Manifesto Antropófago*—undeniably influenced by the European avant-garde, as seen in the direct reference to Blaise Cendrars in the *Manifesto Pau Brasil*—went beyond the construction of a Brazilian identity. The primitive figures in them not as a past to which one would wish to return, but as an ideal transported into the future. Nor can the primitive in that future function as a unified image of an identity, because it figures the positive and the negative at the same time, as much in relation to modernity as to the national past. The nationalism of these examples of the modernist avant-garde entails a transgression and a dislocation of boundaries more than a national discourse that would result in homogeneous and unified identities.

Macunaíma, Allegory of Modernity

The priority of the problem of the national as a specific logic of Brazilian modernism found in Mário de Andrade one of its most paradigmatic examples. Always concerned with what he referred to as "literature of circumstance,"[19] the great majority of his texts in one way or another discuss this problematic. Yet, in addition to the strong presence of this national concern in his poetic and prose texts, and as one of the intellectuals co-opted by the State to work at the very heart of the state bureaucracy, Mário de Andrade carried out a series of cultural projects that are framed within Getúlio Vargas' Estado Novo project to nationalize Brazilian culture. His intellectual trajectory sketches out one of the possible itineraries for Brazilian modernism, from the euphoric avant-garde movements of the 1920s to the institutionalized modernism of the Estado Novo.

Two texts mark the opposite extremes of that itinerary: *Macunaíma*, published in 1928, and considered by some to be the greatest example of the Brazilian *Antropofagia* (Cannibalism) movement, and *A Enciclopédia Brasileira* (The Brazilian Encyclopedia), a report written by Mário de Andrade in his role as civil servant in the Ministry of Education and Culture concerning the elaboration of a national popular encyclopedia that never reached publication. The differences between these two texts are enormous, beginning with their genres: the first, a novel or *rapsodia*; the second, a bureaucratic report. Their differences parallel the dissolution of the modernizing impact of the 1920s avant-garde movements when they are co-opted by the State. However, the persistence in the *Enciclopédia* of certain modernist criteria encased in the national project puts less emphasis on the dissolution of these modernist criteria from their "avant-garde" manifestation to their "nationalist" correction, and more emphasis on the combination or amalgamation of both criteria in each of those moments.

The majority of the readings of *Macunaíma* placed emphasis on the novel as a construction of a national identity. At least up to the analysis by Gilda de Mello e Souza, the book was considered to be one of the most important books of Brazilian National Modernism, highlighting at once the text's modern character and its concern with the construction of a national identity that would be represented in the protagonist of the novel, an Indian of the Tapanhumas tribe who emerges from the jungle to go to the city of São Paulo in search of a talisman, the *muiraquitã*. The text's modernity was seen principally in its collage or bricollage techniques, according to Gilda de Mello e Souza, and in its recourse to and constant problematization of intertextuality as well as its use of indigenous legends and documentary-oriented antimimeticism.

In these readings, nationalism and modernity would seem to split into two separate strategic lines; while certain mechanisms aim at the construction of a national program, others would be responsible for the modern texture of the writing; that is, while the nationalism would be found in the contents or materials, the modernity of the text would be embodied in certain formal strategies and resources. It is possible, moreover, to think that these are precisely the same strategies as the ones that infuse the *rapsodia* with a primitivist air, based on the construction of the protagonist as well as a writing that imitates the "primitive" writing of indigenous legends, drawing in fact on *Von Roraima Zur Orinoco* (From Roraima to the Orinoco) by Koch-Grünberg and on a compilation of Tupí legends recorded in the nineteenth century by Couto de Magalhães, *O Selvagem* (The Savage), in addition to several other texts. That imitation of the writing of Tupí legends can be perceived not only in the narrative structure and character construction, but also in the frequent adoption of a primitivist vocabulary.

The fact that the strategies that are considered modernizing are the same as those that identify the primitivist regimen in the text prompts us to question the use of primitivism as a way of constructing a national identity that is separate, different—or constructed on the basis of its difference—from European modernity. In fact, in several texts Mário de Andrade himself reflected on Macunaíma as a character who would transcend his concern with the national. Considering the work's influence from *Von Roraima Zur Orinoco*, a text treating the vicissitudes of a Venezuelan Indian, the construction of Macunaíma presents him as more Latin American than, strictly speaking, Brazilian, as indicated in the widely known episode in which, having lost his conscience on the island of Marapatá, he *puts on*—this is how the text states it—a Latin American one. But despite an attempt at Panamericanism in that gesture that would truly crystallize in Mário de Andrade's thinking only after the writing of *Macunaíma*, it is ultimately quite clear that—like Musil's man without qualities—"the hero with no character" represents, if he represents anything at all, modern man.[20]

According to Mário de Andrade in a letter:

> Perhaps Macunaíma will acquire that in English, because very secretly it seems to me that the satire, in addition to being generally directed at the Brazilian, of whom it shows some characteristic aspects, systematically hiding the

good ones, what is certain is that it seems to me to be also a more universal satire of contemporary man, principally from the point of view of this itinerant listlessness, these moral notions created the moment any light is thrown on that, which is something I feel and see so much in contemporary man.[21]

Beyond the representative or mimetic character of the primitive as representative of a Brazilian identity, the primitivist scheme has a different function in *Macunaíma*. This scheme can be observed in one of the central episodes, in which the narrative structure of an indigenous legend is used to explain the invention of the automobile.[22] As this legend goes, the automobile had once been a brown jaguar that, escaping from a tigress, ran from the jungle to the sea, eating, as it passed through different parts of Brazil, a motor, some wheels, a few lightning bugs that made for the headlights, and a tin of fuel, transforming ultimately into an automobile.

If, on the one hand, the machine functions in the text as a metonymy for modernity—to the point that, on his arrival in São Paulo, the hero exclaims: "*Eram máquinas e tudo na cidade era só máquina!*" (There were machines and everything in the city was all machine!)[23]—what is certain is that in this episode the machine is associated with Brazilian nature. This operation is constant in the text: the "airplane machine" is a *tuiuiú*, a Brazilian bird; the Smith Wesson "machine" and the watch—memories of the city that Macunaíma takes with him on returning to the jungle—grow from the trees. Even Macunaíma finally decides to travel to Europe to seek, not education, civilization, or modernity, but the talisman that Venceslau Pietro Pietra had taken. He goes to Europe therefore to find there what is his own, what belongs to him and was stolen from him.[24] On the other hand, if we take the character of Venceslau Pietro Pietra as Macunaíma's antagonist and as the representative of Europe and of modernity—he is, as the text indicates, "the capitalist"—we must note that there is also some trading off of roles between him and Macunaíma; as Venceslau collects rocks, which have mythical value in Tupí culture, Macunaíma, in turn, collects machines and invectives in every language.

The episode of the brown jaguar functions as a summary of a nature-machine transformation that, as it is structured on the magical transformism of indigenous legends, incorporates that textuality in order to reverse and dislocate established "identities." In the "legend" of the brown jaguar and in other figurations of modernity in the text, the primitivist scheme functions to displace and dislocate the idea that the machine and technology—modernity—would come from Europe. The primitive presents in that constant dislocation an image of Brazilian modernity. Beyond constructing the identity of a Brazilian culture or people, the primitivism in the novel aims at constructing the identity of a Brazilian modernity, that is, at the specification of what modernity in São Paulo could be as a metonymy for Brazil overall.

The association between nationalism and modernism in the text indicates a kind of nationalism that attempts to comprehend Brazilian and primitive culture as the ambivalent mark of a modernity in which the primitive operates to dismantle the boundaries between the national, or specifically Brazilian, and the modern, or specifically European.

NOTES

1. The anecdote is recounted in José Tinhorão, *Pequena História da Música Popular: Da Modinha a Canção de Protesto* [A Brief History of Popular Music: From *Modinha* to Protest Song] (Petrópolis: Vozes, 1975), pp. 76, 77, which includes other stories about the relationship between tango and samba, with a few errors, as can be verified in its history of tango. For example, citing a newspaper article by Álvaro Moreyra, Tinhorão mentions that Jean Richepin gave a conference at the French Academy about maxixe and later also wrote a comedy about it. Guillermo Gasio published the conference and the play in *Jean Richepin y el Tango Argentino* [Jean Richepin and the Argentine Tango] (Buenos Aires: Corregidor, 1999), and, even if the conference does not make explicit whether its focus is an Argentine or a Brazilian tango, the references to the world of the gauchos make it more possible to associate it with the Argentine tango. Jean Richepin was a French writer born in Argelia. After a few years of living as an "adventurer," in 1876 he published a long poem praising the poetry of vagabonds. That poem, in various ways resonant with *poésie maudite* (accursed poetry), shows Richepin's familiarity with the argot. The book was censored as it was deemed a stimulus to vice and crime, and Richepin was sentenced to one month in prison. In 1908, however, he was named a member of the French Academy, and it is in his status as *académicien* that in 1913 he gave the conference "À Propos du Tango." Although in the history of tango, the anecdote about Richepin figures as an example of the importance that Argentine cultural products receive abroad—especially in Paris, also the capital of cultural modernity—the salvaging of tango that he carries out is grounded in an argument that is rhetorically irrevocable in the context of the Académie: "'In conclusion,' says Richepin, 'what does it matter, after all, that a form of dance had low-class and foreign origins? [. . .] We make everything French, and the dance we like to do also becomes French.'" Gasio, *Jean Richepin*, p. 63.

2. In *Feitiço Decente: Transformações do Samba no Rio de Janeiro (1917–1930)* [Decent Bewitchment: Transformations of Samba in Rio de Janeiro (1917–1930)] (Rio de Janeiro: Jorge Zahar & UFRJ, 2001), Carlos Sandroni makes an analysis of the rhythmic base of the first compositions that were called tango, maxixe, and samba, finding in all three a rhythmic pattern he termed the "paradigm of the *tresillo* (triplet)" that differs from the European rhythmic pattern and which researchers from Brazil and other traditions have strongly associated with music of African origin. Its principal characteristic

is the use of the syncope that at the same time is culturally associated in dance with the mulatto *requebros* (wiggles, swings) and that in tango can be identified in that form's *cortes y quebradas* (cuts and breaks), which refer to dramatic pauses followed by swift turns of the hip in the tango dance. See Sandroni, *Feitiço Decente*, in particular the section "Premissas Musicais" (Musical Premises), pp. 19–38. To be sure, what is known as Argentine tango around the 1920s in Brazil is different from the Brazilian tango, and precisely for that reason the forms are differentiated by adding the country name as adjective in the case of the Brazilian form, an addition that would be considered a redundancy in Argentina.

Ernesto Nazareth wrote several Brazilian tangos, including "Bambino" (Undulant) and "Espalhafatoso" (Extravagant). Alexandre Levy wrote "Brazilian Tango" and "Samba." Gaining entry into semierudite music, according to Mário de Andrade, would seem to have been problematic for Nazareth: "The first time this composer of tangos had the honor of being included in a concert, on the initiative of Luciano Gallet, it was necessary to have the police intervene. Many people were very upset about the fact that they'd dare play this 'low-class music' in the National Institute of Music." See Mário de Andrade, *The Complete Works of Mário de Andrade*, vol. 7: *Música, Doce Música* [Music, Sweet Music] (São Paulo: Martins, 1963), p. 319.

3. Carlos Sandroni and Vicente Rossi coincide in tracing both samba and tango back to that shared root. See Sandroni, *Feitiço Decente*, and Vicente Rossi, *Cosas de Negros* [Black People's Matters] (Buenos Aires: Taurus, 2001). According to Mário de Andrade, the similarities between the Brazilian tango and what Argentines and Uruguayans call tango arise because these genres share an origin in the Cuban habanera. See Mário de Andrade, *Música, Doce Música*, p. 125. That hypothesis is, however, questioned by José Ramos Tinhorão, who holds that the habanera's influence was exclusive to the tangos by Ernesto de Nazareth and did not extend to maxixe in general, whereby he concludes that "in reality there were not one but two creations: a popular one—that of maxixe, emerging little by little in circles of musicians who played choros, as a formal synthesis to accompany a fast style of dance—and another semierudite one—that of Ernesto de Nazareth's tangos, composed for the piano with virtuoso technical refinements, and possibly influenced by the habanera, always more taken advantage of by erudite musicians than by the national maxixe." See Tinhorão, *Pequena História da Música Popular*, p. 67.

The music that is most representative of this proximity, which would be erased with the passage of time, is Lupicínio Rodrigues, a *gaúcho* (South Brazilian) singer who composed tangos as well as sambas. The first carioca samba (samba of Rio de Janeiro) is "Pelo Telefone," by Donga (Ernesto Joaquim Maria dos Santos) and Mauro de Almeida, from 1917, and was registered as a "samba maxixe." For many experts, this composition is not pure maxixe, and without a doubt it is clearly different, as are the rest of the first sambas composed during the 1920s, from the samba that will become famous in the 1930s, what Sandroni calls "Estácio's paradigm" in reference to the Rio de Janeiro neighborhood that was its birthplace. According to Peter Fryer, however, this would not have been the first music to be recorded under the name "samba," for a dozen or so other compositions had claimed the term previously, including a piece called "Brasilianas," played on the piano by João Gualdo Ribeiro in 1910 and Urubu Malandro in 1914. See Peter Fryer, *Rhythms of Resistance: African Musical Heritage in Brazil* (Hanover, CT: Wesleyan University Press, 2000), p. 156.

4. See Caetano Veloso, *Fina Estampa ao Vivo* [Fine Figure, Live], Polygram Latino, 1995 (recording).

5. The album does include a song by Luiz Melodía, "Fadas" (Fairies), dedicated to Astor Piazzolla.

6. The transformations of samba during the Getúlio Vargas period have been lucidly studied. See Maria Isaura Pereira de Queiroz, *Carnaval Brasileiro: O Vivido e o Mito* [Brazilian Carnival: The Lived Experience and the Myth] (São Paulo: Brasiliense, 1992). The study of the political uses of tango has not been systematic, but impressionistic intuitions cut across almost all studies on tango. See Emilio de Ípola, "El Tango en Sus Márgenes" [The Tango in Its Margins], *Punto de Vista* (Buenos Aires) 8, no. 25 (December 1985).

7. Not only do tangos and sambas sing of their own world of the poor outskirts, the poor peripheral hill, the swaggering *compadrito*, and the deceitful *malandro*; but it is also possible to identify an appreciable number of tangos about tango and sambas about samba. There are, moreover, sambas that parody tango, such as "O Pesado 13," which is about "El Penado 14."

8. Other musical genres also cited or parodied tango and samba, as seen in the composition "Le Boeuf sur le Toit" (The Ox on the Roof) by Darius Milhaud, who also composed tangos, or "Tango" by Stravinsky, to name the most well-known examples.

9. Theodor Adorno, "Some Ideas on the Sociology of Music," in *Sound Figures*, trans. Rodney Livingstone (Stanford: Stanford University Press, 1999).

10. Tango, for example, has also been thought of as representative of another national identity, the Uruguayan.

11. Josefina Ludmer was the first Argentine critic to call attention to the importance of the category of use in a cultural criticism, and to elaborate an extremely inspiring definition of such. See Josefina Ludmer, *El Género Gauchesco: Un Tratado sobre la Patria* [The Gaucho Genre: A Treatise on the Motherland] (Buenos Aires: Perfil, 2000; Durham, NC: Duke University Press, 2002).

12. David Lloyd and Paul Thomas state: "Culture produces the consensual ground for the state form of representative democracy by drawing the formal or representative disposition in every individual out of each person's concrete particularity." See *Culture and the State* (London: Routledge, 1997), pp. 14, 15. Following a long-standing tradition in English thought that goes back to Matthew Arnold—whose influential essay, *Culture and Anarchy,* is evoked in the very title that Lloyd and Thomas put to their book— these authors consider that culture fulfills the role of forming citizens for determined States. While the function of the State consists in mediating conflicts between the different interest groups, the function of culture would be to interpellate individuals in the disposition toward disinterested reflection that makes State mediation possible. It is clear that these theorists' point of departure lies with Raymond Williams, whom they nonetheless criticize. Their position against Williams' idea that culture would be

a "dissident element" leads them to propose an opposite vision of culture, where its homogeneity as an instrument of the State would seem to make it an excessively deterministic vision.

13. The classic and influential bibliography on the concept is from Eric Hobsbawm and Terence Ranger, *The Invention of Tradition* (Cambridge: Cambridge University Press, 1983). Toward the end of "Mass-Producing Traditions: Europe 1870–1914," however, Hobsbawm suggests the possibility of studying tango as one episode in the invention of a tradition and as an issue that remains open to debate.

14. In *Hello, Hello Brazil: Popular Music in the Making of Modern Brazil* (Durham, NC: Duke University Press, 2004), Brian McCann, taking as point of departure the indisputable hypothesis of the crucial role of radio, analyzes the nationalization of samba based on the radio programs that made possible such a generalization of samba. The radio indeed generalizes samba but does not make it "national." Nationalization, in the sense of condensation of a sense of the national ascribed to tango and samba transcends radio's influence, as much as that may be its technical condition. For the "declension" of tango during the 1940s and 1950s, see Ípola, "El Tango en Sus Márgenes."

15. The best point of contact, also the one I would have most loved to have witnessed: Carmen Miranda, on her first tour in Buenos Aires in 1931, sang samba in the Broadway theater together with Chico Alves and Mário Reis, for the 6:30 p.m. and 11:30 p.m. shows; Gardel at that time was performing in the same theater, for the 9 p.m. show. See Ruy Castro, *Carmen: Uma Biografía* [Carmen: A Biography] (São Paulo: Companhia das Letras, 2005), p. 71.

16.

Se o Santo Padre soubesse / o gosto que o tango tem / viria do Vaticano / dançar maxixe também.

José Ramos Tinhorão cites a somewhat different version of these quartets, with no mention of tango, that were inserted in a longer composition. See Tinhorão, *Pequena História da Música Popular*, p. 69.

17. Tinhorão (ibid., p. 77), cites an article published by Álvaro Moreyra in the magazine *Fon Fon* 8, no. 14 (April 4, 1914) in which reference is made to a popular French song:

C'est sous le ciel de l'Argentine / où la femme est toujours divine / qu'aux sons de musiques câlines / on dance le *Tango* . . . / Dans le pays brésilien / La Maxixe on dance.

[It's beneath the Argentine sky / where woman is always divine / that, to the sound of affectionate music, / the Tango is danced . . . / In the Brazilian land / it's the Maxixe that is danced.

18. Rossi, *Cosas de Negros*, p. 156.

19. See Simon Frith, *Performing Rites: On the Value of Popular Music* (Cambridge, MA: Harvard University Press, 1996), pp. 269, 270.

20. Cláudia de Matos, *Acertei no Milhar: Samba e Malandragem no Tempo de Getúlio* [I Won the Lottery: Samba and Malandragem in the Age of Getulio] (Rio de Janeiro: Paz e Terra, 1982); Jorge Luis Borges, *Evaristo Carriego* (Buenos Aires: Gleizer, 1930); 2nd edition, 1955.

21. The difference between the musical styles of Firpo's and Canaro's orchestras gave rise to two modalities for performing tango that bore marked contrasts and that were from then on called the *tendencia tradicional* (traditional tendency) and the *tendencia evolucionista* (evolutionary tendency). Firpo's style was characterized by an essentially melodic form of expression, whereas Canaro's presents a marked accentuation of the rhythm. According to Luis Adolfo Sierra, *Historia de la Orquesta Típica* [History of the Autochthonous Orchestra] (Buenos Aires: Corregidor, 1997), p. 74:

> In Francisco Canaro there always existed a certain unalterable lack of concern regarding orchestral resources of the harmonious type; he infused the groups under his direction with a modality of marked rhythmic accentuation, though with denser sonority and less rapidness in the tempo than evinced by primitive tango's modality; an undisputed artifice of what is known as *marcación cuadrada* (squared marking), to the sacrifice even of the sense of melody as something that could be sung; all of this within the frame of a concept of tango essentially as a music to dance to, having already rectified the initial rhythmic division of two by four (a mistaken term that still prevails in literature on tango) with the correct marking of four by eight. In Roberto Firpo, on the other hand, there always predominated a decided inclination towards essentially melodic forms of expression; it is to his innovative and aesthetically minded motivations to which we owe the definitive incorporation of the piano in tango orchestras; he introduced the treatment of a solid, flexible, agile and cushioned rhythmic base, with a slow accentuation that looked zealously after the sonorous balance without excesses or effectivist and antimusical strategies; special attention to elegant management of tones grounded in the subtle intentions of impeccable good taste; preeminence given to the singing strings and the linking of sounds; an image, lastly, of the orchestra with a permanent atmosphere of compact sonority, though perfectly apt for dancing.

22. Comparativism has been criticized as a tool that presumed a notion of Central Europe as the model, above all in comparative literature, which arose in the postwar years among European exiles in the United States. Studies on alternative modernities also took a European model as origin from which the supposed alternative modernities would have been a kind of divergence, not to mention how much of this can be applied also to the study of Latin American avant-garde movements or Latin American modernisms, if not that of Romanticisms, Naturalisms, and so on. One of the most recent manifestations of this polemic took place as from Franco Moretti's project to accomplish a universal history of the novel with his new Center for the Study of the Novel at Stanford University, which sets itself the goal of carrying out a reconnaissance of the novel's functioning throughout the world, focusing on the work of critics from each of the national traditions, operating a bit like native informers, to supply a sort of "raw material" for the theorist (Moretti, or any theorist centered in a university with the requisite resources, obviously a North American or European one). See Franco Moretti, "Conjectures on World Literature," *New Left Review* 1 (2000), pp. 54–68; Jonathan Arac, "Anglo-Globalism?" *New Left Review* (July–August 2002); and Gayatri Spivak, *Death of*

a Discipline (New York: Columbia University Press, 2003), among others. The journal *New Left Review* published various other articles that create this polemic.

The discipline of Area Studies, in contrast, was questioned for one of its fundamental notions, that the world can be divided into homogeneous areas, and above all for representing a type of thinking that, by concentrating on self-contained entities, obstructed reflection on the transfers and movements between those areas, constitutive also of cultural forms and of problematics that Area Studies would have overlooked because of its own epistemological organizational structure.

23. In spite of having reflected much more on European literature than on Latin American literature (outside of the Brazilian category), Candido's thinking is ultimately fundamental for the construction of thought on Latin American literatures. See Adriana Amante and Florencia Garramuño, "Partir de Candido" [Candido as Point of Departure], in *Antonio Candido y los Estudios Latinoamericanos* [Antonio Candido and Latin American Studies], ed. Raúl Antelo, (Pittsburgh: Pittsburgh University Press, 2001).

24. Antonio Candido, "Literatura Comparada" [Comparative Literature], in *Recortes* (São Paulo: Companhia das Letras, 1996).

25. See Sandroni, *Feitiço Decente*, and Hermano Vianna, *O Mistério do Samba* [The Mystery of Samba] (Rio de Janeiro: Jorge Zahar & UFRJ, 1995).

PART I, CHAPTER 1

1. The nation, Etienne Balibar points out, is a kind of community that is created by erasing and extirpating other kinds of existing communities. See Balibar, "The Nation Form," in Etienne Balibar and Immanuel Wallerstein, *Race, Nation, Class: Ambiguous Identities* (London, New York: Verso, 1991). This explains the strong intolerance within Latin American nations toward any seed or rough draft of another community grouping, the existence of which was presumed always to represent a threat to the constitution of the nation. A text in which that intolerance is expressed with great horror—ratified at first by the narrator himself and only toward the end of the text rejected by him—is *Os Sertões* [Rebellion in the Backlands], by Euclides da Cunha. For the vision of samba as a community ritual, see Júlio Ribeiro, *A Carne* [The Flesh] (São Paulo: Martin Claret, 1999); for that of tango, Vicente Rossi, *Cosas de Negros* [Black People's Matters] (Buenos Aires: Taurus, 2001).

2.

En Francia lo han transformado / y lo llaman *le tango* / puede ser que allí resulte / digno de Madame Argot / que era capaz de bailarse / la Marcha de Ituzaingó / Richepin ha defendido / hasta en la Academia el tango / (para mí que está chiflado / desde la punta hasta el mango). / ¡Dejad que bailen el tango / donde ha nacido: en el Congo!

3. Perloff points out: "Perhaps a more satisfactory critique of primitivism and its analogs would begin with the recognition that primitivisms, like the modernisms to which they are related, can only be plural." Marjorie Perloff, "Tolerance and Taboo," in *Poetry On and Off the Page* (Evanston, IL: Northwestern University Press, 1998), p. 48.

4. Regarding Lunfardo, Antonio Dellepiane wrote a renowned essay titled *El Idioma*

del Delito [The Language of Delinquency] (Buenos Aires: Mirasol, 1894/1967), wherein, citing Lombroso, he writes the following on the topic of argots:

> Criminals [says Lombroso] create their own special language that has many points of contact with the languages of savage tribes because, in reality, they are savages lost in the midst of today's flourishing civilization, because they are men who have, given their regressive inheritance, gone back to the state of the primitive barbarian. If the criminal is a savage, it is natural that he would think and feel the way a savage does, and that his language, which is the manifestation of his mind and his heart, would offer clear analogies to the language of primitive or savage peoples. (p. 51)

The book, as can be observed in this quotation, is a perfect example of nineteenth-century primitivism in its negative assessment. At the same time, in his comparison between slang and what he calls "decadent and symbolist literature," he also outlines an early theory on the usefulness of primitivism for aesthetic thought:

> The characteristics we have pointed out in decadentist works, the swelling, the bombast, the nervousness [. . .] in its phrasing, are the very same ones offered by a criminal's literary productions. These shared traits of decadentist and criminal literature have induced some minds to presume a cerebral analogy, a psychical kinship between the representatives of these groups. Both literatures would thus be the clear and patent manifestations of a shared neurosis, an identical mental imbalance, equally shown in symbolists and in criminals. (p. 51)

Among his examples, he cites Rubén Darío and Jean Richepin (pp. 65, 66). Even though he chooses to reject this hypothesis, he nonetheless affirms a strong formal relationship between Lunfardo and modernist language.

5. The *Marcha de Ituzaingó* [March of Ituzaingó] is performed by military bands to announce the arrival of the president of the Argentine republic at official events.

6.

> El tango no es tampoco nuestro, sólo nos pertenecen los nuevos cortes que se le da al bailarlo, pues bien sabe todo el mundo que este es un baile de negros. En África se bailaba entre tribus de diferentes figuras y existía el tango mexicano, el cubano y el brasileño que éstos denominaban "Condesa", "Pasa mi sargento". ¿Y quién no recuerda, de los de mis tiempos, aquellas sociedades de candombes?
>
> Al ritmo del tambor y de otros instrumentos iban adelante con requiebros y meneos los negros ejecutando al compás de esta música el tiempo del tango.

Cited by Oscar Zucchi, *El Tango, el Bandoneón y Sus Intérpretes* [Tango, the Bandoneón, and Its Musicians], vols. 1 and 2 (Buenos Aires: Corregidor, 1998), p. 111.

7. For an inspiring analysis of this and other illustrations related to tango, see Marta Savigliano, *Tango and the Political Economy of Passion* (Boulder, CO: Westview Press, 1995), pp. 30–40.

8. From the pages of none other than the journal *Martín Fierro*, Ricardo Güiraldes claims Fígari for the avant-garde, appointing him a "true painter of things our own." See *Martín Fierro* 8/9. The article's sequel in the next issue features Emilio Pettoruti, named "one of the criollo avant-garde." I analyze some of Pettoruti's paintings of tango and the above-mentioned article "Pettoruti" in "Primitive Avant-Garde Artists" (this volume). In

Un Triángulo Crucial: Borges, Güiraldes y Lugones [A Crucial Triangle: Borges, Güiraldes and Lugones] (Buenos Aires: Eudeba, 1999), p. 16, Ivonne Bordelois relates that Ricardo Güiraldes' father sold a collection of European paintings to buy works by Fígari.

9. For a detailed analysis on the figuration of tango in the Argentine avant-garde, see Edgardo Dieleke, *Los Tangos de la Vanguardia: Una Perspectiva Diferente sobre la Lógica de Funcionamiento de la Vanguardia Argentina* [The Tangos of the Avant-Garde: A Different Perspective on the Logic of Argentine Avant-Garde Functioning], thesis for the Licenciatura degree (Buenos Aires: Universidad de San Andrés, 2002).

10. Freyre's reassessment of the African legacy is also credited with fixing samba in the national psyche. Freyre participated widely in the gatherings of Rio de Janeiro's bohemian set, where the formation of the urban carioca samba took place. See Hermano Vianna, *O Mistério do Samba* [The Mystery of Samba] (Rio de Janeiro: Jorge Zahar & UFRJ, 1995).

11. The bibliography on the relationship between what is African and what is national in the Brazilian tradition is extensive. Some of the most interesting texts are Flora Süssekind, *O Negro como Arlequim* [The Negro as Harlequin] (Rio de Janeiro: Achiamé, 1982), and Lilia Moritz Schwartz, *O Espetáculo das Raças* [The Spectacle of Races] (São Paulo: Companhia das Letras, 1993).

12. *Diário do Congresso Nacional* [National Congress Newspaper], November 8, 1914, p. 2789. The reception Rui Barbosa refers to was organized by Nair de Teffé, first lady to President Marshal Hermes da Fonseca.

13. See Vianna, *O Mistério do Samba.*

14. Cited by Rossi in *Cosas de Negros* [Black People's Matters], p. 169.

15. According to Caetano Veloso: "First the theater and later the radio and the record album gave birth to successive generations of arrangers, singers, composers, and instrumentalists who created a *tamed* and refined samba, especially as from the 1930s." See Veloso, *Verdade Tropical* [Tropical Truth] (São Paulo: Companhia das Letras, 1997), p. 37 (emphasis mine). And Tinhorão:

> The history of the carioca samba is, thus, the history of the ongoing social ascent of a genre of popular urban music, in a phenomenon similar in all respects to jazz in the United States. Fixed as a musical genre by composers in the city's lower classes, starting from motifs still cultivated toward the end of the nineteenth century by blacks hailing from rural zones, samba created a base of percussion instruments that shifted into the domain of the middle class, which dressed it up later with stereotypical orchestras and launched it as dance and music for ballrooms. From that moment on, as the 1930s progressed, several types of samba arose, according to the social group being performed for: the grandchildren of the blacks from the Saúde area came to the hills surrounding Rio de Janeiro, drawn by the value of the urban center, and they continued cultivating the *batucado* samba later known as the "samba of the hills"; the lower middle class adhered to the syncopated samba (ballroom samba); the higher echelons discovered the samba-song with a view to making it the equivalent of the foxtrot swing performed by orchestras of international profiles in dimly lit nightclubs.

See José Ramos Tinhorão, *Pequena História da Música Popular: Da Modinha à Canção de Protesto* [A Brief History of Popular Music: From *Modinha* to Protest Song] (Petrópolis: Vozes, 1975).

16. *PBT*, April 4, 1914.

17. In *Una Modernidad Periférica: Buenos Aires 1920–1930* [A Peripheral Modernity: Buenos Aires 1920–1930] (Buenos Aires: Nueva Visión, 1988), pp. 22, 23, Beatriz Sarlo examines the changes in advertising during those decades, signaling personal hand soap as one of the products that makes its appearance in advertising in this period. The lyrics of one tango speak specifically to the lack of hygiene associated with tango. Titled *Entrada Prohibida* [No Entry Allowed], it was written not coincidentally in the cabaret environment, according to Gobello, a "territory that was difficult for the lower-class malefactor to gain entry to"):

> De L'Abbaye la piantaron / y la razón no le dieron / pero después le dijeron / que fue por falta de higiene, / pues la pobrecita tiene / una costumbre asquerosa: / que no se lava la cosa / para no gastar en jabón. / Rajá de aquí, / andate a pastorear, / piantá de acá / que no te doy tecor. / Y si querés volver a figurar / Lavate bien pa no pasar calor.
>
> [From L'Abbaye they shooed her away / and did not say why / but later they did tell her / it was due to lack of hygiene / because the poor girl had / a quite disgusting habit: / she didn't wash herself down there / to save on the cost of soap. / Get out of here, / go take a hike, / shoo and scram / I won't pay you any mind. / And if you want back in / Clean yourself to not catch such heat.]

José Gobello, *Las Letras de Tango de Villoldo a Borges* [Tango Lyrics from Villoldo to Borges] (Buenos Aires: La Brújula, 1966), p. 10.

In *Civilization and Its Discontents*, Freud states:

> Dirtiness of any kind seems to us incompatible with civilization. We extend our demand for cleanliness to the human body too. We are astonished to learn of the objectionable smell which emanated from the Roi Soleil, and we shake our heads on the Isola Bella when we are shown the tiny washbasin in which Napoleon made his morning toilet. Indeed, we are not surprised by the idea of setting up the use of soap as an actual yardstick for civilization.

See Sigmund Freud, *Civilization and Its Discontents*, trans. James Strachey (New York: Norton, 1962), p. 40. First published in 1930, its ideas and the title itself provide historical reference to the unstable meanings of civilization and culture during the period of the nationalization of tango and samba, and not only in Latin America.

18. Note that *matchicha* is the Spanish translation of *maxixe*.

19. H. Dias da Cruz, quoted by Raúl Antelo, *Literatura em Revista* [Literature in Review] (São Paulo: Ática, 1984), p. 141.

20. José Ramos Tinhorão, *Música Popular: Um Tema em Debate* [Popular Music: A Topic of Debate] (São Paulo: Editora 34, 1997), p. 17.

21. The cartoon, published in 1920, had appeared previously in *Judge*, of New York. On the topic of dances like tango and maxixe and their association with modernity in São Paulo in the 1920s, see Nicolau Sevcenko, *Orfeu Extático na Metrópole: São Paulo, Sociedade e Cultura nos Frementes Anos Veinte* [Orpheus Ecstatic in the Metropolis: São

Paulo, Society and Culture in the Bustling Twenties] (São Paulo: Companhia das Letras, 1992), pp. 89–95.

22. The iconography of tango that appears on the covers of the printed scores is often delineated with the art nouveau features that prevailed as a graphic style during this period. I lament not having worked in detail on the rich corpus of analysis those music scores present.

23. Béatrice Humbert, "El Tango en París de 1907 a 1920" [The Tango in Paris from 1907 to 1920], in *El Tango Nómade* [Nomadic Tango], ed. Ramón Pelinski (Buenos Aires: Corregidor, 2000), pp. 114, 115.

24. See Rachel Valença, *Carnaval* [Carnival] (Rio de Janeiro: Rio Arte & Relume Dumará, 1996).

25. In *O Globo* on February 7, 1931, p. 8, a request appears for radio clubs to broadcast this music "to expand the diffusion of carnival sambas."

26. A carnival *bloco* (block) is a group of people who parade in the carnival in an organized way, generally wearing the same costumes and performing choreographies that were practiced in advance.

27. *O Globo*, February 11, 1931, p. 8.

28.

Dizem que Cristo / nasceu em Belém / a história se enganou / Cristo nasceu na
Bahia, meu bem / e o baiano criou / na Bahia tem vatapá / na Bahia tem caruru /
moqueca e arroz-de-auçá / manga, laranja e caju / Cristo nasceu na Bahia, meu
bem / isto sempre hei de crer / Bahia é terra santa, também / baiano santo há de ser.

In reality this is a maxixe, composed in 1926, that the musical revue "Tudo Preto" (All Black) later incorporated. It is supremely interesting for pursuing the relationship between samba, the avant-garde, and the search for radical transformations for Brazilian society. In 1924, Sinhô, *"o Rei do Samba"* (the King of Samba), traveled to São Paulo on the invitation of the Clube de Antropofagia in order to present his samba "Eu Ouço Falar" (The Rumor Goes), also known as "Seu Julinho" in support of the presidential candidacy of Júlio Prestes. After the event, Tarsila do Amaral and Oswald de Andrade hosted a party in Sinhô's honor, and the latter, in gratitude, dedicated that samba "to Dr. Oswald de Andrade and Our Lady of Brazil, Tarsila" (Abel Cardoso Júnior, record cover of *Sinhô*). For an analysis of the relationship between the avant-garde, tango, and samba, see "Primitive Avant-Garde Artists" (this volume).

29. For an analysis of this primitivism, see "Appendix: Primitive Savages" (this volume).

30. Mário de Andrade, *Ensaio sobre a Música Brasileira* [Essay on Brazilian Music] (São Paulo: Martins, 1962), p. 58.

31. Not only did Adorno place both extremes on the same level of comparison, but he also, even in the highest expression of musical modernism according to his own parameters, perceived the manifestation of a content as "somewhat savage." He states in *Philosophy of Modern Music*:

The origin of atonality as the fulfilled purification of music from all conventions contains by its very nature elements of barbarism. In Schoenberg's outbursts—often hostile to culture—this purification repeatedly causes the surface to tremble. The dissonant chord, by comparison with consonance, is not only the more differentiated and progressive; but furthermore, it sounds as if it had not been completely subdued by the ordering principle of civilization, as if it were older than tonality itself. [. . .] At first the complex chords strike the naïve ear as "false," as an inability to do things correctly, in the same manner that the layman finds radical graphics "misdrawn." Progress itself in its passionate protest against conventions has something of the child—a regressive tendency.

Theodor Adorno, *Philosophy of Modern Music*, trans. Anne G. Mitchell and Wesley V. Blomster (New York: Seabury Press, 1973), pp. 40, 41.

32. Nationalist impulse arising so much in popular music that in this period defines a great quantity of national genres—tango, samba, ballenato, etcetera—as in erudite music, also marked by a nationalizing tendency. See Ana Maria Ochoa, *Músicas Locales en Tiempos de Globalización* [Local Forms of Music in Globalized Times] (Buenos Aires: Norma, 2003), and Mário de Andrade, *Pequena História da Música* [Small History of Music]. São Paulo: Martins, 1944.

33. Darius Milhaud, *Notes sans Musique* [Notes without Music] (París: Julliard, 1949), pp. 93, 94. On nationalism in the music of the 1920s, see de Andrade, *Pequena História da Música*.

34. Oscar Zucchi, *El Tango, el Bandoneón y sus Intérpretes* [Tango, the Bandoneón and Its Musicians], vols. 1 and 2 (Buenos Aires: Corregidor, 1998), and Luis Adolfo Sierra, *Historia de la Orquesta Típica* [History of the Autochthonous Orchestra] (Buenos Aires: Corregidor, 1997).

35. The incorporation of the *bandoneón* into tango occurred around 1900. According to Oscar Zucchi:

[T]he *bandoneón* has an extremely striking acoustic duality: opening the bellows, its sound is bright and clear, but closing them it sounds harsh, muffled and contentious, as if beatitude and villainy were wrestling it out inside it. The *bandoneón* makes it possible, in addition, to play melodies or accompaniments with either hand, and the sound volume can rise or fall in the middle of playing a phrase, allowing for the full range of tones.

Zucchi, *El Tango*, p. 27. On the evolution of tango music, see also Robert Farris Thompson, *Tango: The Art History of Love* (New York: Pantheon Books, 2005).

36. See Gobello, *Las Letras de Tango*, p. 9.

37. Marta Savigliano, *Tango and the Political Economy of Passion* (Boulder, CO: Westview Press, 1995), p. 110.

38. Rossi, *Cosas de Negros*, p. 234.

39. Ezequiel Martínez Estrada, *Radiografía de la Pampa* [X-Ray of the Pampa] (Buenos Aires: Sudamericana, 1970), p. 221.

40. Borges, above all in *Evaristo Carriego*, makes reference to a state of the tango prior to the time he writes in, the 1930s. His preference is almost always for an earlier tango previous to the more accentuated influence of immigration in its compositions, perceived as primitive in relation to the tango that will be converted into a national symbol. Martínez Estrada, by contrast, denies an evolution of tango, seeing in its trans-

formations during the early decades of the twentieth century the manifestation of an original essence that has gradually come to show itself.

41. In strictly formalist and musical terms, many consider "Pelo Telefone" (By Phone) to be the first samba. For others, it is not samba at all, but rather maxixe, just as "Mi Noche Triste" (My Sad Night) inaugurates for many the tango song that is in many ways different from the so-called true tango of the brothels and the poor outskirts of the city. The polemics and the disputes about these diverse forms are endless in the Brazilian bibliography, and often extremely interesting. Like Sandroni, I prefer to view the nationalization of samba as a moment in a process that includes the appearance in the nineteenth century of other musical forms—maxixe, Bahian samba, carioca samba, choro, Brazilian tango. From a strictly formalist point of view, nonetheless, one must recognize that samba, as a genre, as it is known today, was born no earlier than in the 1930s.

42. See Carlos Sandroni, *Feitiço Decente: Transformações do Samba no Rio de Janeiro (1917–1930)* [Decent Bewitchment: Transformations of Samba in Rio de Janeiro [1917–1930] (Rio de Janeiro: Jorge Zahar & UFRJ, 2001), p. 210.

43. Ibid., pp. 221, 222.

44. Carmen Miranda, "Recensamento" (Census), on the album *A Pequena Notável*.

45.

Em 1940 / lá no morro começaram o recenseamento / e o agente recenseador / esmiuçou a minha vida / que foi um horror / e quando viu a minha mão sem aliança / encarou para a criança / que no chão dormia / e perguntou se meu moreno era decente / se era do batente ou se era da folia.

Obediente como a tudo que é da lei / fiquei logo sossegada e falei então: / O meu moreno é brasileiro, é fuzileiro, / é o que sai com a bandeira do seu batalhão! / A nossa casa não tem nada de grandeza / nós vivemos na fartura sem dever tostão / tem um pandeiro, um cavaquinho, um tamborim / um reco-reco, uma cuíca e um violão.

Fiquei pensando e comecei a descrever / tudo, tudo de valor / que meu Brasil me deu / um céu azul, um Pão de Açúcar sem farelo / um pano verde e amarelo / tudo isso é meu! / Tem feriado que pra mim vale fortuna / a Retirada da Laguna vale um cabedal! / Tem Pernambuco, tem São Paulo, tem Bahia / um conjunto de harmonia que não tem rival.

46. The history of the modernization of Rio de Janeiro during the first decades of the twentieth century is fraught with violence and small popular revolts against state intervention in public space as well as state intercession in the private sphere. "*O bota abaixo*" (the demolition)—the popular appellation for the urban modernization that Mayor Pereira Passos carried out and that demolished not only historic buildings to widen the city's narrow streets, but also hills perceived as intervening in the carioca landscape—was resisted by the lower-class population through organized demonstrations. The most famous of the popular riots was known as "Revolta da vacina," when the population of Rio de Janeiro rebelled, in 1904, against mandatory smallpox vaccination.

47. Matos, *Acertei no milhar*, p. 41.

48. See Carmen Miranda, "Gente Bamba," on the album *O Que É Que a Baiana Tem?* [What Does the Bahian Woman Have?] (Rio de Janeiro: Odeon, 1966).

49. According to Antonio Risério, Doryval Caymmi "brings dissonance and other different conquests of European impressionism to the Bahian samba," *Caymmi, uma Utopia de Lugar* [Caymmi, a Uptopia of Place] (São Paulo: Perspectiva, 1993, p. 15). Caymmi himself writes: "I, on my own, always had a tendency to alter perfect chords. I'd take one finger off a string and place it on another one, looking for a different harmony. I always prefer sevenths, ninths, chord inversions." Quoted by Risério, ibid.

PART I, CHAPTER 2

1. The history of persecution and criminalization for tango and for samba coincide at more than one point. The historical strength and credibility of these discourses has been called into question by various texts, Brazilian as well as Argentine. See Carlos Sandroni, *Feitiço Decente: Transformaçoes do Samba no Rio de Janeiro (1917–1930)* [Decent Bewitchment: Transformations of Samba in Rio de Janeiro (1917–1930)] (Rio de Janeiro: Jorge Zahar & UFRJ, 2001), and Vianna, *O Mistério do Samba.*

2. The topos of the desert for Argentina and of the jungle for Brazil often functions to postulate an emptiness that should be filled and modified. On the functioning of this contrast in two specific places, the Amazon and Patagonia, see *Margens/Márgenes* 4 (2005).

3. As was indicated in footnote 40 in part 1, chapter 1, for many who study it this primitive samba has little to do with the samba that is converted into the music of the nation in the 1930s. As a cultural phenomenon, however, these first references bear fundamental importance in the constitution of a cultural representation of samba and of music with syncretic characteristics. The first appearance of the word *samba* seems to be in a quartet by Brother Miguel do Sacramento Lopes Gama, published in *O Carapuceiro* [The Hooded Man]. See Sérgio Cabral, *As Escolas de Samba do Rio de Janeiro* [Rio de Janeiro's Samba Schools] (Petrópolis: Lumiar, 1996). In 1888 a novel by Júlio Ribeiro was published, *A Carne* [The Flesh], that included a representation of a rural samba. This description gave rise to the first composition of erudite music to take the name *samba*, for the last of the four movements of *Suite Brésilienne*, composed by Alexandre Levy. See David Appleby, *The Music of Brazil* (Austin: University of Texas Press, 1989), p. 85. Already in 1906, João do Rio, in his *Kósmos* chronicles was using the word *samba* to designate the forms of music sung at carnival. For the first appearances of the term, see Sandroni, *Feitiço Decente*, chapter 2.

4. Regarding Alencar and the importation of the novel, the best articles—and, moreover, those which provide perspectives on many opposing aspects—are the following: by Roberto Schwarz, "A Importação do Romance em Alencar" [The Importing of the Novel in Alencar], in *Ao Vencedor as Batatas* [To the winner, the Potatoes] (São Paulo: Editora 34, 2000) and Silviano Santiago, "Liderança e Hierarquia em Alencar" [Leadership and Hierarchy in Alencar], in *Vale Quanto Pesa* [Worth Its Weight] (Rio de Janeiro: Paz e Terra, 1982). On *O Cortiço* and its overflow, see Antonio Candido, "De Cortiço a Cortiço" [From Slum to Slum], in *O Discurso e a Cidade* [The Discourse and

the City] (São Paulo: Duas Cidades, 1993); and, above all, the aforementioned article by Araripe Júnior, which not only positions Azevedo as an original creator, but also elaborates the first theoretical treatment of the construction of a tropical style, based on this novel. See Tristão de Alencar Araripe Júnior, "Estilo Tropical" [Tropical Style], in *Obra Crítica* [Critical Works], vol. 2 (Rio de Janeiro: Casa de Rui Barbosa, 1958–1970). For a lucid commentary on this article and its importance in Brazilian literary historiography, see Roberto Ventura, *Estilo Tropical: História Cultural e Polêmicas Literárias no Brasil, 1870–1914* [Tropical Style: Cultural History and Literary Polemics of Brazil, 1870–1914] (São Paulo: Companhia das Letras, 1991).

5. See Sandroni, *Feitiço Decente*, p. 92.

6. Toward the end of the 1880s, samba was effectively identified with a dance typical of African blacks and mulattos, but it had not been postulated as a specifically national characteristic as it would be in *O Cortiço*. Unmistakably at issue in this case is a sort of metaphorical extension of that which is considered typically Brazilian.

7. In the center of Rio de Janeiro at the end of the century, before Pereira Passos's reform, businesses, residences, and tenement houses were intermixed. Hermano Vianna, *O Mistério do Samba* [The Mystery of Samba] (Rio de Janeiro: Jorge Zahar & UFRJ, 1995), p. 21. We can make note of the description in *O Cortiço*: "Just about that time, a small hotel was also sold on the right and a mere few meters away; thus the entire left flank of the building, some twenty meters, looked out with their nine windowsills on the innkeeper's property." Aluísio Azevedo, *O Cortiço* [The Slum] (São Paulo: Ática, 1997), p. 18. Antonio Candido signals the coexistence of the different social classes as one of the great differences between the Brazilian novel and its European "model"; the primitive stage of capitalist accumulation that Brazil was in during that period made it appropriate for Azevedo to place in one and the same novel the exploiters and the exploited, whereas the level of differentiation in French society in the same era required Zola to produce separate works for treatment of these agents, though they pertained to the same cycle. See Candido, "De Cortiço a Cortiço"; for an analysis of this article, see Roberto Schwarz, "Adequação Nacional e Originalidade Crítica" [National Adequation and Critical Originality] in *Seqüencias Brasileiras* [Brazilian Sequences] (São Paulo: Companhia das Letras, 1999).

8. "*O Cortiço* Será a Psicologia do Tumulto." Araripe Júnior, "Estilo Tropical."

9. From a structuralist perspective, Sant'Anna reads *O Cortiço* as a system of transformations. See Affonso Romano de Sant'Anna, *Análise Estrutural de Romances Brasileiros* [Structural Analysis of Brazilian Novels] (Petrópolis: Vozes, 1979).

10. Azevedo, *O Cortiço*, p. 198.

11.

Naquela mulata estava o grande mistério, a síntese das impressões que ele recebeu chegando aqui: ela era a luz ardente do meio-dia; ela era o calor vermelho das sestas da fazenda; era o aroma quente dos trevos e das baunilhas, que o atordoara nas matas brasileiras; era a palmeira virginal e esquiva que se não torce a nenhuma outra planta; era o veneno . . . para lhe cuspir dentro do sangue uma centelha daquele amor setentrional, uma nota daquela música feita de gemidos de prazer. Ibid., p. 73.

12. On romanticism and its construction of national primitivism, see Antonio Candido, *Formação da Literatura Brasileira* [Formation of Brazilian Literature] (Belo Horizonte: Itatiaia, 1957/1981).

13. Almost all the critiques of *O Cortiço*, grounded in differing critical ideologies, point out this persistence of romanticism in Azevedo.

14. Azevedo, *O Cortiço*, p. 175 (emphasis mine).

15. In this novel by Aluísio Azevedo one can see something that Antonio Candido pointed out in another novel by Azevedo (and that, on the other hand, is usually a characteristic of naturalist fiction): in these books, "primary importance is no longer accorded to the individual drama, which now appears as mere appendage to a collective struggle." See Candido, "Introdução."

16. "O sangue da mestiça reclamou os seus direitos de apuração, e Rita preferiu no europeu o macho de raça superior." Azevedo, *O Cortiço*, p. 151.

17. Flora Süssekind, *O Brasil Não É Longe Daqui* (Brazil Is Not Far from Here) (São Paulo: Companhia das Letras, 1990); and Ventura, *Estilo Tropical*, p. 60. There is a translation into Spanish of the first chapter of this book in Adriana Amante and Florencia Garramuño, *Absurdo brasil: Polémicas en la cultura brasileña* (Absurd Brazil: Polemics in Brazilian Culture) (Buenos Aires: Biblos, 2000).

18. Ventura, *Estilo Tropical*, pp. 67, 68.

19. The appeal appears in *Martín Fierro* (second period), 1, no. 4 (May 15, 1924); Güiraldes' response in the following issue, no. 5–6 (June 15, 1924).

20. Ivonne Bordelois points out: "'My entire oeuvre has been nothing but one long *Cencerro de Cristal*,' Güiraldes will say many years later. It is key to recognize that the phrase . . . means, in reality, that *Cencerro de Cristal* contains, in latent form and among other traits, the indications of that project which *Don Segundo Sombra* will be the confirmation and final justification of." *Genio y Figura de Ricardo Güiraldes* [The Genius and Figure of Ricardo Güiraldes] (Buenos Aires: Eudeba, 1966), p. 48.

21. For a contemporary definition of these descriptions, see José M. Ramos Mejía, *Las Multitudes Argentinas: Estudio de Psicología Colectiva* [The Argentine Multitudes: A Study of Collective Psychology] (Buenos Aires: Belgrano, 1977), pp. 214, 215.

22. See Marta Savigliano, *Tango and the Political Economy of Passion* (Boulder, CO: Westview Press, 1995), pp. 114–25.

23. It is interesting to observe, however, that Güiraldes was an excellent tango dancer and that from very early on, five years of age, he already knew how to play, on the guitar, a few chords of "El Queco et la Milonga." Roberto Selles, "El Tango y Sus Dos Primeras Décadas (1880–1900)" [Tango and Its First Two Decades (1880–1900)], in *La Historia del Tango* [The History of Tango], vol. 2 (Buenos Aires: Corregidor, 1980).

24. Regarding the ambiguities in *El Cencerro de Cristal* and in Güiraldes' writing in general, see Bordelois, *Genio y Figura de Ricardo Güiraldes*; Eduardo Romano, "Introducción," in Ricardo Güiraldes, *Don Segundo Sombra* (Buenos Aires: Colihue, 1985); and Francine Masiello, *Lenguaje e Ideología* [Language and Ideology] (Buenos Aires: Hachette, 1988).

25. See Jorge Luis Borges, "Ascendencias del Tango" [Tango's Origins], in *El Idioma*

de los Argentinos [The Language of the Argentines] (Madrid: Alianza, 1995), p. 105 and "Leopoldo Lugones," in *Sur* 8, no. 41 (February 1938), published together in *Borges en Sur: 1931–1980* [Borges in *Sur*: 1931–1980] (Buenos Aires: Emecé, 1999).

PART I, CHAPTER 3

1.

Pesadez de los tangos ingleses, alemanes, deseo, espacio mecanizado por fracs que ni siquiera pueden exteriorizar su sensibilidad, plagio de tangos parisinos e italianos, parejas moluscas, felinidad y salvajismo argentino idiotamente ablandados, morfinizados, pesados. Poseer una mujer no es frotarse con ella, sino penetrarla. ¡Bárbaros! ¿Una rodilla entre los muslos? ¡Vamos, hombre, si hacen falta dos! ¡Bárbaros! Sí, seamos bárbaros. Hijas del tango y de sus lentos soponcios, ¿creéis que es divertido mirarse mutuamente en la boca y tratarse recíprocamente los dientes como dos dentistas alucinados?

—¿Hay que arrancarlo? ¿Emplomarlo? / ¿Pensáis que es gracioso tirabuzonearse el uno al otro para destapar el espasmo de vuestra pareja sin que podáis llegar jamás? ¿O de mirar la punta de vuestro calzado como zapateros hipnotizados? [. . .]

Tristán e Isolda retardan su espasmo para excitar al rey Marc [. . .] miniatura de angustias sexuales, chupetín de deseo, lujuria al aire libre, delirium tremens, manos y pies de alcoholizado; minicoito de cinematógrafo, vals masturbado. ¡Uf! Hijas diplómatas de piel. ¡Viva la salvajada de una posesión brusca, la toma de una danza muscular exaltante y fortificante! Tango y tangaje de veleros, estallad de ternura y de imbecilidad lunar. Tango, tango, tangaje a vomitar. Tango, lento y paciente funeral del sexo muerto. Se trata por cierto de religión, moral y mojigatería; estas tres palabras no tienen ningún sentido para nosotros. Pero es en nombre de la salud, de la fuerza, de la voluntad, de la virilidad que nosotros abucheamos el tango y sus debilidades pasatistas.

E. T. Marinetti, "A bas le tango et Parsifal," 1923; quotation and Spanish translation by Béatrice Humbert, "El tango en París de 1907 a 1920" [The Tango in Paris from 1907 to 1920], in *El Tango Nómade* [Nomadic Tango], ed. Ramón Pelinski (Buenos Aires: Corregidor, 2000).

2. On the importance of primitivism in the critique of the European avant-garde, see, among others, Hal Foster, "The 'Primitive' Unconscious of Modern Art, or White Skin Black Masks," in *Recodings: Art, Spectacle, Cultural Politics* (Seattle: Bay Press, 1985); James Clifford, "On Ethnographic Surrealism," *Comparative Studies in Society and History* 23, no. 4 (1981); and Rosalind Krauss, *The Originality of the Avant Garde and Other Modernist Myths* (Cambridge, MA: MIT Press, 1985).

3. For a new and extremely interesting perspective on defining the Latin American avant-garde movements, focused on architecture but also including a detailed analysis of the process of tango, see Adrián Gorelik, *Das Vanguardas à Brasília: Cultura Urbana e Arquitetura na América Latina* [From the Avant-Garde to Brasília: Urban Culture and Architecture in Latin America] (Belo Horizonte: UFMG, 2005).

4. One exception is José Ramos Tinhorão's perspective, as can be read as much in *História Social da Música Popular Brasileira* [Social History of Brazilian Popular Music] (São Paulo: Editora 34, 1998) as in *Pequena História da Música Popular: Da Modinha à Canção de Protesto* [A Brief History of Popular Music: From Modinha to Protest Song] (Petrópolis: Vozes, 1975) and *Música Popular: Um Tema em Debate* [Popular Music: A Topic of Debate] (São Paulo: Editora 34, 1997).

5. Marta Savigliano, *Tango and the Political Economy of Passion* (Boulder, CO: Westview Press, 1995), p. 82.

6. Ibid., p. 137.

7. James Clifford states: "Another crucial outgrowth of ethnographic surrealism is third world modernism and nascent anticolonial discourse." "On Ethnographic Surrealism," p. 546, note 18.

8. Peter Osborne, *Philosophy in Cultural Theory* (London: Routledge, 2000), pp. 59, 60. Also see Osborne, *The Politics of Time* (London: Verso, 1995).

9. Within these same coordinates Raúl Antelo analyzes the following exquisite paragraph written by Oliverio Girondo:

Una noche en que mi abuelo (Tatata como le decíamos nosotros) se encontraba indispuesto la llama a mi abuela (mamá Pepa) que se encontraba en el cuarto contiguo y cuando se le acerca a la cama le pregunta: "¿Mearé o tomaré agua?" y dice Antelo: "He aquí una auténtica escena primaria de la escritura de Oliverio. Se trata de una disyuntiva, un dilema, estructura agónica de la modernidad periférica. Esa alternativa de dos puntas oscila entre expulsar e incorporar".

[One night when my grandfather (Tatata as we called him) was indisposed, he called my grandmother (mama Pepa) who was in the next room, and when she approached his bed he asked her: "Will I pee or will I drink some water?" and Antelo says: "Here we have an authentic first scene of Oliverio's writing. At issue here is a dilemma, a quandary, the agonic structure of the periphery's modernity. That alternative between two extremes oscillates between expelling and incorporating."]

See Raúl Antelo, "Introducción del coordinador" [Editor's Introduction], in Oliverio Girondo, *Obra Completa* [Complete Works] (Madrid: ALLCA XX, 1999), p. xxxviii.

10. I would not want to introduce a new dichotomy, now between European and Latin American primitivism, in order to replace the first one. In fact, certain primitivisms of the Old World also appealed to the national past, such as Russian primitivism and its recuperation of peasant art and icons. This latter, however, is in a certain sense also peripheral to the historical avant-garde. For a detailed study of the different nativisms of the nineteenth century, see Edward Said, *Culture and Imperialism* (New York: Vintage Books, 1994), pp. 220–38.

11. Partha Chatterjee, *Nationalist Thought and the Colonial World: A Derivative Discourse?* (London: Zed for the United Nations University, 1986), p. 18.

12. In an extremely interesting and inspiring analysis of the primitivism of the *Martin Fierro* group, Adriana Armando and Guillermo Fantoni seem to prefer this homologation. See Girondo, *Obra Completa*, p. 480.

13. Antonio Candido, *Literatura e sociedade: Estudos de teoria e história literaria*

[Literature and Society: Studies on Literary Theory and History] (São Paulo: T. A. Queiroz, 2000), p. 121.

14. Haroldo de Campos, "Prefácio" [Preface], in *Poesias Reunidas* [Collected Poems], by Oswald de Andrade (Rio de Janeiro: Civilização Brasileira, 1971).

15. Several texts by Mário de Andrade can be read from this perspective. One of them shows collaboration with the visual arts avant-garde in a single book: *Poemas da Negra* [The Black Woman's Poems] is made up of twelve love poems published in *Remate de Males* [Culmination of Evils] (1930) together with drawings specially made for that edition by Emiliano Di Cavalcanti. See Mário de Andrade, *Poesias Completas* [Complete Poems], critical edition by Diléa Zanotto Manfio (Belo Horizonte: Itatiaia; São Paulo: Editora da Universidade de São Paulo, 1987).

16. For the formulation of this questioning, see Hal Foster, "Who's Afraid of the Neo-Avant-Garde?" in *The Return of the Real* (Cambridge, MA: MIT Press, 1996), p. 10, and the classic and fundamental work by Rosalind Krauss, *The Originality of the Avant-Garde and Other Modernist Myths* (Cambridge, MA: MIT Press, 1985); for the Brazilian articulation of this problem, see Silviano Santiago, "Permanência do discurso da tradição no modernismo brasileiro" [The Permanence of the Discourse of Tradition in Modernism], in *Cultura Brasileira: Tradição/Contradição* [Brazilian Culture: Tradition/Contradition], ed. Adauto Novaes (Rio de Janeiro: Jorge Zahar, 1987).

17. See Santiago, "Permanência do discurso."

18. See Gorelik, *Das Vanguardas à Brasília*, pp. 25, 26.

19. Peter Osborne, *Philosophy in Cultural Theory*, p. 60.

20. See "Appendix: Primitive Savages" (this volume).

21. See Jorge Luis Borges, *Evaristo Carriego* (Buenos Aires: Gleizer, 1930), p. 27.

22. In the period during which Borges wrote the first edition of *Evaristo Carriego*, the music of the River Plate was in constant effervescence. Pedro Henríquez Ureña gave a conference in 1929 titled "Música popular de América" [Popular Music of America] in which he apologized for not discussing all American music. Among the limits on his parameters, he notes: "the first was easy: to not talk about the River Plate, just as one would not take owls to Athens or oranges to Paraguay." See Pedro Henríquez Ureña, *Ensayos* [Essays], critical edition by José Luis Abellán and Ana María Barrenechea (Madrid: ALLCA XX, 2000), p. 627.

23. The 1955 edition also presents other changes. It adds five chapters: "Stories of Horsemanship," "The Dagger," "Prologue to a Publication by Evaristo Carriego," "History of Tango," and "Two Letters." "History of Tango" rewrites and combines two texts that Borges had included in *El Idioma de los Argentines* [The Language of the Argentines]: "The Origins of Tango" and "Men Fought." At the same time, *Evaristo Carriego* had been a continuation and rewriting of the text in *El Tamaño de Mi Esperanza* [The Size of My Hope], "Carriego y el Sentido del Arrabal" [Carriego and the Meaning of the Periphery] and is the text that Borges promised in that work: "This very brief discourse has its watchword and I must return to it someday, if only to sing its praises." Jorge Luis Borges, *El Tamaño de Mi Esperanza* (Buenos Aires: Seix Barral, 1993), p. 31.

24. Borges, *Evaristo Carriego*, 1955 edition, pp. 125, 160; 1930 edition, pp. 139, 160.

25. Borges, *Evaristo Carriego*, 1955 edition, note 1, pp. 124, 159.

26. Borges, *Evaristo Carriego*, in *Obras Completas* [Complete Works] (Buenos Aires: Emecé, 1989), p. 159.

27. Ibid., p. 168.

28. Partha Chatterjee warns of the dangers of considering too seriously the exigencies of nationalism as an exclusively political movement (*Nationalist Thought*, p. 216), pointing out that Hindu nationalism establishes its own sovereign domain within colonial society dividing the world of institutions and practices into two domains, the spiritual and the material. This distinction provides one of the possible ways of reading the opposition between the nationalism of Lugones, so much more institutional or "material," and that of Borges.

29. *Nosotros*, year 19, vol. 49, no. 191 (April 1925). In *Textos Recobrados: 1919–1929* [Recovered Texts: 1919–1929] (Buenos Aires: Emecé, 1997), p. 207.

30. A typical strategy of Borges the nationalist, according to Jorge Panesi. See *Críticas* [Critiques] (Buenos Aires: Norma, 2000), p. 123: "En Borges, los héroes o los arquetipos de subjetividad, además de escasos, son sospechosos, espurios, se los erige como varones ejemplares para ejercer inmediatamente sobre ellos la reticencia. Rosas o Carriego, Quevedo u Oscar Wilde soportan el fervor admirativo no menos que la apasionada discusión intelectual de sus defectos." (In Borges, the heroes or the archetypes of subjectivity, in addition to being scarce, are suspect and illegitimate; they are set up as exemplary men only to have reticence immediately applied to them. Rosas or Carriego, Quevedo or Oscar Wilde endure fawning fervor no less than impassioned intellectual deliberations on their defects.)

31. Borges, *Evaristo Carriego*, p. 168.

32. *Translator's note:* It is an unsuual matter for a poem by such an internationally renowned poetic genius as Borges not to have been translated by any of the professionals who worked with him or the corpus of his work. Hence, I have produced a simple English version for the purposes of *Primitive Modernities*, at least for linguistic comprehension purposes, and duly apologize for the lack of better poetic instincts.

Quejumbre mora / bordeando oscuramente ambas eternidades / del cielo gigantesco y de las leonadas arenas, / llevada con horror de alfanjes heroicos / a los límpidos prados andaluces / desgarrándose como una hoguera por las malezas del tiempo, / entre los siglos escurriéndose / quemando las vihuelas en llamarada de jácaras / hasta el milagro de la gesta de Indias / cuando los castellanos / saqueadores de mundos / iban robando tierras de albur al poniente. / Desmelenada por la pampa, / trasegada de guitarra criolla en guitarra, / entreverándose con la pena / de avillanda gente quichua / descoyuntándose con la insolencia del puerto, / otra vez picota de arrufianados vivires / y humilladero de mujeres malas, / ha logrado ahondar con tal virtud en nuestra alma / que si de nochecita una ventana / la regala en sonora generosidad a la calle / el caminante / siente como si le palparan el corazón con la mano.

Borges, *Textos Recobrados*, p. 165. The text was published in *Fervor de Buenos Aires* [Fervor of Buenos Aires] (Buenos Aires: Imprenta Serantes, 1923; author's edition).

33. Borges, *Evaristo Carriego*, p. 161.

34. Mário de Andrade and Manuel Bandeira, *Correspondência* [Correspondence] (São Paulo: Editora da Universidade de São Paulo, 2000), p. 84.

35. Ibid., p. 88. Below the poem's title, depending on how it appears in a given edition of *Clã do Jabotí*, the year 1923 is included. See Mário de Andrade, *Poesias Completas* [Complete Poems], critical edition by Diléa Zanotto Manfio (Belo Horizonte: Itatiaia; São Paulo: Editora da Universidade de São Paulo, 1987), p. 163. The title of the book also specifies this kind of encounter, observable in several of the poems included in it. In a 1928 letter to Drummond, Mário de Andrade explains: "Clã é reunião" (Clan is reunion). De Andrade and Bandeira, *Correspondência*, p. 88.

36.
A princípio fiquei enojado. / Tanta vulgaridade! / Tanta gritaria! / Minha frieza
bruma de paulista.

De Andrade and Bandeira, *Correspondência*, p. 88.

37.
Minha frieza de paulista / policiamentos interiores / temores da exceção . . .

Mário de Andrade, *Poesias Completas*, p. 163.

38. This ethnographic diction will be, given the rest, a general trait of almost all of *Clã do Jabotí* and marks in addition an entire zone of Brazilian modernism within which one could mention Manuel Bandeira, primarily in *Carnaval* [Carnival], or Raúl Bopp in *Cobra Norato* [Black Snake], among other works.

39. See Davi Arrigucci, *Humildade, Paixão e Morte: A Poesia de Manuel Bandeira* [Humility, Passion and Death: The Poetry of Manuel Bandeira] (São Paulo: Companhia das Letras, 1990).

40. See Roberto Schwarz, "O Psicologismo na Poética de Mário de Andrade" [Psychologism in the Poetics of Mário de Andrade], in *A Sereia e o Desconfiado* [The Siren and the Incredulous Man] (Rio de Janeiro: Paz e Terra, 1981), p. 15.

41. "A vida moderna desvairia o poeta [. . .] e este transfere seu desvairismo para a vida moderna." João Luis Lafetá, "A Representação do Sujeito Lírico na *Paulicéia Desvairada*" [The Representation of the Lyrical Subject in *Hallucinated City*], *Revista da Biblioteca Mário de Andrade* (São Paulo) 51 (1993), p. 79.

42.
Em baixo do Hotel Avenida em 1923 / na mais pujante civilização do Brasil / os
negros sambando em cadência. / Tão sublime, tão áfrica! / A mais moça bulcão
polido ondulações lentas lentamente / com as arrecadas chispando raios glaucos
ouro na luz peluda de pó. / Só as ancas ventre dissolvendo-se em vaivéns de ondas
em cio. / Termina se benzendo religiosa talqualmente num ritual. / E o bombo
gargalhante de tostões / sincopa a graça danada.

Mário de Andrade, "Prefácio Interessantíssimo [Most Interesting Preface], in *Paulicéia Desvairada* (1922), *Poesias Completas* [Complete Poems].

43.

E a multidão compacta se aglomera aglutina / mastiga em aproveitamento brincadeiras / asfixias desejadas delírios sardinhas desmaios / serpentinas serpentinas cores luzes sons / e sons!

Ibid.

44.

Ora, se em vez de unicamente usar versos melódicos horizontais [. . .] fizermos que se sigam palavras sem ligação imediata entre si: estas palavras, pelo fato mesmo de se não seguirem intelectual, gramaticalmente, se sobrepõem umas às outras, para a nossa sensação, formando, não mais melodias, mais harmonias.

Ibid., p. 68.

45. Ibid., p. 69. The arpeggio is a chord, the notes of which are played successively and not simultaneously and in a rapid fashion, which differentiates it from a chord (in which the notes are played simultaneously) and a spread chord (in which the notes are played successively but in a slower fashion). The arpeggio functions as a single note (in terms of the rhythm), but in that unit each note maintains a certain individuality, its own specific tone.

46. A comparison of the different figurations of the primitive in *Clã do Jabotí* [Clan of the Turtle] and *Feuilles de Route* [Road Map] by Blaise Cendrars exceeds the parameters of this chapter, although the problems set forth there do not. It is important to recall that both texts arose on the basis of the famous "viagem da descoberta do Brasil" (voyage of the discovery of Brazil) the modernists carried out, together with Cendrars, in 1924.

47.

El primitivo le gusta a uno por lo que tiene de primitivo y no por lo que no tenemos de primitivos. Lo que nos gusta en el primitivo es que es síntesis, es realismo, es deformación, es símbolo. En el arte del primitivo hay un abandono de las particularidades y una revivificación sistemática de los valores esenciales, religión, belleza, política, sociedad, verdad, bondad, amor, etc., etc.

Mário de Andrade, *El Paulista de la Calle Florida* [The Man from São Paulo on Florida Street], ed. and trans. Raúl Antelo (Buenos Aires: Iracema Collection, Centro de Estudios Brasileños, 1979), p. 114.

48. "Sem nós a Europa não teria sequer a sua pobre declaração dos direitos do homem." Oswald de Andrade, *Manifesto Antropófago* (Cannibalist Manifesto), in *A Utopia Antropofágica* [The Cannibalist Utopia] (São Paulo: Globo, 1990), p. 48.

49.

Brasil amado não porque seja minha patria / pátria é acaso de migrações e do pão-nosso onde Deus der . . . / Brasil que eu amo porque é o ritmo do meu braço aventuroso, / o gosto dos meus descansos, / o balanço das minhas cantigas amores e danças. / Brasil que eu sou porque é a minha / expressão muito engraçada, / Porque é o meu sentimento pachorrento, / Porque é o meu jeito de ganhar dinheiro, de comer e de dormir.

Mário de Andrade, *Poesias Completas*, p. 162.

50. For the classic text regarding the relationship between particularism and universalism, see Ernesto Laclau, *Emancipación y Diferencia* [Emancipation and Difference] (Buenos Aires: Nueva Visión, 1996). On that text and that relationship, see also Judith Butler, "Restaging the Universal: Hegemony and the Limits of Formalism," in *Contingency, Hegemony, Universality: Contemporary Dialogues on the Left*, ed. Judith Butler, Ernesto Laclau, and Slavoj Žižek (London and New York: Verso, 2000), p. 42. On this text and on Joan Wallach Scott, *Only Paradoxes to Offer: French Feminists and the Rights of Man* (Cambridge, MA: Harvard University Press, 1997), Butler points out: "Indeed, it seems to me that most minority rights struggles employ both particularist and universalist strategies at once, producing a political discourse that sustains an ambiguous relation to Enlightenment notions of universality." Butler cites thereafter the text by Paul Gilroy, *The Black Atlantic: Modernity and Double Consciousness* (Cambridge, MA: Harvard University Press, 1992).

51. Many other artists of the Argentine and Brazilian avant-garde have produced paintings and drawings about tango and samba, such as Lasar Segall and Xul Solar.

52. Cecília Meireles, *Batuque, Samba e Macumba: Estudos de Gesto e Ritmo, 1926–1934* [Batuque, Samba and Macumba: Studies on Gesture and Rhythm, 1926–1934] (Rio de Janeiro: FUNARTE, 1983). An article in the newspaper *A Nação* announces "a interessantíssima exposição de Cecília Meireles fixando os ritmos do samba através de uma grande coleção de desenhos, aquarelas e estudos, bem como as figuras típicas da baiana e do bamba" (the extremely interesting exhibition by Cecília Meireles, fixing the rhythms of samba in a large collection of designs, watercolors, and studies, as well as of autocthonous figures of the Bahian woman and the Bamba). The exhibit was accompanied by a presentation of the samba "school" or group, "Escola da Portela."

53. Páulo Reis (1994) says: "Él sólo rompería con la gran influencia del cubismo de Picasso (y eventualmente de Braque) cuando vuelve al Brasil y decide hacer una radiografía de nuestro pueblo, transformando mulatas en madonas" (He would only break with the great influence of the cubism of Picasso [and eventually Braque] when he returns to Brazil and decides to make an x-ray of our people, transforming mulatas into Madonnas"). See Paulo Reis, "Di Cavalcanti" in *Jornal do Brasil*, July 6, 1994. For a reading of Di Cavalcanti's painting as an insert within *Rappel a l'ordre*, see Carlos Zilio, *A Querela do Brasil: A Questão da Identidade na Arte Brasileira; A Obra de Tarsila, Di Cavalcanti e Portinari* [The War for Brazil: The Question of Identity in Brazilian Art; the Work of Tarsila, Di Cavalcanti and Portinari] (Rio de Janeiro: Relume Dumará, 1997); and Tadeu Chiarelli, "Entre Almeida Jr. e Picasso," in *Arte Internacional Brasileira* (São Paulo: Lemos, 1999).

54. See Carlos Zilio, *A Querela do Brasil*.

55. One can see a similar operation in relation to samba in the xylography titled "Samba" by Lasar Segall.

56. Rosalind Krauss, *Los Papeles de Picasso* [The Picasso Papers] (Barcelona: Gedisa, 1999), p. 30.

57. The relationship between Di Cavalcanti and Almeida Júnior has been the focus of work by Chiarelli, "Entre Almeida Jr. e Picasso."

58. Ibid., p. 63.

59. See Mário de Andrade, *Aspectos das Artes Plásticas* (São Paulo: Martins, 1963), p. 47.

60. Carmen Miranda used this costume, dressed as a typical Bahian woman, in the film *Banana da Terra* [Banana from the Land] (1939), although for that period the costume had been used already by several singers and dancers in cabarets. See José Ramos Tinhorão, *História Social da Música Popular Brasileira* [Social History of Brazilian Popular Music] (São Paulo: Editora 34, 1998).

61. "En el carnaval carioca, innegablemente licencioso y grosero, como en todas partes en la expansión de personas habitualmente civilizadas, el carnaval de los negros guarda aun aspecto único de respeto, elegancia y digamos incluso de distinción artística sorprendente." Meireles, *Batuque, Samba e Macumba*, p. 62.

62.

Perto do bar-restaurante da Praia da Freguesia, os falsos grã-finos mostram seu nojo pelo carnaval da negrada, sentando de pijama nas cadeiras do passeio, com a garotada fantasiada de índio, choramingando em redor. Foi aí que passou um bando de sujos com tamborim, três cuícas e uma gaita de bôca fazendo solo: cantavam o chorinho mais bonito dêste ano:

—Lá vem a lua lá no céu surgindo. . . .
—E o que é que eu tenho com isso?
Um senhor de barbicha pôs a mão em concha atrás da orelha, escutou a cantiga e ficou danado:
—Isso é verso futurista! Ó xentes, até em samba já dá verso futurista!

Rachel de Queiroz, "Carnaval na Ilha do Governador" [Carnival on "Ilha do Governador"], in *Rio de Janeiro em Prosa e Verso* [Rio de Janeiro in Prose and Verse], by Manuel Bandeira and Carlos Drummond de Andrade (Rio de Janeiro: José Olympio, 1965), p. 253.

PART II, CHAPTER 1

1. See Flora Süssekind, *O Brasil Não É Longe Daqui* [Brazil Is Not Far from Here] (São Paulo: Companhia das Letras, 1990); Adolfo Prieto, *Los Viajeros Ingleses y la Emergencia de la Literatura Argentina, 1820–1850* [British Travelers and the Emergence of Argentine Literature, 1820–1850] (Buenos Aires: Fondo de Cultura Económica, 1990). Adriana Amante focused on Rosas' political exiles in Rio de Janeiro in "La Literatura del Exilio en el Brasil en la Época de Rosas" [The Literature of Exile in Brazil during the Age of Rosas], doctoral dissertation, Facultad de Filosofía y Letras, UBA, Buenos Aires, 2006. Laura Malosetti Costa, in *Los Primeros Modernos: Arte y Sociedad en Buenos Aires a Fines del Siglo XIX* [The First Moderns: Art and Society in Buenos Aires at the End of the XIX Century] (Buenos Aires: Fondo de Cultura Económica, 2001), studied the voyages of visual artists at the end of the nineteenth century, and Beatriz Colombi, in *Viaje Intelectual: Migraciones y Desplazamientos en América Latina (1880–1915)* [Intellectual Voyage: Migrations and Displacements in Latin America 1880–1915)] (Rosario: Beatriz Viterbo, 2004), studied diverse intellectual voyages between 1880 and 1915.

2. See Marta Savigliano, *Tango and the Political Economy of Passion* (Boulder, CO: Westview Press, 1995), p. 251. Also see Juan Corradi, "How Many Did It Take to Tango? Voyages of Urban Culture in the Early 1900s," in Vera Zolberg and Joni Maya Cerbo (eds.), *Outsider Art: Contesting Boundaries in Latin America Contemporary Culture* (Cambridge: Cambridge University Press, 1997); and Eduardo Berti, "Primer Tango en París" [First Tango in Paris], *La Nación* (Buenos Aires), Suplemento Cultura (December 9, 2001).

3. See Luis Adolfo Sierra, *Historia de la Orquesta Típica* (History of the Autochthonous Orchestra) (Buenos Aires: Corregidor, 1997); and Sérgio Cabral, "Les Batutas em Paris" [The Batutas in Paris] in *Pixinguinha: Vida e Obra* [Pixinguinha: Life and Works] (Petrópolis: Lumiar, 1997). Regarding Arnaldo Guinle and his financing of Os Oito Batutas and of Villa-Lobos, see Carlos Sandroni, *Feitiço Decente: Transformações do Samba no Rio de Janeiro (1917–1930)* [Decent Bewitchment: Transformations of Samba in Rio de Janeiro [1917–1930]] (Rio de Janeiro: Jorge Zahar & UFRJ, 2001), p. 116; Cabral, *Pixinguinha*, pp. 72 and 73.

4. In Argentina commercial agencies had even been created to contract tango musicians to send to Europe. See Francisco Canaro, *Mis Memorias: Mis Bodas de Oro con el Tango* [My Memoirs: My Golden Anniversary with Tango] (Buenos Aires: Corregidor, 1999) and Enrique Cadícamo, *Mis memorias* [My Memoirs] (Buenos Aires: Corregidor, 1995).

5. Quoted by Annateresa Fabris, in *Candido Portinari* (São Paulo: EDUSP, 1996).

6. See Diana Wechsler, "Portinari en la Cultura Visual de los Años Treinta: Estéticas del Silencio, Silenciosas Declamaciones" [Portinari in the Visual Culture of the Thirties: Aesthetics of Silence, Silent Recitations], in *Candido Portinari y el Sentido Social del Arte* [Candido Portinari and the Social Meaning of Art], ed. Andrea Giunta (Buenos Aires: Siglo XXI, 2005).

7. In the case of tango and of samba or maxixe, the most imperious exigency is the one that demands adaptation to a certain idea of what is typical and autochthonous abroad, which for the musicians entails not only a process of self-exoticization but also a clear distancing from the "truth" of those musical forms. Tango musicians, for example, were obliged in Paris to dress up as gauchos in order to overcome restrictions imposed by the French musicians' union, which allowed orchestras with non-French musicians to perform only if the piece was "an autochthonous number." According to Francisco Canaro, in typically narcissistic style, he himself conceived of the formula for the costume. See Francisco Canaro, *Mis Memorias* [My Memoirs].

8. See Oswald de Andrade, *Manifesto da Poesia Pau Brasil: A Utopia Antropofágica* [Pau Brasil Manifesto: The Cannibalist Utopia] (São Paulo: Globo, 1990); Spanish translation: *Escritos Antropófagos* [Cannibalist Writings], selection, chronology, and epilogue by Gonzalo Aguilar and Alejandra Laera (Buenos Aires: Corregidor, 2001). Oswald de Adrade's *Manifesto* is from 1924, the same year as André Breton's *Surrealist Manifesto*.

9. *Carta de Tarsila à família* [Letter from Tarsila to her family], Paris, October 8, 1923, cited by Aracy Amaral, *Tarsila: Sua Obra e Seu Tempo* [Tarsila: Her Oeuvre and Her Era] (São Paulo: Editora 34 & EDUSP, 2003), p. 119. The compulsion to acquire the

maximum possible signs of European modernity appears frequently, as much in the letters and telegrams of Oswald de Andrade as in those of Tarsila do Amaral. See ibid.

10. Hermano Vianna showed that this collaboration arose also at the social margins of national space in his work on the points of contact between modernists and samba artists in Rio de Janeiro. André Gardel worked on the formal connections between Manuel Bandeira and Sinhó, and Santuza Cambria Naves worked on the points of contact between modernists and popular music. See Hermano Vianna, *O Mistério do Samba* [The Mystery of Samba] (Rio de Janeiro: Jorge Zahar & UFRJ, 1995); Santuza Cambraia Naves, *O Violão Azul: Modernismo e Música Popular* [The Blue Guitar: Modernism and Popular Music] (Rio de Janeiro: Fundação Getúlio Vargas, 1998); and André Gardel, *O Encontro entre Bandeira e Sinhô* [The Meeting of Bandeira and Sinhô] (Rio de Janeiro: Prefeitura da Cidade do Rio de Janeiro, Secretaría Municipal de Cultura, Departamento Geral de Documentação e Informação Cultural, Divisão de Editoração, 1996). See also Manuel Bandeira, "Sinhó, Traço de União" [Sinhó, a Unifying Element], in *Rio de Janeiro em Prosa e Verso* [Rio de Janeiro in Prose and Poetry], ed. Manuel Bandeira and Carlos Drummond de Andrade, vol. 5. (Rio de Janeiro: José Olympio, 1965).

11. Oswald de Andrade, *Serafim Ponte Grande*, in *Obras Completas* [Complete Works, vol. 2 (Rio de Janeiro: Civilização Brasileira, 1972), p. 131. This prologue is famous because it marked the beginning of the deep self-criticism that Oswald de Andrade carried out in regard to his participation in modernism; self-criticism, moreover, according to Silviano Santiago in absentia in his conference in Belo Horizonte, "O Caminho Percorrido," almost contemporaneous with the self-criticism of modernism realized by Mário de Andrade, "O Movimento Modernista." While in the prologue to *Serafim Ponte Grande*, Oswald de Andrade renounces his most strongly modernist phase, in the conference he recuperates modernism in his nationalist phase without the self-criticism he had expressed in the prologue to *Serafim*. As Silviano Santiago states, Oswald de Andrade chooses to celebrate another twenty years, those of modernism's turn toward nationalism. See Silviano Santiago, "Sobre Plataformas e Testamentos" [On Platforms and Testaments], in *Ponta de Lança* [Spearhead] by Oswald de Andrade (São Paulo: Globo, 2004), later reproduced in his *Ora Direis, Puxar Conversa!* [And Now You Will Say, Spark Conversation!] (Belo Horizonte: UFMG, 2006).

Oswald was not the only one to brandish a strong self-criticism regarding the functioning of the avant-garde in the Brazilian context. Mário de Andrade too, in his famous essay "O Movimento Modernista," of 1942, launched one of the saddest epitaphs of his generation. Despite the differences in these criticisms, they share the same horizon: that of the avant-garde's exhaustion, in relation to which its combination to an authoritarian state is no secondary matter.

12. Amaral, "Correspondência," pp. 410, 411.

13. Ibid.

14. Paulo Renato Gueriós, "Heitor Villa-Lobos e o Ambiente Artístico Parisiense: Convertendo-se em um Músico Brasileiro" [Heitor Villa-Lobos and the Artistic Context in Paris: Becoming a Brazilian Musician], *Mana* 9, no. 1 (2003), p. 92.

15. Francisco Canaro, *Mis Memorias* [My Memoirs], "Sentimiento Gaucho" [Gau-

cho Feeling] is from 1924, with music composed by Rafael and Francisco Canaro and lyrics by Juan Andrés Caruso:

> En un viejo almacén del Paseo Colón / donde van los que tienen perdida la fe, / todo sucio, harapiento, una tarde encontré / a un borracho sentado en oscuro rincón. / Al mirarle sentí una profunda emoción / porque en su alma un dolor secreto adiviné

> y, sentándome cerca, a su lado, le hablé, / y él, entonces, me hizo esta cruel confesión. / Ponga, amigo, atención. / Sabe que es condición de varón el sufrir . . . / La mujer que yo quería con todo mi corazón / se me ha ido con un hombre que la supo seducir / y, aunque al irse mi alegría tras de ella se llevó, / no quisiera verla nunca . . . Que en la vida sea feliz / con el hombre que la tiene pa' su bien . . . o qué sé yo.

> Porque todo aquel amor que por ella yo sentí / lo cortó de un solo tajo con el filo'e su traición . . .

> Pero inútil . . . No puedo, aunque quiera, olvidar / el recuerdo de la que fue mi único amor. / Para ella ha de ser como el trébol de olor / que perfuma al que la vida le va a arrancar. / Y, si acaso algún día quisiera volver / a mi lado otra vez, yo la he de perdonar. / Si por celos a un hombre se puede matar / se perdona cuando habla muy fuerte el querer / a cualquiera mujer.

> [In an old grocery on Paseo Colón / where the ones who've lost their faith go, / all dirty and in rags, one afternoon I found / a drunkard sitting in a dark corner. / When I saw him I felt a deep emotion / because in his soul I guessed a secret pain

> and, sitting nearby, at his side, I spoke to him, / and he, then, told me this cruel confession. / Pay attention, friend. / You know it's a man's fate to suffer . . . / The woman I loved with all my heart / went off with another man who knew how to seduce her / and, though when she left she took my joy with her, / I would never want to see her again . . . May she be happy in life / with the man who has her for her own good . . . or what do I know.

> Because all that love I felt for her / was cut with a single blow by the blade of her betrayal . . .

> But it's useless . . . I can't, even if I wanted to, forget / the memory of what was my only love. / For her it must have been like a pretty flower / that offers its perfume to the one who's going to cut its life short. / And if someday she might want to come back / to be at my side again, I will have to forgive her. / If one can kill out of jealousy toward another man, / one can forgive when love speaks so strongly, / no matter what kind of woman it is.]

The novel *Don Segundo Sombra*, by Güiraldes, was published in 1926. In 1969 Manuel Antín made the film *Don Segundo Sombra*, adapting the novel for the big screen. For tango, see *Los Clásicos Argentinos* [The Argentine Classics], vol. 4.

16. Emilio Pettoruti, *Un Pintor ante el Espejo* [A Painter before the Mirror] (Buenos Aires: Librería Histórica, 2004), p. 116.

17. See Sven Olov Wallenstein, "Object-Form and Commodity Form (Art for Art's Sake, Money for God's Sake)," *Subsol* 2. Available online at <http://subsol.c3.hu/subsol_2/contributors3/wallensteintext.html>.

18. Walter Benjamin, "False Criticism," in *Selected Writings*, vol. 2, 1927–1934, trans. Rodney Livingstone and others; ed. Michael W. Jennings, Howard Eiland, and Gary Smith (Cambridge, MA: Belknap Press/Harvard University, 1999).

19. Walter Benjamin, *The Arcades Project*, trans. Howard Eiland and Kevin McLaughlin (Cambridge, MA: Belknap Press of Harvard University, 1999), p. 37.

20. Jon Roberts, "After Adorno Art, Autonomy, and Critique." Available online at <http://www.apexart.org/residency/roberts.htm>.

21. Ibid.

22. On uneven modernization, see Julio Ramos, *Desencuentros de la Modernidad en América Latina* [Disencounters of Modernity in Latin America] (Mexico City: Siglo 21, 1989); on the artistic and literary market, see Silviano Santiago, "História de um Livro" [History of a Book], in *Macunaíma* by Mário de Andrade (Brasilia: Archives, 1988); and Sérgio Miceli, *Nacional Estrangeiro* [National Foreigner] (São Paulo: Companhia das Letras, 2003).

23. Gueriós, *Heitor Villalobos e o Ambiente Artístico Parisiense*, p. 92.

24. Paul Poiret was also the designer of preference for Isadora Duncan, Sarah Bernhardt, and other celebrities. In *Nacional Estrangeiro*, p. 129, Miceli points out: "Tarsila y Oswald estaban iniciando una sociedad amorosa y de trabajo que repercutiría sobre la producción de ambos. En función de la disponibildad de recursos a su alcance, viabilizaron un proyecto artístico-literario semiempresarial, con sede en París a lo largo de la década de 1920, que tenía a los maestros literarios y plásticos franceses como modelos y al mercado metropolitano como espacio privilegiado de difusión." (Tarsila and Oswald were beginning a romantic and profesional liaison that would have repercussions in both artists' production. With the resources they had at hand, they forged a semientrepreneurial artistic-literary project, with its headquarters in Paris through the 1920s, which had French master writing and painting instructors as models and the metropolitan marketplace as its privileged sphere of dissemination.)

25.

Caipirinha vestida por Poiret / a preguiça paulista reside nos teus olhos / que não viram Paris nem Picadilly / nem as exclamações dos homens em Sevilha / à tua passagem entre brincos.

Locomotivas e bichos nacionais / geometrizam as atmosferas nítidas / Congonhas descora sob o pálio das procissões de Minas.

A verdura no azul klaxon / cortada / sobre a poeira vermelha.

Arranha-céus / fordes / viadutos / um cheiro de café / no silêncio emoldurado.

See Oswald de Andrade, *Pau Brasil*, facsimile edition of 1925, Paris: Sans Pareil, included in *Caixa Modernista*, ed. Jorge Schwarz (São Paulo: EDUSP; Minas: UFMG, Imprensa Oficial, 2003), p. 75. The book's first edition, produced in Paris in 1925, features illustrations by Tarsila do Amaral.

26. One of do Amaral's illustrations for the first edition of *Pau Brasil* is precisely a drawing of a locomotive, done with a majority of curved lines, placed in the book after the poem titled "Metalurgica." See Oswald de Andrade, *Pau Brasil*, pp. 50, 51.

27. The magazine was published between May 15, 1922, and January 1923, and its main collaborators were Guilherme de Almeida, Mário de Andrade, Oswald de Andrade, Rubens Borba de Andrade, Luís Aranha, and Sérgio Milliet. Sérgio Buarque de Holanda was their correspondent in Rio de Janeiro. The editorial text of the first issue ends with a mention of the Batutas. It states:

> 19th century—Romanticism, Ivory Tower, Symbolism. Later, the international fireworks of 1914. For almost 130 years now humanity has been having tantrums. The rebellion is fair. We want to construct happiness. The farce itself, the burlesque, does not repel us, just as it did not repel Dante, Shakespeare, or Cervantes. Soaked, congested, rheumatized by a tradition of artistic tears, we have decided. Surgical procedure. Extirpation of tear glands. Age of the 8 Batutas, of the Jazz Band, of Chicarrão, of Charlie (Chaplin), of Mutt & Jeff. Age of laughter and of sincerity. Age of construction. Age of KLAXON.

See *Klaxon* 1 (May 15, 1922). Chicarrão was a famous Brazilian clown, and it is worth remembering that another famous clown, Piolim, took part in the Week of Modern Art representing Circo. On Piolim, see Tarsila do Amaral, "Trajetória do Circo," *Diário de São Paulo*, September 23, 1936, cited in Amaral, *Tarsila*, p. 155.

28. Several studies have emphasized the importance of the rise of coffee that occurred on the international market during the first decades of the twentieth century as a driving factor of industrial development and wealth that strongly influenced—specifically in the generation of resources for the *Week of Modern Art* in São Paulo—the emergence of Brazilian modernism. See Miceli, *Nacional Estrangeiro*, and Roberto Schwarz, "A Carroça, o Bonde, e o Poeta Modernista" [The Cart, the Tram, and the Modernist Poet], in *Que Horas São?* [What Time Is It?] (São Paulo: Companhia das Letras, 1997) (included in English in *Misplaced Ideas*), among others. One of the first modernist journals, *Terra Roxa e Outras Terras* [Red Earth and Other Lands], emphasizes that importance in its title in reference to the dark red soil suitable for the cultivation of coffee and located in the province São Paulo. The journal was released in 1926, directed by A. C. Couto de Barros and Antonio de Alcântara Machado, and had the participation of Oswald de Andrade and Mário de Andrade. Also in the famous prologue to *Serafim Ponte Grande*, already mentioned for its criticism of the bourgeois and oligarchic complicity of modernism, this journal appears metonymically indicated by way of coffee. The text reads: "The assessment of coffee's value was an imperialist maneuver. So was la Poesia Pau Brasil. This had to fall with the bugle-calls of the crisis. Just as almost all Brazilian 'avant-garde' literature collapsed, being provincial and suspect, if not thinly exhausted and reactionary. Of my own participation, this book is left. A document. An illustration." See Oswald de Andrade, *Serafim Ponte Grande*, p. 133.

29. I borrow the expression from Aracy Amaral, "Tarsila," in *Tarsila do Amaral* (Buenos Aires: Ediciones Banco Velox, 1998).

30. On collage in Oswald de Andrade, see Antonio Candido, "Estouro e Liberta-ção" [Explosion and Liberation], in *Vários Escritos* [Sundry Writings] (São Paulo: Duas Cidades, 1995), and Haroldo de Campos, "Prefácio" [Preface], in *Poesias Reunidas* [Collected Poems], by Oswald de Andrade (Rio de Janeiro: Civilização Brasileira, 1971).

31. For inspiring analyses of collage, see Marjorie Perloff, "A Invenção da Collagem" [The Invention of Collage], in *O Momento Futurista* [The Futurist Moment] (São Paulo: EDUSP, 1993); and Krauss, *Los Papeles de Picasso*.

32. See, in Amaral, "Tarsila," p. 184, the testimony offered by Georgina Malfatti: "Me acuerdo de ella en el teatro Trocadero, con una capa roja, con forro de satén blanco, un sombrero de lentejuelas, grande y negro. En París, donde las personas se visten discre-tamente, era una sensación la vanidad de Tarsila vestida por Poiret, al lado de Oswald, de camisa púrpura" (I remember her at the Trocadero Theater, wearing a red cape with a white satin lining and a large black sequined hat. In Paris, where people dress discreetly, it was quite a sensation, the vanity of Tarsila in a Poiret design, next to Oswald in a purple shirt.)

33. Oscar Terán used the term "*modernos intensos*" (intense moderns) for those Ar-gentine intellectuals who, during the 1920s, allowed for a toning down of the "overly monolithic [image] of the sentiment of bonanza and moderationism of those years" to include in that image an intellectual constellation that was "vague and of blurred, im-precise boundaries," composed of those authors who, like Roberto Arlt, appear as mod-ern critics of the destructive effects of modernism itself. See Oscar Terán, "Modernos Intensos en los Veinte" [Intense Moderns in the Twenties], *Prismas* 1 (1997), pp. 91–104.

34. According to the renowned and marvelous quote from *Capital*:

A commodity appears, at first sight, a very trivial thing, and easily understood. Its analysis shows that it is, in reality, a very queer thing, abounding in metaphysical subtleties and theological niceties. So far as it is a value in use, there is nothing mys-terious about it, whether we consider it from the point of view that by its properties it is capable of satisfying human wants, or from the point that those properties are the product of human labour. [. . .] But, so soon as it steps forth as a commodity, it is changed into something transcendent. It not only stands with its feet on the ground, but, in relation to all other commodities, it stands on its head, and evolves out of its wooden brain grotesque ideas, far more wonderful than "table-turning" ever was.

See Karl Marx, *Capital*, trans. Samuel Moore and Edward Aveling; ed. Frederick Engels; online version: Marx/Engels Internet Archive (marxists.org) 1995, 1999: Capital, vol. 1, Part 1, Ch. 1, Section 4. The original quote in Spanish is taken from: Karl Marx, *El Capi-tal*, tomo 1, vol. 1 (Mexico City: Siglo 21, p. 87).

35. Tarsila do Amaral, in Amaral, "Tarsila."

36. Tom Nairn, *Faces of Nationalism: Janus Revisited* (London and New York: Verso, 1997), p. 71.

37. Cadícamo, *Mis Memorias*, p. 130.

38.

Tirao por la vida de errante bohemio / estoy, Buenos Aires, anclao en París. / Cubi-erto de males, bandeado de apremio, / te evoco, desde este lejano país. / Contemplo

la nieve que cae blandamente / desde mi ventana, que da al bulevar: / las luces roji-
zas, con tono muriente, / parecen pupilas de extraño mirar.

Lejano Buenos Aires, ¡qué lindo has de estar! / Ya van para diez años que me viste
zarpar . . . / Aquí, en este Montmartre, faubourg sentimental, / yo siento que el re-
cuerdo me clava su puñal.

¡Como habrá cambiado tu calle Corrientes! . . . /¡Suipacha, Esmeralda, tu mismo
arrabal! . . . / Alguien me ha contado que estás floreciente / Y un juego de calles se
da en diagonal . . . / ¡No sabés las ganas que tengo de verte! / Aquí estoy varado, sin
plata y sin fe . . . / ¡Quién sabe una noche me encane la muerte / Y, chau Buenos
Aires, no te vuelva a ver!

39.
Disseram que eu voltei americanizada / com o burro do dinheiro / que estou muito
rica / que não suporto mais o breque do pandeiro / e fico arrepiada ouvindo uma
cuíca
e disseram que com as mãos / estou preocupada / e corre por aí / que eu sei certo
zum zum / que já não tenho molho, ritmo, nem nada / e dos balangandans já não
existe mais nenhum

Mas pra cima de mim, pra que tanto veneno? / eu posso lá ficar americanizada? / eu
que nasci com o samba e vivo no sereno / topando a noite inteira a velha batucada
/ nas rodas de malandro minhas preferidas / eu digo mesmo eu te amo, e nunca I
love you / enquanto houver Brasil / na hora da comida / eu sou do camarão enso-
padinho com chuchu!

"South American Way" is a samba-rumba, composed by Jimmy McHugh and Al Dubin
especially for the musical *Street of Paris,* which was the show of Carmen Miranda's debut
on Broadway. See Ruy Castro, *Carmen: Uma biografia* [Carmen: A Biography] (São
Paulo: Companhia das Letras, 2005), p. 203.

PART II, CHAPTER 2

1. See chapter 2 (this volume) on Araripe Júnior's notion of tropical style elaborated
on the basis of *O Cortiço* [The Slum], by Aluísio Azevedo.

2. Manuel Gálvez as much as Marques Rebelo inserts these novels, functioning almost like national literary maps, into a general plan for narrative that is based on the
accumulation of different narrative geographical spaces more than on narrative problems. Gálvez' and Marques Rebelo's narrative plans are set forth as "occupation of territory," according to María Teresa Gramuglio's expression for referring to Gálvez' plan.
See María Teresa Gramuglio, "Novela y Nación en el Proyecto Literario de Manuel
Gálvez" [Novel and Nation in the Literary Project of Manuel Gálvez], in *Historia Crítica
de la Literatura Argentina* [Critical History of Argentine Literature], ed. María Teresa
Gramuglio, vol. 6: *El Imperio Realista* [The Realist Empire] (Buenos Aires: Emecé, 2002),
p. 147. For the author's formulation of his plan, see Manuel Gálvez, *En el Mundo de los
Seres Ficticios* [In the World of Fictitious Beings] (Buenos Aires: Hachette, 1962); and the
Preface to *Nacha Regules* (Buenos Aires: Pax, 1922). In 1944, Rebelo collected his chroni-

cles in a book titled *Cenas da Vida Brasileira: Suíte n° 1* [Scenes from Brazilian Life: Suite no. 1], which functions simultaneously as title for the chronicles and the collection of all his works, which included the novels he had written up to that point, among them, *A Estrela Sobe,* in addition to the chronicles he had published in the pro-Vargas magazine *Cultura e Política* [Culture and Politics]. For Marques Rebelo's plan, see Raúl Antelo, "As Marcas de Rebelo" [The Marks of Rebelo], in *Literatura em Revista* [Literature in Review] (São Paulo: Ática, 1984).

3. In *La Novelística de Manuel Gálvez* [The Novel of Manuel Gálvez] (Santa Fe: Facultad de Filosofía y Letras, Universidad del Litoral, 1965), p. 22, Norma Desinano points out that already in Gálvez' first two novels "the characteristics of his style are observable, characteristics that will be sustained with only slight variations in the rest of his work. This first phase can be defined as rich in documentary elements that totally supersede the literary ones; description prevails over plot, and characters and situations are subordinated to the author's decision to show rather than to tell."

4. The radio appears in this novel with a very important structural function—one could even almost think of it as another character. The radio played a decisive role in the diffusion and constitution of samba as symbol of national identity. See Brian McCann, *Hello, Hello Brazil: Popular Music in the Making of Modern Brazil* (Durham: Duke University Press, 2004).

5. See Manuel Gálvez, *Nacha Regules* (Buenos Aires: Centro Editor de América Latina, 1968), pp. 147, 148. On the world of prostitution in Buenos Aires at the beginning of the twentieth century, see Donna Guy, *Sex and Danger in Buenos Aires* (Lincoln: University of Nebraska Press, 1991). The story of the *milonguita* was also represented in the cinema; the most representative film is that called, precisely, *Milonguita*, directed by José Bustamante y Ballivián, with Ignacio Corsini and María Ester Lerena, released in 1922.

6. See Néstor Pinsón, "Mi Noche Triste, el Tango Canción" [My Sad Night, the Tango Song]. Available online at <www.todotango.com.ar>.

7.

Mina que te manyo de hace rato / perdonáme si te bato / de que yo te vi nacer . . . / Tu cuna fue un conventillo / alumbrado a querosén.

8.

Justo a los catorce abriles / te entregastes a las farras, / las delicias de un gotán . . . / te gustaban las alhajas, / los vestidos a la moda / y las farras de champán.

Luego fuiste la amiguita / de un vejete boticario, / y el hijo de un comisario / todo el vento te sacó . . . / Empezó tu decadencia, / las alhajas amuraste / y un bulincito alquilaste / en una casa e' pensión.

Te hiciste tonadillera, / pasaste ratos extraños / y a fuerza de desengaños / quedaste sin corazón.

9.

Fue tu vida como un lirio . . . / de congojas y martirio / sólo un peso te agobió . . . / no tenías en el mundo ni un consuelo / el amor de tu madre te faltó. / Fuiste papusa del fango / y las delicias de un tango / te arrastraron del bulín / los amigos te engru-pieron / y ellos mismos te perdieron / noche a noche en el festín.

Mina que te manyo de hace rato, / perdonáme si te bato
de que yo te vi nacer . . . / Tu cuna fue un conventillo / alumbrado a querosén. /
Justo a los catorce abriles / te entregastes a las farras, / las delicias de un gotán . . . /
te gustaban las alhajas, / los vestidos a la moda / y las farras de champán.

10. The recording was made in Buenos Aires in 1924, Odeon recording number 18116 2435, with the accompaniment of José "El Negro" Ricardo and Guillermo D. Bar-bieri. This tango had been debuted by Luisa Morotti in the performance of the *sainete* (comedy sketch, short farce), "Un Programa de Cabaret," written by Contursi himself in collaboration with Enrique P. Maroni, July 4, 1924.

11.
Yo quiero un cotorro / que tenga balcones, / cortinas muy largas / de seda crepé
. . . / Mirar los bacanes / pasando a montones, / pa ver si algún reo / me dice: ¡Qué hacé! . . .

Yo quiero un cotorro / con piso encerado, / que tenga alfombrita / para caminar. /
Sillones de cuero todo *reempujado* / y un loro atorrante / que sepa cantar . . .

Yo quiero una cama / que tenga acolchado . . . / y quiero una estufa / pa entrar en calor . . . / que venga el mucamo / corriendo apurado / y diga: ¡Señora! /¡Araca! Está el Ford . . .

12.
[Por eso la mina, aburrida / de aguantar la vida que le di, / cachó el baúl una noche / y se fue cantando así:]

Yo quiero un cotorro / que tenga balcones, / cortinas muy largas / de seda crepé, /
mirar los bacanes / pasando a montones, / pa'ver si algún reo / me dice:qué hacé!

Yo quiero un cotorro / con piso encerado, / que tenga alfombrita / para caminar. /
Sillones de cuero / todo repujado / y un loro atorrante / que sepa cantar.

[Pero qué me dicen de las pretensiones de esta milonga? / Un loro, sillones rempujados, un Ford . . . / Y yo sin poder acertar un ganador, seco, y en la vía! /
Y al final de cuentas me sale con que:]

Yo quiero una cama / que tenga acolchado,
y quiero una estufa / pa' entrar en calor,
que venga el mucamo / corriendo apurado
y diga . . . ¡Señora! /¡Araca! Está el Ford . . ."

[Salute Garibaldi, / que este muerto lo aguante otro / lo que soy yo, largo . . .]

13.
Che Madame que parlás en francés / ahora te causa risa mi chamuyo de revés / pero algún día volverás desengañada y sin fe / y entonces seré yo quien te diga / che, muñeca brava, qué hacés.

Che madame que parlás en francés / y tirás ventolina a dos manos / que cenás
con champagne bien frappé / y en el tango enredás tu ilusión / sos un biscuit de
pestañas muy arqueadas / muñeca brava bien cotizada / sos del trianon de vill / que
vampiresa juguete de ocasión / tenés un canba que te hace gustos / y veinte abriles
que son ligeros / y bien repleto tu monedero pa patinarlo de norte a sur / te baten
todos muñeca brava / porque a los giles mareás sin grupo / para mí sos siempre la
que no supo / guardar un cacho de amor de juventud
/ de mí que siempre soñé con tu cariño / y allá en el barrio te amé de niño / pero pa
que viá decirte cosas viejas / si ya cambiaste muñeca el corazón.

14. For a reading of *Nacha Regules* as "urban cartography," see María Teresa
Gramuglio, "Novela y Nación en el Proyecto Literario de Manuel Gálvez."

15. Rebelo, *Nacha Regules*, p. 123.

16.

Pero aquellos círculos infernales no eran para que impunemente los recorriera el
primer venido. Montsalvat debió soportar burlas, humillaciones, insultos. En algu-
nas casas le sacaron dinero; en una le robaron. Más de una vez no le permitieron
entrar, y le cerraron la puerta arrojándole dicterios y palabrotas.

Ibid., p. 125.

17.

[E]ra una vieja casa de familia, democratizada en inquilinato; la pieza, en el piso alto
y sobre la calle, fue tomada inmediatamente por Monsalvat. Y así, cuando apareció
en el cuarto de su amiga, ya era habitante de la casa.

Ibid., p. 144.

18. Arnedo le tomó la mano al tiempo que le *clavaba los ojos* y le ordenaba:
—¡Quédese!
—Pueden venir. . . .
—No me importa. La he visto y me he vuelto loco—exclamó él, con simulado
    arrebato—.

19.

El malevo había clavado los ojos en los de Linda y parecía como que quisiera *penetrarla*. Ella resistió un momento aquella mirada dominadora, negra, brutal, aquella
mirada *que golpeaba en sus ojos femeninos como una cosa material, que penetraba en
su rostro como dos cortafierros*, que tenía un no sabía ella qué de incomprensible, de
fatal, de espantosamente perturbador.

Manuel Gálvez, *Historia de Arrabal* [A History of the Periphery] (Buenos Aires: Deucalión, 1956), p. 27.

20. A film was made based on the novel by Bruno Barreto in 1974.

21. "[L]a forma que cabe en la relación entre escritor y realidad es la de fijar aquello
que no puede ser aprehendido: las instantáneas. Al no poder narrar—el tiempo fue abo-
lido—, se describe la vida social." Raúl Antelo, "As Marcas de Rebelo" (p. 128). Renato
Codeiro Gomes *also* pointed out how much of the chronicle there is in Marques Rebelo's
fiction in "Marques Rebelo, Cronista de uma Cidade" [Marques Rebelo, Chronicler of a

City] *Marques Rebelo: Melhores Crônicas* [Marques Rebelo: The Best Chronicles], edited by Renato Codeiro Gomes (São Paulo: Global, 2004), p. 8.

22. On this aspect, see Adonias Filho, "Introdução" [Introduction], in *A Estrela Sobe* [The Star Is Rising], by Marques Rebelo (Rio de Janeiro: Nova Fronteira, 1986), and Gomes, "Marques Rebelo."

23. "aquel que enaltece las virtudes del propio gênero." See also Luíz Tatit, *O Século da Canção* [The Century of the Song] (São Paulo: Ateliê, 2004), p. 155:

> Es generalmente en el samba-samba que el compositor exhibe sus malabarismos con la melodía y la letra, una reportándose a la otra en una adecuación que, de cierto modo, simboliza la plena integración de la música con la 'musa inspiradora'. Son canciones que asocian el canto rítmico con la danza de las jóvenes (sambas, morenas, bahianas) con lugares típicamente brasileños ('Rio', 'Bahía'), con los instrumentos musicales (*violão, cavaquinho, pandeiro, tamborim*).
>
> [It is generally in the samba-samba that the composer exhibits his juggling with the melody and the lyrics, a mutual interchange in an adaptation that, in a certain way, symbolizes the full integration of the music with the 'muse of inspiration.' These are songs that associate rhythmic singing with the dance the young people are doing (sambas, morenas, bahianas) with typically Brazilian places ['Rio', 'Bahia'], with the musical instruments as well [guitar, *cavaquinho, pandeiro*, tambourine].

24. Carlos Sandroni points out in *Feitiço Decente*, p. 159: "El momento en el que se instaura esa identidad entre sambista y malandro es, como ya habrá notado el lector, el mismo en el que ocurrió la mudanza estilística que nos ocupa." (The moment in which that identity connecting *sambista* and *malandro* is instated is, as the reader must have noted already, the same one in which the stylistic shift, of interest to us here, also occured). Cláudia de Matos had already observed this on writing that "la noción de malandro está asociada a la de sambista desde los años de 1920. La asociación es simultánea al proceso de derivación del samba hacia su versión rítmica 'moderna', aquella que se divulgó a partir de fines de la década de 1920 en las creaciones de la gente de Estácio" (the notion of the *malandro* is associated with that of the *sambista* starting in the 1920s. The association is simultaneous with the process of samba's development toward its "modern" rhythmic version, that which was divulged starting at the end of the 1920s in the creations of Estácio's people). Cláudia de Matos, *Acertei no Milhar: Samba e Malandragem no Tempo de Getúlio* [I Won the Lottery: Samba and Malandragem in the Age of Getulio] (Rio de Janeiro: Paz e Terra, 1982), p. 41. What is especially interesting is the relationship between *malandro* samba or samba-samba with modernity.

25. See "Céu no Chão" [Sky on the Ground], "1933," in Gomes, *Marques Rebelo*.

26. Ibid., p. 72. The inverse could be proposed for the relationship between *Nacha Regules* and tango: even though the tangos about the *milonguita* had already established a "tradition" by the time Gálvez' novel was published (between 1917 and 1919 there are several tangos of this type), his novel seems to anticipate other tangos that had not been written yet: "Galleguita" [Little Spanish/Galician Girl], for example, would not be composed until 1915; "Madame Ivonne" in 1933.

27. "Vai como uma cega por entre a multidão. É a multidão que a leva, que a arrasta, como uma corrente irresistível, que a deixa sem destino em todas as esquinas." Marques Rebelo, *A Estrela Sobe*, p. 82.

28. "Aqui termino a história de Leniza. Não a abandonei, mas, como romancista, perdi-a. Fico, porém, quantas vezes, pensando nessa pobre alma tão fraca e miserável quanto a minha. Tremo: que será dela, no inévitavel balanço da vida, se não descer do céu uma luz que ilumine o outro lado das suas vaidades?" (Ibid., p. 115.)

29. "Dando o que pôde, o autor lamenta profundamente a debilidade das suas forças para um trecho tão forte como este e como a maioria dos que se seguem. Em compensação absteve-se de lançar mão de recursos mistifantes para uso de lectores ingênuos." (Ibid., footnote 6, p. 101.)

30. "Quando o garçom chegava com o serviço, ela saía. Mário Alves atirou dois milréis na mesa e foi-lhe atrás. Caíram na multidão. Era noite fechada. Fulgiam anúncios luminosos. Os bondes apinhados, lotados os ônibus. Estrugem buzinas, estampidos, campainhas, rangem freios, descem portas de aço com estrépito de metralhadoras. Há o tropel e o vozear dos transeuntes, o alarido sensacional dos vendedores de jornais, um cheiro quente de gasolina. E eles caminham, o mais depressa que podem, através da onda humana. Não falam. Vem uma esquina. O sinal fechou como um olho de sangue. Leniza sentiu as pernas bambas. Sentiu uma coisa passar-lhe pela vista como uma mancha, uma nuvem cheia de pontos luminosos." (Ibid., p. 62.)

31. According to Leo Bersani, realist narration is an "exercise of containment." He points out: "A good part of the realist novelist's imaginative energies—no matter what his intentions may be—is devoted to sparing his society the pain of confronting the shallowness of its order and the destructiveness of its appetites." See Leo Bersani, *A Future for Astyanax* (Boston, Toronto: Little, Brown, 1976), p. 61.

PART II, CHAPTER 3

1. Villiers de l'Isle Adam, *Tomorrow's Eve*, trans. Robert Martin Adams (Urbana: University of Illinois Press, 2001); Villiers de l'Isle Adam, *L'Eve Future* (Paris: Gallimard, 1993). Note that the English translation reads "ten minutes" whereas the Spanish version reads "six minutes."

2. André Bazin, *What Is Cinema?* trans. Hugh Gray (Berkeley: University of California Press, 1972), p. 21.

3. Jacques Rancière, *The Politics of Aesthetics: The Distribution of the Sensible*, trans. Gabriel Rockhill (London: Continuum, 2004), pp. 32–33; *La División de lo Sensible* (Salamanca: Consorcio Salamanca, 2002), pp. 53–55.

4. See Bazin, *What Is Cinema?*; Noël Burch, *El Tragaluz del Infinito* [The Infinite Skylight] (Madrid: Cátedra, 1987).

5. Moreover, that relationship with popular culture can be read also in the older antecedent of an attempt to reproduce movement based on photography. This is the well-known invention created by Muybridge, who, financed by a millionaire lover of horse racing, developed a form of multiple photography whereby he was able to capture for the first time the movement of a horse, demonstrating with a single throw of the

dice how much the representational arts had invented, how much the effect of the real is more about effect than it is about the real, and how much of reality is hidden to the naked eye. For a comparative analysis of Muybridge's invention and the aesthetic transformations that it presumes, see David Oubiña, *El Silencio y Sus Bordes* [Silence and Its Edges], doctoral dissertation, Facultad de Filosofía y Letras, UBA, 2005.

6. Noël Burch points out that the primitive technology of cinema did not allow for more than a kind of potpourri, very close to popular forms. See his *El Tragaluz del Infinito*, p. 62.

7. In 1937 another *Nobleza Gaucha* [Peasant/Cowboy Nobility] was filmed, this one with a screenplay by Homero Manzi and Hugo MacDougall, and music by Sebastián Piana. There too one recognizes the influence of tango.

8. Stanley Cavell states: "the aesthetic possibilities of a medium are not givens. [. . .] The first successful movies [. . .] were not applications of a medium that was defined by given possibilities, but the creation of a medium by their giving significance to specific possibilities." See Stanley Cavell, *The World Viewed* (Cambridge, MA: Harvard University Press, 1979), pp. 31, 32.

9. Regarding these issues, see José Agustín Mahieu, *Breve Historia del Cine Argentine* [A Brief History of Argentine Cinema] (Buenos Aires: Eudeba, 1966); Jorge Miguel Couselo et al., *Historia del Cine Argentine* [History of Argentine Cinema] (Buenos Aires: Centro Editor de América Latina, 1984); and Ana María López, "Of Rhythms and Borders" (1985), in *Everynight Life*, ed. Celeste Delgado and José Muñoz (Durham, NC: Duke University Press, 1997). In relation to the case of Brazil, see Maria Rita Galvão and Carlos Roberto de Souza, "Cinema Brasileiro: 1930–1964" [Brazilian Cinema: 1930–1964], in *História Geral da Civilização Brasileira* [General History of Brazilian Civilization], by Sérgio Buarque de Holanda, vol. 4 (Rio de Janeiro: Bertrand, 1989).

10. Domingo Di Núbila, *La Época de Oro: Historia del Cine Argentino* [The Golden Age: History of Argentine Cinema] (Buenos Aires: Ediciones del Jilguero, 1998).

11. The *chanchada* is a popular comedy with musical interludes (see Alex Viany, Jean-Claude Bernardet, and Paulo Emílio Salles Gomes) which, having arisen around the 1940s, had its apogee in the 1950s. According to Ronsângela de Oliveira Dias, that popularity is based on a hybridization with the Hollywood musical. See Rosângela de Oliveira Dias, *O Mundo como Chanchada: Cinema e Imaginário das Classes Populares na Década de 50* [The World as *Chanchada*: Cinema and the Imaginary of the Popular Classes in the 1950s] (Rio de Janeiro: Relume Dumará, 1993), p. 53.

12. Concerning these aspects, see Sérgio Augusto, *Este Mundo É um Pandeiro: A Chanchada de Getúlio a JK* [This World Is a *Pandeiro* (Tambourine): The *Chanchada* from Getúlio to JK] (São Paulo: Companhia das Letras, 2001), pp. 91–93; and Brian McCann, *Hello, Hello, Brazil: Popular Music in the Making of Modern Brazil* (Durham, NC: Duke University Press, 2004), p. 138.

13. Enrique Susini, César José Guerrico, and Luis Romero Carranza—called "Los Locos de la Azotea" [The Madmen of the Terrace] because they had broadcast the first radio transmission from the terrace of the Coliseo theater—founded the company, "Radio Cinematográfica Lumiton." See María Valdez, "La Radio en el Cine" [The Radio

in Film], in *Cine Argentino: Industria y Clasicismo* [Argentine Cinema: Industry and Classicism] by Claudio España (Buenos Aires: Fondo Nacional de las Artes, 2000).

14. Cited in Randal Johnson and Robert Stam (eds.), *Brazilian Cinema* (Austin: University of Texas Press, 1988), p. 25.

15. For a detailed treatment of Cinema Novo and its connections with previous Brazilian cinema, see Ismail Xavier, *O Cinema Brasileiro Moderno* [Modern Brazilian Cinema] (São Paulo: Paz e Terra, 2001), and his introduction to Glauber Rocha, *Revolução do Cinema Novo* [Revoultion in the Cinema Novo Movement] (São Paulo: Cosac & Naify, 2004). In *Este Mundo É um Pandeiro*, pp. 27, 28, Sérgio Augusto sees the relationship between Cinema Novo and the *chanchada* as a kind of "openly oedipal" relationship, between rejection and acceptance, according to the different directors of Cinema Novo. The *chanchada* was harshly criticized by Glauber Rocha in *Revolução do Cinema Novo*, although it was also vindicated by some of the movement's members because of its popular and national character. *Macunaíma* is a clear example of the reappropriation in Cinema Novo of certain traits of the *chanchada*, starting with use of the same actor (Grande Otelo), who had been until then the great actor of the Brazilian *chanchadas*. Sérgio Augusto, in *Este Mundo é um Pandeiro*, pp. 70–74, examines a certain "universality" of the *chanchada* in the different national traditions of musical comedies, and qualifies Romero and Gardel's films as equivalents of the Brazilian *chanchadas*.

16. Some facts indicate that *Los caballeros de cemento* [The Cement Knights] was already finished before production was begun on *Tango!* See España, *Cine Argentino.*

17. *Luces de Buenos Aires* premiered in 1931 and was made by Paramount in Paris, directed by a Chilean filmmaker, Adelqui Millar. Its screenwriters were Manuel Romero and Luis Bayón Herrera. It is the first film made by Gardel, with the exception of *Flor de Durazno* [Peach Blossom] in which he participates only episodically. According to Collier, this film and those that follow it were made by Gardel with the intention of achieving international fame. See Simon Collier, "Carlos Gardel and the Cinema," in *The Garden of Forking Paths: Argentine Cinema*, ed. John King and Nissa Torrents (London: British Film Institute, 1988), pp. 173–214.

18. Peter Brooks relates the birth of melodrama with a reaction against the desacralization that "both asserted the need for some version of the Sacred and offered further proof of the irremediable loss of the Sacred in its traditional, categorical, unifying form." Within this reaction, melodrama's structure of opposites and its clear distinction of a moral universe would serve, according to Brooks, the need to purge the social order. See Peter Brooks, *The Melodramatic Imagination: Balzac, Henry James, Melodrama and the Mode of Excess* (New Haven: Yale University Press, 1984), pp. 14–20.

19. In 1917, only 2 of the 24 songs recorded by Gardel were tangos; in 1925, this number surpassed 63, out of a total 90 recorded songs. See Carlos Gardel, *Compilación poética* [Compiled Poems], ed. Pedro Arias and Leonardo Capristo (Buenos Aires: Corregidor, 2003).

20. This negotiation is framed in a series of disputes between geographical and cultural categories that can be seen in many tangos whose peasant origin is plainly evident, especially in tangos by Agustín Bardi, such as "El Abrojo" (Thistle), "El Rodeo"

(The Rodeo), and "El Tauro" (The Taurus), and by José Martínez, such as "Expresión Campera" [Countryside Expression] or "El Palenque" [The Tethering Post]. Indeed, the tango that seems to have been the first to cross the ocean, "La Morocha" [The Dark-Haired Girl], is much nearer to the criollo world than to Lunfardo:

> Yo soy la morocha, / la más agraciada, / la más renombrada / de esta población. / Soy la que al paisano / muy de madrugada / brinda un cimarrón. /
>
> Yo, con dulce acento, / junto a mi ranchito, / canto un estilito / con tierna pasión, / mientras que mi dueño / sale al trotecito / en su redomón. /[. . .] Soy la gentil compañera / del noble gaucho porteño, / la que conserva el cariño / para su dueño. / [. . .] En mi amado rancho, / bajo la enramada, /en noche plateada, / con dulce emoción, / le canto al pampero, / a mi patria amada / y a mi fiel amor.
>
> [I am the dark-haired girl, / the most attractive, / the most renowned / of this village. / I'm the one who the peasant / in the wee hours / offers a toast of bitter mate tea.
>
> I, with a sweet accent, / near my little hut, / sing an *estilito* / with tender passion, / while my owner / goes at a trot / on his half-trained horse. / [. . .] I am the gentle partner / of the noble *porteño* gaucho, / the one who saves her affections / for her owner. / [. . .] In my beloved hut, / under the arbour / on silvery nights, / with sweet emotion / I sing to the wind, / to my beloved country / and to my faithful love.]

These tangos are violently opposed to the interpretation of that first nationalism that saw tango as something absolutely different—even as spurious, and therefore worthy of rejection—from the criollo world. For this position, see Leopoldo Lugones, *El payador* [The Folksinger/Minstrel] (Caracas: Biblioteca Ayacucho, 1991), and Ezequiel Martínez Estrada, *Radiografía de la Pampa* [X-Ray of the Pampa] (Buenos Aires: Sudamericana, 1970).

21. There is in the history of tango a chronology that extends from the danced tango to the tango song with which the film is working. The first tangos, associated with life in bordellos, were for dancing. They had no lyrics, or, if there were lyrics, they were reduced to just a few verses. Often, lyrics were written significantly later for the music, and in many cases various sets of lyrics were associated with the same tango tune. The shift from the danced tango to the tango song, dated in 1917 with "Mi Noche Triste" by Contursi and associated with Carlos Gardel—and at the same time his own shift from being a singer of folk or peasant songs in the Gardel-Razzano duo to being a soloist tango singer—is seen as one of the more necessary stages in order for tango to become accepted by the middle and upper classes. The displacement from the bodies and the choreography seen as very indecent until that time, and the greater preponderance that is now given the song, which is only listened to and not danced to, is considered one of the first steps in the "cleansing of tango." See Roberto Selles, "El Tango y Sus Dos Primeras Décadas (1880–1900)" [The Tango and Its First Two Decades], in *La Historia del Tango* [The History of Tango], vol. 2 (Buenos Aires: Corregidor, 1980). The *casitas* or *garçonnières* (bachelors' rented rooms), intimately related to the history of tango, were apartments or houses where men of the upper class held their "*farras*" (a Lunfardo term for "parties"). They represent a first step toward the upper class which to that point had only

connected with tango in their incursions downwards on the social scale, in bordellos. The *garçonières* mark tango's first shift from the poor outskirts to the city center, but it is a displacement that keeps itself to the private sector still. The shift from the tango of the poor outskirts to the public center is a different step, one that does not however replace the *casita* but rather that is superimposed on it and coexists with it. The relationship "*casita*-bordello-downtown theater" in the history of tango is clearly depicted in the film.

22. Beatriz Sarlo, *Borges, un Escritor de las Orillas* [Borges, a Writer on the Shores] (Buenos Aires: Ariel, 1995).

23. Regarding the relationship between the films with Carmen Miranda and the "good-neighbor policy," see Eneida Maria de Souza, "Nem Samba nem Rumba" [Neither Samba nor Rumba], in *Crítica Cult* (Belo Horizonte: Editora da Universidade Federal de Minas Gerais, and Antonio Pedro Tota, *O Imperialismo Sedutor* [The Seductive Imperialism] (São Paulo: Companhia das Letras, 2000). According to Luiz Herique Saia:

> Down Argentine Way, filmed completely inside a studio, was so artificial that the neon sign on the boat that Carmen sings on in Buenos Aires presents her in English instead of Spanish. Argentines, offended, attacked the cinema where the film was being projected, and Nelson Rockefeller, who commanded one of the most agile arms of the Good Neighbor Policy, took U$S40,000 out of the CIA coffers and ordered Darryl F. Zanuck, the film's producer, to redo all the scenes that Argentines had judged offensive.

This, however, is not confirmed in other texts about the film. Ruy Castro, in *Carmen: Uma Biografia* [Carmen: A Biography], points out however that the film was made before the good-neighbor policy was approved as law. When the Argentine Censorship Committee prohibited the projection of *Down Argentine Way* in the country and the government of President Ramón Castillo made an official protest, the office of the Coordinator of Inter-American Affairs (the CIAA, not the CIA) convinced Zanuck to redo some scenes, although these were only redone in the version for Argentina, whereas in other countries the original copy continued being shown. See Ruy Castro, *Carmen: Uma biografia* [Carmen: A Biography] (São Paulo: Companhia das Letras, 2005), pp. 265–67.

24. This is the same song that Carmen Miranda will sing in the Casino da Urca in the performance of her first return to Brazil in 1935, and it will be the origin of the whistling and rejection from the audience of the Rio de Janeiro elite present in the casino that night. To that rejection, Carmen Miranda will answer with the song "Disseram que eu Voltei Americanizada" [They Say I Came Back Americanized].

25. Walter Benjamin, "La Obra de Arte en la Época de su Reproductibilidad Técnica" and "Pequeña Historia de la Fotografía," in *Discursos Interrumpidos I* [Interrupted Speeches I] (Buenos Aires: Taurus, 1989). (English translation: "The Work of Art in the Age of Mechanical Reproduction" and "Short History of Photography," available in *The Work of Art in the Age of Its Technological Reproducibility, and Other Writings on Media*, eds. Michael W. Jennings, Brigid Doherty, and Thomas Y. Levin (Cambridge, MA: Harvard University Press).

26. Renato Ortiz, *Otro Territorio* [Another Territory], Buenos Aires: Universidad Nacional de Quilmes, 2002, pp. 82–84.

APPENDIX

1. Gilberto Freyre, *Casa Grande e Senzala* (Rio de Janeiro: José Olympio, 1978); English version: *The Masters and the Slaves*, translated by Samuel Putnam (Berkeley: University of California Press, 1986).

2. Hannah Arendt, *The Origins of Totalitarianism* (New York: Harcourt Brace Jovanovich, 1973), pp. 161, 162.

3. I mention *O Guesa* [The Errant One] as the beginning of this productive figuration of the primitive because this text—while inscribed within Brazilian Romanticism due to its era as well as its representation of similar traits and problematics—nonetheless presents a marginal position in relation to the aforementioned movement, and to a certain point even parodies Romanticism itself. It does so because it is a *canto epico* (epic song) that neither constructs unified national identities nor believes in them (see, on this issue, Flora Süssekind, *O Brasil Não É Longe Daqui* [Brazil Is Not Far from Here] (São Paulo: Companhia das Letras, 1990), p. 76, and because of the figuration itself of the primitive as an Indian who has lost all "primogenial" identity. It does not seem coincidental to me that it should be precisely a text that clearly articulates the contradictions of modernity—recall the section "O Inferno em Wall Street" (Hell on Wall Street)—that would be the beginning of this tradition of the dislocated primitive as a figure of Brazilian modernity.

4. Romantic Indianism also needs a dislocation, but in this case one of the white or European in Indian territory. In this way, at least, is Alencar's Indianism constructed, as much in *Iracema* as in *O Guarani* [The Guarani]

5. Oswald de Andrade, *A Utopia Antropofágica* [The Cannibalist Utopia] (São Paulo: Globo, 1990), p. 52.

6.

> Num dos últimos domingos vi passar pela Avenida Central um carroção atulhado de romeiros da Penha: e naquele amplo *boulevard* esplêndido, sobre o asfalto polido, contra a fachada rica dos prédios altos, contra as carruagens e carros que desfilavam, o encontro do velho veículo, em que os devotos bêbedos urravam, me deu a impressão de um monstruoso anacronismo: era a resurreição da barbaria—era uma idade selvagem que voltava, como uma alma selvagem do outro mundo, vindo perturbar e envergohnar a vida da idade civilizada . . . Ainda se a orgia desbragada se confinasse ao arraial da Penha! Mas não! Acabada a festa, a multidão transborda como uma enchurrada vitoriosa para o centro da urbs.

Olavo Bilac, "Crónica" [Chronicle], *Revista Kosmos* (October 1906).

7. The vision of the modernization of Rio de Janeiro as a displacement and dislocation is clear in various texts, many of which make reference to that which in popular language is called "*o bota abaixo*" (the demolition) that Pereira Passos' reform carried out, and that would construct none other than the Central Avenue that Bilac refers to in the quotation, now Rio Branco Avenue. The extreme of dislocation that modernization signified in Rio de Janeiro was manifested in the destruction of the Morro do Castelo, located in the very center of the city. Today, in that zone, one finds the MEC—epitome

of architectural modernism—and Praça Paris (Paris Square) in a notably French style with the exception that it looks upon Guanabara Bay instead of the Seine.

8. The following chronicle by Benjamin Constallat, published in the *Gazeta de Notícias* (News Gazette) reviewing the first performance of the Oito Batutas in the Automóvil Club in 1919 registers the impact and novelty of that performance in the uniquely Brazilian setting of the period:

> It was a true scandal when, four years ago, the Oito Batutas made their appearance. They were Brazilian musicians who had come to sing Brazilian things! And in the middle of the Avenue, in all that quietude, in the midst of those anemic youths, frequenters of cabarets, who only speak French and dance Argentine tangos! In the midst of the internationalism of French seamstresses, Italian bookstores, Spanish ice cream parlors, American automobiles, Polish women, cosmopolitan and idiotic snobbery.

Quoted by Josué de Barros, *Carmen Miranda: Vida, Glória e Morte* [Carmen Miranda: Life, Glory and Death] (Rio de Janeiro: Companhia Brasileira de Artes Gráficas, n.d.), p. 72.

9. I take the concept of the misplaced from Roberto Schwarz, as he developed it in "Las Ideas Fuera de Lugar" [Misplaced Ideas], in Adriana Amante and Florencia Garramuño, *Absurdo Brasil: Polémicas en la Cultura Brasileña* [Absurd Brazil: Polemics in Brazilian Culture] (Buenos Aires: Biblos, 2000).

10. That reading of primitivism as a collision comes from a reading of the avant-garde paradigm as a break with tradition and with the past, which Rosalind Krauss (in *The Originality of the Avant-Garde*) as well as Raymond Williams have dismantled. Williams especially, in "The Politics of Modernism," separates out the different ideological positions that a primitivist appeal could have according to its specific articulations.

11. This reading is not exclusive to the Brazilian tradition, though perhaps in this tradition it has manifested with clearer delineations. Several Latin American avant-garde movements share different manifestations of this nationalism, among which the Mexican case is one of the most evident. Appeals to the national can also be found elsewhere, as in the journal *Martín Fierro* and in the writings of Jorge Luis Borges in Buenos Aires, though it has also been possible to observe nationalism as a frame for modernism in other "marginal" traditions, especially in the Irish case—Yeats and Joyce—but also in the case of Russian primitivism. See Edward Said, *Culture and Imperialism* (New York: Vintage Books, 1994).

12. See Antonio Candido, "Literatura e Cultura de 1900 a 1945 (Panorama para Estrangeiros)" [Literature and Culture from 1900 to 1945 (Panorama for Foreigners)], in *Literatura e Sociedade: Estudos de Teoria e História Literária* [Literature and Society: Studies in Literary Theory and History] (São Paulo: T. A. Queiroz, 2000), p. 121.

13. See Hal Foster, "The 'Primitive' Unconscious of Modern Art, or White Skin Black Masks," in *Recodings: Art, Spectacle, Cultural Politics* (Seattle: Bay Press, 1985), p. 183.

14. Roberto Schwarz, "A Carroça, o Bonde e o Poeta Modernista" [The Cart, the Tram, and the Modernist Poet], in *Que Horas São?* [What Time Is It?] (São Paulo: Companhia das Letras, 1997). (Included in English in *Misplaced Ideas*.)

15. See Matei Calinescu, *Five Faces of Modernity* (Durham, NC: Duke University Press, 1987).

16. This is the same problematic analyzed in relation to the figuration of the primitive in Borges and in Mário de Andrade. See "Primitive Avant-Garde Artists" (this volume).

17. "Contra o Padre Vieira. Autor do nosso primeiro empréstimo, para ganhar comissão. O rei-analfabeto dissera-lhe: ponha isso no papel mas sem muita lábia. Fez-se o empréstimo. Gravou-se o açúcar brasileiro. Vieira deixou o dinheiro em Portugal e nos trouxe a lábia." Oswald de Andrade, *Manifesto Antropófago* [Cannibalist Manifesto], in *A Utopia Antropofágica* [The Cannibalist Utopia] (São Paulo: Globo, 1990), p. 48.

18. "Queremos a Revolução Caraíba. Maior que a Revolução francesa. A unificação de todas as revoltas eficazes na direção do homem. Sem nós a Europa não teria sequer a sua pobre declaração dos direitos do homem." Ibid., p. 48. English translation attributed to David Treece, as cited in Lúcia Sá, *Rainforest Literatures: Amazonian Texts and Latin American Culture* (Minneapolis: University of Minnesota Press, 2004).

19. See, for example, "O Movimento Modernista" [The Modernist Movement], in *Aspectos da Literatura Brasileira* [Aspects of Brazilian Literature] (São Paulo: Livraria Martins, 1974).

20. In regard to this episode on the island, see Raúl Antelo, *Na Ilha de Marapatá* [On the Island of Marapatá] (São Paulo: Hucitec, 1986).

21.

Isso talvez o *Macunaíma* ganhe em inglês porque muito secretamente o que me parece é que a sátira além de dirigível ao brasileiro em geral, de que mostra alguns aspectos característicos, escondendo os aspectos bons sistematicamente, o certo é que me pareceu também uma sátira mais universal ao homen contemporâneo, principalmente sob o ponto de vista desta sem-vontade itinerante, destas noções morais criadas no momento de a realizar, que sinto e vejo tanto no homem de agora.

Mário de Andrade, *Macunaíma*, p. 510.

22. Ibid., pp. 129–31.

23. Ibid, p. 40.

24. To get the talisman, moreover, he must enter into dealings with the prostitutes of São Paulo, all of whom are Polish, French, or Asian. As Donna Guy has shown in the case of Buenos Aires, prostitution was one sphere where the majority of illegal immigration circulated. The prostitute is a figure of transit and transfer—as can be seen, for example, in the paintings of Lasar Segall in Brazil, and in his entire series on "O Mangue"—not only of the transit that presumes the movement from Europe to America, but also the transit between public and private space that is made manifest in the quasioxymoron *"mujer pública"* (public woman, prostitute), as well as the transfer the exchange itself presupposes.

BIBLIOGRAPHY

Adorno, Theodor Wiesengrund. *Sound Figures*, translated by Rodney Livingstone. Stanford, CA: Stanford University Press, 1999.

———. *The Culture Industry*, edited and with an introduction by J. M. Bernstein. London, New York: Routledge, 2001.

———. *Filosofia da Nova Música*. São Paulo: Perspectiva, 2004. Translated by Anne G. Mitchell and Wesley V. Blomster as *Philosophy of Modern Music* (New York: Seabury Press, 1973.)

Altman, Rick. "The American Film Musical: Paradigmatic Structure and Mediatory Function." In *Genre: The Musical. A Reader*, edited by Rick Altman. London: Routledge, 1981.

Amante, Adriana. "La Literatura del Exilio en el Brasil en la Época de Rosas" [The Literature of Exile in Brazil during the Age of Rosas]. Doctoral dissertation, Facultad de Filosofía y Letras, Universidad de Buenos Aires, 2006.

———. "Partir de Candido" [Candido as Point of Departure]. In *Antonio Candido y los Estudios Latinoamericanos* [Antonio Candido and Latin American Studies], edited by Raúl Antelo. Pittsburgh: Pittsburgh University Press, 2001.

———, and Florencia Garramuño. *Absurdo Brasil: Polémicas en la Cultura Brasileña* [Absurd Brazil: Polemics in Brazilian Culture]. Buenos Aires: Biblos, 2000.

Amaral, Aracy. *Boletim* 33 (São Paulo: Secretaria da Cultura, Ciência e Tecnologia, Pinacoteca do Estado, October 1976).

———. *Tarsila: Sua Obra e Seu Tempo* [Tarsila: Her Ouevre and Her Era]. São Paulo: Editora 34 & EDUSP, 2003.

Andrade, Mário. *Aspectos das Artes Plásticas* [Aspects of the Visual Arts]. São Paulo: Martins, 1963.

———. *Aspectos da Música Brasileira* [Aspects of Brazilian Music]. São Paulo: Martins, 1991.

———. *Ensaio sobre a Música Brasileira* [Essay on Brazilian Music]. São Paulo: Martins, 1962.

———. "O Movimento Modernista" [The Modernist Movement]. In *Aspectos da Literatura Brasileira* [Aspects of Brazilian Literature]. São Paulo: Livraria Martins, 1974.

———. *Música, Doce Música* [Music, Sweet Music], vol. 7 of *The Complete Works of Mário de Andrade*. São Paulo: Martins, 1963.

———. *Pequena História da Música* [Brief History of Music]. São Paulo: Martins, 1944.

———. *Poesias Completas* [Complete Poems], critical edition by Diléa Zanotto Manfio. Belo Horizonte: Itatiaia; São Paulo: Editora da Universidade de São Paulo, 1987.

———. *Querida Henriqueta* [Dear Henriqueta], edited by Abigail de Oliveira. Letters from Mário de Andrade to Henriqueta Lisboa. Rio de Janeiro: José Olympio, 1990.

———, and Manuel Bandeira. *Correspondência* [Correspondence], compilation, translation, and notes by Marcos Antonio de Moraes. São Paulo: Editora da Universidade de São Paulo, 2000.

Andrade, Oswald de. *A Utopia Antropofágica* [The Cannibalist Utopia]. São Paulo: Globo, 1990.

———. *Escritos Antropófagos* [Cannibalist Writings], selection, chronology, and epilogue by Gonzalo Aguilar and Alejandra Laera. Buenos Aires: El Cielo por Asalto, 1993; 2nd ed., Buenos Aires: Corregidor, 2001.

———. *Pau Brasil*. Facsimile edition of the 1925 original. Paris: Sans Pareil. Included in *Caixa Modernista*, ed. Jorge Schwarz (São Paulo, Minas Gerais: EDUSP, UFMG, Imprensa Oficial, 2003).

———. *Serafim Ponte Grande*. In *Obras Completas* [Complete Works], vol. 2. Rio de Janeiro: Civilização Brasileira, 1972.

Antelo, Raúl. "Ser, Dever Ser e Dizer: Pelas Costas" [To Be, Should Be, and to Say: The Backside of Things] Mimeo.

———. *El Paulista de la Calle Florida* [The Man from São Paulo on Florida Street], edited and translated by Raúl Antelo. Buenos Aires: Iracema, Centro de Estudios Brasileños, 1979.

———. *Literatura em Revista* [Literature in Review]. São Paulo: Ática, 1984.

———. *Na Ilha de Marapatá* [On Marapatá Island] (São Paulo: Hucitec, 1986).

Appleby, David. *The Music of Brazil*. Austin: University of Texas Press, 1989.

Arac, Jonathan. "Anglo-Globalism?" *New Left Review* (July–August 2002).

Araripe Júnior, Tristão de Alencar. "Aluísio Azevedo: O Romance no Brasil (1888)" [Aluísio Azevedo: The Novel in Brazil [1888]]. In *Obra Crítica* [Critical Works], vol. 2. Rio de Janeiro: Casa de Rui Barbosa, 1958–1970.

———. "Estilo Tropical: A Fórmula do Naturalismo Brasileiro (1888)" [Tropical Style: The Formula of Brazilian Naturalism (1888)]. In *Obra Crítica* [Critical Works], vol. 2. Rio de Janeiro: Casa de Rui Barbosa, 1958–1970.

Archetti, Eduardo P. "El Tango Argentino" [The Argentine Tango]. In *América Latina: Palavra, Literatura, Sociedade* [Latin America: Word, Literature, Society], by Ana Pizarro. Memorial, Campinas: UNICAMP, 1994.

Arendt, Hannah. *The Origins of Totalitarianism*, translated by Guillermo Solana. New York: Harcourt Brace Jovanovich, 1973. Originally cited in the Spanish translation: *Los Orígenes del Totalitarismo* (Madrid: Taurus, 1974).)

Armando, Adriana y Guillermo Fantoni. "El Primitivismo Martinfierrista: De Girondo a Xul Solar" [The Primitivism of the Martin Fierro Avant-Garde Group: From Girondo to Xul Solar]. In *Obra Completa* [Complete Works], by Oliverio Girondo, critical edition by Raúl Antelo. Madrid: ALLCA XX, 1999.

Arrigucci, Davi. *Humildade, Paixão e Morte: A Poesia de Manuel Bandeira* [Humility, Passion and Death: The Poetry of Manuel Bandeira]. São Paulo: Companhia das Letras, 1990.

Assunçao, Fernado. *El Tango y Sus Circunstancias* [Tango and Its Circumstances]. Buenos Aires: El Ateneo, 1984.

Augusto, Sérgio. "Hollywood Looks at Brazil: From Carmen Miranda to *Moonraker*." In *Brazilian Cinema*, edited by Randal Johnson and Robert Stam. Austin: University of Texas Press, 1988.

———. *Este Mundo É um Pandeiro: A Chanchada de Getúlio a JK* [This World Is a *Pandeiro* (Tambourine): The *Chanchada* from Getúlio to JK]. São Paulo: Companhia das Letras, 2001.

Azevedo, Aluísio. *O Cortiço* [The Slum]. São Paulo: Ática, 1890/1997.

Bandeira, Manuel. "Sinhó, Traço de União" [Sinhó, A Unifying Element]. In Manuel Bandeira and Carlos Drummond de Andrade, *Rio de Janeiro em Prosa e Verso* [Rio de Janeiro in Prose and Verse], vol. 5. Rio de Janeiro: José Olympio, 1965.

Barros, Josué de. *Carmen Miranda: Vida, Glória e Morte* [Carmen Miranda: Life, Glory and Death]. Rio de Janeiro: Companhia Brasileira de Artes Gráficas, n.d.

Barros, Orlando de. "A Companhia Negra de Revistas Contra os Foros da Civilização" [The *Companhia Negra de Revistas* Against Civilization's Forums]. *Margens/ Márgenes* 3 (July 2003).

Balibar, Etienne, and Immanuel Wallerstein. *Race, Nation, Class: Ambiguous Identities*. London, New York: Verso, 1991.

Bazin, André. *What Is Cinema?* Berkeley: University of California Press, 1972.

Benjamin, Walter. "False Criticism." In *Selected Writings*, vol. 2: *1927–1934*, translation by Rodney Livingstone and others; edited by Michael W. Jennings, Howard Eiland, and Gary Smith. Cambridge, MA: Belknap Press/Harvad University, 1999.

———. *The Arcades Project*, translation by Howard Eiland and Kevin McLaughlin. Cambridge, MA: Belknap Press of Harvard University Press, 1999.

———. "La Obra de Arte en la Época de Su Reproductibilidad Técnica" and "Pequeña Historia de la Fotografía." In *Discursos Interrumpidos I*. Buenos Aires: Taurus, 1989. Translated by Jesús Aguirre. "The Work of Art in the Age of Mechanical Reproduction" and "Brief History of Photography," in *The Work of Art in the Age of Its Techno-*

logical Reproducibility, and Other Writings on Media, edited by Michael W. Jennings, Brigid Doherty, and Thomas Y. Levin (Cambridge, MA: Harvard University Press, 2008).

Bernstein, J. M. "Introduction." In *The Culture Industry*, by Theodor Wiesengrund Adorno. London, New York: Routledge, 2001.

Berti, Eduardo. "Primer Tango en París" [First Tango in Paris]. *La Nación* (Buenos Aires), Suplemento Cultura, December 9, 2001.

Bhabha, Homi K. "DissemiNation: Time, Narrative and the Margins of the Modern Nation." In *Nation and Narration*. London, New York: Routledge, 1990.

Bilac, Olavo. "Crónica" [Chronicle] (October 1906).

Bordelois, Ivonne. *Genio y Figura de Ricardo Güiraldes* [The Genius and Figure of Ricardo Güiraldes]. Buenos Aires: Eudeba, 1966.

Borges, Jorge Luis. "Ascendencias del Tango" [Tango's Origins]. In *El Idioma de los Argentinos* [The Language of the Argentines]. Madrid: Alianza, 1995.

———. *Borges en Sur: 1931–1980* [Borges in Sur: 1931–1980]. Buenos Aires: Emecé, 1999.

———. *Evaristo Carriego*. Buenos Aires: Gleizer, 1930/1955.

———. *Evaristo Carriego*. In *Obras Completas* [Complete Works]. Buenos Aires: Emecé, 1974.

———. Discusión. In *Obras Completas* [Complete Works]. Buenos Aires: Emecé, 1974.

———. El jardín de senderos que se bifurcan. In *Obras Completas*. Buenos Aires: Emecé, 1974.

———. *El Tamaño de Mi Esperanza* [The Size of My Hope]. Buenos Aires: Seix Barral, 1993.

———. *Textos Recobrados: 1919–1929* [Recovered Texts: 1919–1929]. Buenos Aires: Emecé, 1997.

———, and Silvina Bullrich. *El Compadrito: Su Destino—Sus Barrios—Su Música* [The *Compadrito*: His Destiny—His Neighborhoods—His Music]. Buenos Aires: Compañía Fabril Editora, 1968.

Bosi, Alfredo. "La Parábola de las Vanguardias Latinoamericanas" [The Parabola of Latin American Avant-Garde Movements]. In *Las Vanguardias Latinoamericanas: Textos Programáticos y Críticos* [The Latin American Avant-Garde Movements: Programmatic and Critical Texts], by Jorge Schwarz. Madrid: Cátedra, 1990.

Brennan, Timothy. "The National Longing for Form." In *Nation and Narration,* Homi K. Bhabha. London, New York: Routledge, 1990.

Brooks, Peter. *The Melodramatic Imagination: Balzac, Henry James, Melodrama, and the Mode of Excess*. New Haven, CT: Yale University Press, 1984.

Burch, Noël. *El Tragaluz del Infinito* [The Infinite Skylight]. Madrid: Cátedra, 1987.

Bürger, Peter. *Theory of the Avant-Garde*. Minneapolis: University of Minnesota Press, 1984.

Butler, Judith. "Restaging the Universal: Hegemony and the Limits of Formalism." In *Contingency, Hegemony, Universality: Contemporary Dialogues on the Left*, edited by Judith Butler, Ernesto Laclau, and Slavoj Žižek. London, New York: Verso, 2000.

Cabral, Sérgio. *As Escolas de Samba do Rio de Janeiro* [Rio de Janeiro's Samba Schools]. Petrópolis: Lumiar, 1996.

———. *Pixinguinha: Vida e Obra* [Pixinguinha: Life and Works] (Petrópolis: Lumiar, 1997).

Cadícamo, Enrique. *Mis Memorias* [My Memoirs]. Buenos Aires: Corregidor, 1995.

Calinescu, Matei. *Five Faces of Modernity*. Durham, NC: Duke University Press, 1987.

Campos, Haroldo de. "Prefácio" [Preface]. In *Poesias Reunidas* [Collected Poems], by Oswald de Andrade. Rio de Janeiro: Civilização Brasileira, 1971.

Canaro, Francisco. *Mis Memorias: Mis Bodas de Oro con el Tango* [My Memoirs: My Golden Anniversary with Tango] (Buenos Aires: Corregidor, 1999).

Candido, Antonio. "Literatura e Cultura de 1900 a 1945 (Panorama para Estrangeiros)" [Literature and Culture from 1900 to 1945 (Panorama for Foreigners)]. In *Literatura e Sociedade: Estudos de Teoria e História Literária* [Literature and Society: Studies in Literary History and Theory]. São Paulo: T. A. Queiroz, 2000.

———. "De Cortiço a Cortiço" [From Slum to Slum]. In *O Discurso e a Cidade* [The Discourse and the City]. São Paulo: Duas Cidades, 1993.

———. "Estouro e Libertação" [Explosion and Liberation]. In *Vários Escritos* [Some Writings]. São Paulo: Duas Cidades, 1995.

———. "Introdução" [Introduction]. In *Filomena Borges*, by Aluísio Azevedo. São Paulo: Martins, 1960.

———. "Literatura Comparada" [Comparative Literature]. In *Recortes* [Clippings]. São Paulo: Companhia das Letras, 1996.

———. *Literatura e Sociedade: Estudos de Teoria e História Literária* [Literature and Society: Studies in Literary History and Theory]. São Paulo: T. A. Queiroz, 2000.

Cardoso Júnior, Abel. *Carmen Miranda: A Cantora do Brasil* [Carmen Miranda: The Singer of Brazil]. São Paulo: self-published edition, 1978.

Castro, Ruy. *Carmen: Uma biografia* [Carmen: A Biography]. São Paulo: Companhia das Letras, 2005.

Cavell, Stanley. *The World Viewed*. Cambridge, MA: Harvard University Press, 1979.

Chatterjee, Partha. "Whose Imagined Community?" In *Mapping the Nation*, edited by Gopal Balakrishnan. London, New York: Verso, 1996.

———. *Nationalist Thought and the Colonial World: A Derivative Discourse?* London: Zed for the United Nations University, 1986.

Chiarelli, Tadeu. "Entre Almeida Jr. e Picasso" [Between Almeida Jr. and Picasso]. In *Arte Internacional Brasileira* [International Brazilian Art]. São Paulo: Lemos, 1999.

Clifford, James. "On Ethnographic Surrealism." *Comparative Studies in Society and History* 23, no. 4 (1981).

Collier, Simon. "Carlos Gardel and the Cinema." In *The Garden of Forking Paths: Argentine Cinema*, edited by John King and Nissa Torrents. London: British Film Institute, 1988.

Colombi, Beatriz. *Viaje intelectual: Migraciones y desplazamientos en América Latina (1880–1915)* [Intellectual Voyage: Migrations and Displacements in Latin America (1880–1915)]. Rosario: Beatriz Viterbo, 2004.

Corradi, Juan. "How Many Did It Take to Tango? Voyages of Urban Culture in the Early 1900s." In *Outsider Art: Contesting Boundaries in Latin American Contemporary Culture,* edited by Vera Zolberg and Joni Maya Cerbo. Cambridge, MA: Cambridge University Press, 1997.

Couselo, Jorge Miguel et al. *Historia del Cine Argentino* [History of Argentine Cinema]. Buenos Aires: Centro Editor de América Latina, 1984.

Crow, Thomas. *Modern Art in the Common Culture.* New Haven, CT: Yale University Press, 1998. Originally cited in the Spanish translation: *El Arte Moderno en la Cultura de lo Cotidiano,* translated by Joaquín Chamorro Mielke (Madrid: Akal, 2002).

Dellepiane, Antonio. *El Idioma del Delito* [The Language of Delinquency]. Buenos Aires: Mirasol, 1894/1967.

Dias, Rosângela de Oliveira. *O Mundo como Chanchada: Cinema e Imaginário das Classes Populares na Década de 50* [The World as *Chanchada*: Cinema and the Imaginary of the Popular Classes in the 1950s]. Rio de Janeiro: Relume Dumará, 1993.

Dieleke, Edgardo. *Los Tangos de la Vanguardia: Una Perspectiva Diferente sobre la Lógica de Funcionamiento de la Vanguardia Argentina* [The Tangos of the Avant-Garde: A Different Perspective on the Logic of Argentine Avant-Garde Functioning]. Thesis for the Licenciatura (Undergraduate) Degree, Buenos Aires, Universidad de San Andrés, 2002.

Di Núbila, Domingo. *La época de Oro: Historia del Cine Argentino* [The Golden Age: History of Argentine Cinema]. Buenos Aires: Ediciones del Jilguero, 1998.

España, Claudio. "El Cine Sonoro y Su Expansión" [Sound Movies and Their Expansion]. In *Historia del Cine Argentino* [History of Argentine Cinema], by José Miguel Cosuelo, et al. Buenos Aires: Centro Editor de América Latina, 1992.

Fabris, Annateresa. *Candido Portinari.* São Paulo: EDUSP, 1996.

Ferrer, Horacio. "Gardel y Su Mito" [Gardel and His Myth]. In *La Historia del Tango: Tomo Extra* [The History of Tango: Extra Volume], by Juan Carlos Martini Real, Francisco García Jiménez et al. Buenos Aires: Corregidor, 1977.

———. *El Libro del Tango: Crónica y Diccionario. 1950–1977* [The Book of Tango: Chronicle and Dictionary. 1950–1977]. Buenos Aires: Galerna, 1977.

———, and Oscar Del Priore. *El Inventario del Tango* [The Tango Inventory]. Buenos Aires: Fondo Nacional de las Artes, 1999.

Foot Hardman, Francisco. *Nem Pátria nem Patrão! Vida Operária e Cultura Anarquista no Brasil* [Neither Fatherland nor Boss! The Workers' Life and Anarchist Culture in Brazil], São Paulo: Brasiliense, 1983.

Foster, Hal. "The 'Primitive' Unconscious of Modern Art, or White Skin Black Masks." In *Recodings: Art, Spectacle, Cultural Politics*. Seattle: Bay Press, 1985.

———. "Who's Afraid of the Neo-Avant-Garde?" In *The Return of the Real*. Cambridge: MIT Press, 1996.

Freud, Sigmund. *Civilization and Its Discontents*, translated by James Strachey. New York: W. W. Norton, 1962. Originally cited in the Spanish translation: *El Malestar de la Cultura* (Madrid: Alianza, 1988).

Freyre, Gilberto. "Acerca da Valorização do Preto" [On the Valorization of Blacks]. In *Diario de Permambuco, Tempo de Aprendiz* [Diary of Pernambuco, Time of Apprenticeship]. São Paulo: IBRASA, 1979.

———. *Casa Grande e Senzala*. Rio de Janeiro: José Olympio, 1978.

———. *The Masters and the Slaves*, translated by Samuel Putnam. Berkeley: University of California Press, 1986.

Frith, Simon. *Performing Rites: On the Value of Popular Music*. Cambridge, MA: Harvard University Press, 1996.

Fryer, Peter, *Rhythms of Resistance: African Muscial Heritage in Brazil*. Hanover, CT: Wesleyan University Press, 2000.

Galvão, Maria Rita, and Carlos Roberto de Souza. "Cinema Brasileiro: 1930–1964" [Brazilian Cinema: 1930–1964]. In *História Geral da Civilização Brasileira* [General History of Brazilian Civilization], by Sérgio Buarque de Holanda, vol. 4. Rio de Janeiro: Bertrand, 1989.

Gálvez, Manuel. *Historia de Arrabal* [A History of the Periphery]. Buenos Aires: Deucalión, 1956.

———. *En el Mundo de los Seres Ficticios* [In the World of Fictitious Beings]. Buenos Aires: Hachette, 1962.

———. *Nacha Regules* (Buenos Aires: Pax, 1922; Buenos Aires: Centro Editor de América Latina, 1968).

García Jiménez, Francisco. *Historia de Medio Siglo: 1880–1930* (History of a Half-Century: 1880–1930). Buenos Aires: Eudeba, 1964.

Gardel, André. *Compilación Poética* [Compiled Poems], edited by Pedro Arias and Leonardo Capristo. Buenos Aires: Corregidor, 2003.

———. *O encontro entre Bandeira e Sinhô* [The Meeting of Bandeira and Sinhô]. Rio de Janeiro: Prefeitura da Cidade do Rio de Janeiro, Secretaria Municipal de Cultura, Departamento Geral de Documentação e Informação Cultural, Divisão de Editoração, 1996.

Gasio, Guillermo. *Jean Richepin y el Tango Argentino* [Jean Richepin and the Argentine Tango]. Buenos Aires: Corregidor, 1999.

Gilroy, Paul. *The Black Atlantic: Modernity and Double Consciousness*. Cambridge, MA: Harvard University Press, 1992.

Girondo, Oliverio. *Obra completa* [Complete Works]. Madrid: ALLCA XX, 1999.

Gomes, Renato Cordeiro. "Céu no Chão" [Sky on the Ground]. In *Marques Rebelo: Melhores Crônicas* [Marques Rebelo: The Best Chronicles], edited by Renato Cordeiro Gomes. São Paulo: Global, 2004.

———. "Marques Rebelo, Cronista de uma Cidade" [Marques Rebelo, Chronicler of a City]. In *Marques Rebelo: Melhores Crônicas* [Marques Rebelo: The Best Chronicles], edited by Renato Cordeiro Gomes. São Paulo: Global, 2004.

Gorelik, Adrián. *Das Vanguardas à Brasília: Cultura Urbana e Arquitetura na América Latina* [From the Avant-Garde to Brasília: Urban Culture and Architecture in Latin America]. Belo Horizonte: UFMG, 2005.

———. *La Grilla y el Parque* [The Grid and the Park]. Bernal: Universidad Nacional de Quilmes, 1988.

Gramsci, Antonio. *Literatura y vida nacional* [Literature and National Life]. Mexico City: Juan Pablos Editor, 1976.

Gramuglio, María Teresa. "La Persistencia del Nacionalismo" [The Persistence of Nationalism]. *Punto de Vista* 50 (November 1994), pp. 23–27.

———. "Novela y Nación en el Proyecto Literario de Gálvez" [Novel and Nation in Gálvez' Literary Project]. In *Historia Crítica de la Literatura Argentina* [Critical History of Argentine Literature], edited by María Teresa Gramuglio, vol. 6: *El Imperio Realista* [The Realist Empire]. Buenos Aires: Emecé, 2002.

Grossberg, Lawrence. "Identity and Cultural Studies—Is That All There Is?" In *Questions of Cultural Identity*, edited by Stuart Hall. London, Thousand Oaks, New Delhi: Sage, 1996.

Gueriós, Paulo Renato. "Heitor Villa-Lobos e o Ambiente Artístico Parisiense: Convertendo-se em um Músico Brasileiro" [Heitor Villa-Lobos and the Artistic Context in Paris: Becoming a Brazilian Musician]. *Mana* 9 (1), 2003.

Güiraldes, Ricardo. *El Cencerro de Cristal* [The Crystal Cowbell]. Buenos Aires: Losada, 1952.

———. *Raucho*. Buenos Aires: Losada, 1956.

Guy, Donna. *Sex and Danger in Buenos Aires*. Lincoln: University of Nebraska Press, 1991.

Hall, Stuart. "The Local and the Global: Globalization and Ethnicity." In *Culture, Globalization and the World System*, edited by A. King. London: Macmillan, 1991.

Henríquez Ureña, Pedro. *Ensayos* [Essays], critical edition by José Luis Abellán and Ana María Barrenechea. Madrid: ALLCA XX, 2000.

Hewitt, Andrew. *Fascist Modernism: Aesthetics, Politics and the Avant-garde*. Stanford, CA: Stanford University Press, 1993.

Hobsbawm, Eric. *Uncommon People: Resistance, Rebellion and Jazz*. London, Werdenfeld and Nicholson, 1998.

———, and Ranger, Terence. *The Invention of Tradition*. Cambridge: Cambridge University Press, 1983.

Humbert, Béatrice. "El Tango en París de 1907 a 1920" [The Tango in Paris from 1907 to 1920]. In *El Tango Nómade* [Nomadic Tango], edited by Ramón Pelinski. Buenos Aires: Corregidor, 2000.

Ípola, Emilio de. "El Tango en Sus Márgenes" [The Tango in Its Margins]. *Punto de Vista* 8 (25), Buenos Aires: December 1985.

Jitrik, Noé. "Papeles de Trabajo: Notas sobre Vanguardismo Latinoamericano" [Working Papers: Notes on the Latin American Avant-Garde]. *Revista de Crítica Literaria Latinoamericana* 15 (1982), pp. 13–24.

———. "Poesía Argentina entre dos Radicalismos" [Argentine Poetry between Two Radicalisms]. In *Ensayos y Estudios de Literatura Argentina* [Essays and Studies on Argentine Literature]. Buenos Aires: Galerna, 1971.

Johnson, Randal, and Robert Stam (eds.). *Brazilian Cinema*. Austin: University of Texas Press, 1988.

Kracauer, Sigfried. *Theory of Film: The Redemption of Physical Reality*, introduction by Miriam Bratu Hansen. Princeton, NJ: Princeton University Press, 1997.

Krauss, Rosalind. *The Originality of the Avant-Garde and Other Modernist Myths*. Cambridge, MA: MIT Press, 1985.

———. *The Picasso Papers*. Cambridge, MA: MIT Press, 1999. Originally cited in the Spanish translation: *Los Papeles de Picasso*, translated by Mireya Reilly de Fayard (Barcelona: Gedisa, 1999).

Laclau, Ernesto. *Emancipación y Diferencia* [Emancipation and Difference]. Buenos Aires: Nueva Visión, 1996.

Lafetá, João Luís. *1930: A Crítica e o Modernismo* [1930: Criticism and Modernism]. São Paulo: Duas Cidades, 2000.

———. "A Representacão do Sujeito Lírico na *Paulicéia Desvairada*" [The Representation of the Lyrical Subject in *Hallucinated City*]. *Revista da Biblioteca Mário de Andrade* (São Paulo) 61 (1993).

Lima Barreto, Afonso Henriques de. *Clara dos Anjos*. São Paulo: Brasiliense, n.d.

López, Ana María. "Of Rhythms and Borders." In *Everynight Life*, edited by Celeste Delgado Muñoz and José Muñoz. Durham, NC: Duke University Press, 1997.

Lloyd, David, and Paul Thomas. *Culture and the State*. London: Routledege, 1997.

Ludmer, Josefina. *El Género Gauchesco: Un Tratado sobre la Patria* [The Gaucho Genre: A Treatise on the Motherland]. Buenos Aires: Perfil, 2000; Durham: Duke University Press, 2002.

Lugones, Leopoldo. *El Payador* [The Folksinger/Minstrel]. Caracas: Biblioteca Ayacucho, 1991.

Mahieu, José Agustín. *Breve Historia del Cine Argentino* [Brief History of Argentine Cinema]. Buenos Aires: Eudeba, 1966.

Malosetti Costa, Laura. *Los Primeros Modernos: Arte y Sociedad en Buenos Aires a Fines del Siglo XIX* [The First Moderns: Art and Society in Buenos Aires at the End of the 19th Century]. Buenos Aires: Fondo de Cultura Económica, 2001.

Marques Rebelo. *A Estrela Sobe* [The Star Is Rising]. Rio de Janeiro: Nova Fronteira, 1986.

Martínez Estrada, Ezequiel. *Radiografía de la Pampa* [X-Ray of the Pampa]. Buenos Aires: Sudamericana, 1970.

Marx, Karl. *Capital*, translation by Samuel Moore and Edward Aveling; edited by Frederick Engels; on-line version: Marx/Engels Internet Archive (marxists.org) 1995, 1999. (Originally cited in the Spanish version: *El Capital*. Mexico City: Siglo XXI, 1987.)

Masiello, Francine. *Lenguaje e Ideología* [Language and Ideology]. Buenos Aires: Hachette, 1988.

Matamoro, Blas. *La Ciudad del Tango: Tango Histórico y Sociedad* [The City of Tango: Historical Tango and Society]. Buenos Aires: Galerna, 1982.

Matos, Claudia de. *Acertei no Milhar: Samba e Malandragem no Tempo de Getúlio* [I Won the Lottery: Samba and *Malandragem* in the Age of Getulio]. Rio de Janeiro: Paz e Terra, 1982.

McCann, Brian. *Hello, Hello Brazil: Popular Music in the Making of Modern Brazil*. Durham, NC: Duke University Press, 2004.

Meireles, Cecília. *Batuque, Samba e Macumba: Estudos de Gesto e Ritmo, 1926–1934* [Batuque, Samba and Macumba: Studies on Gesture and Rhythm, 1926–1934]. Rio de Janeiro: FUNARTE, 1983.

Mendes, Murilo. "Di Cavalcanti." *A Manhã: Suplemento Letras e Artes* (Rio de Janeiro), February 6, 1949.

Miceli, Sérgio. *Nacional Estrangeiro* [National Foreigner]. São Paulo: Companhia das Letras, 2003.

Moretti, Franco. "Conjectures on World Literature." *New Left Review* 1 (2000), pp. 54–68.

———. "More Conjectures." *New Left Review* 2 (April 2003).

Nairn, Tom. *Faces of Nationalism: Janus Revisited*. London and New York: Verso, 1997.

Naves, Santuza Cambraia. *O Violão Azul: Modernismo e Música Popular* [The Blue Guitar: Modernism and Popular Music]. Rio de Janeiro: Fundação Getúlio Vargas, 1998.

Nunes, Benedito. "Antropofagia ao Alcance de Todos" [Cannibalism for Everyone]. In *A Utopia Antropofágica* [The Cannibalist Utopia], by Oswald de Andrade. São Paulo: Globo, 1990. Originally published in *O Globo*, February 11, 1931.

Ochoa, Ana Maria. *Músicas Locales en Tiempos de Globalización* [Local Forms of Music in Globalized Times]. Buenos Aires: Norma, 2003.

Ortiz, Renato. *A Consciencia Fragmentada* [The Fragmented Conscience]. São Paulo: Paz e Terra, 1980.

———. *Otro Territorio* [Another Territory]. Buenos Aires: Universidad Nacional de Quilmes, 2002.

Osborne, Peter. *Philosophy and Cultural Theory*. London: Routledge, 2000.
———. *The Politics of Time*. London: Verso, 1995.
Oubiña, David. *El Silencio y Sus Bordes* [Silence and Its Edges]. Doctoral dissertation, Buenos Aires, Facultad de Filosofía y Letras, Universidad de Buenos Aires, 2005.
Pacheco, Jaci. *Carmen Miranda*. Rio de Janeiro: Pensa, 1955.
Panesi, Jorge. "Borges Nacionalista: Una Identidad Paradójica" [Nationalist Borges: A Paradoxical Identity]. In *Identidade e Representação* [Identity and Representation], edited by Raúl Antelo. Florianópolis: Universidade Federal de Santa Catarina, 1994.
Parker, Richard. *Bodies, Pleasures, and Passions: Sexual Culture in Contemporary Brazil*. Boston: Beacon Press, 1991.
Pinsón, Néstor. "Mi Noche Triste, el Tango Canción" [My Sad Night, the Tango Song]. Available online at <www.todotango.com.ar>.
Pedrosa, Mário. "Forma e Percepção Estética" [Form and Aesthetic Perception]. In *Textos Escolhidos II* [Selected Texts II], edited by Otília Arantes. São Paulo: EDUSP, 1996, p. 100.
Pereira de Queiroz, Maria Isaura. *Carnaval Brasileiro: O Vivido e o Mito* [Brazilian Carnival: The Lived Experience and the Myth]. São Paulo: Brasiliense, 1992.
Perloff, Marjorie. "Tolerance and Taboo." In *Poetry On and Off the Page*. Evanston, IL: Northwestern University Press, 1998.
Pettoruti, Emilio. *Un Pintor ante el Espejo* [A Painter before the Mirror]. Buenos Aires: Libéria Histórica, 2004.
Prieto, Adolfo. *Los Viajeros Ingleses y la Emergencia de la Literatura Argentina, 1820–1850* [British Travelers and the Emergence of Argentine Literature, 1820–1850]. Buenos Aires: Fondo de Cultura Económica, 1990.
Queiroz, Rachel. "Carnaval na Ilha do Governador" [Carnival on "Ilha do Governador" Island]. In *Rio de Janeiro em Prosa e Verso* [Rio de Janeiro in Prose and Verse], by Manuel Bandeira and Carlos Drummond de Andrade. Rio de Janeiro: José Olympio, 1965.
Ramos, Julio. *Desencuentros de la Modernidad en América Latina* [Disencounters of Modernity in Latin America]. Mexico City: Siglo XXI, 1989.
Ramos Mejía, Juan José. *Las Multitudes Argentinas: Estudio de Psicología Colectiva* [The Argentine Multitudes: A Study of Collective Psychology]. Buenos Aires: Belgrano, 1977.
Rancière, Jacques. *The Politics of Aesthetics: The Distribution of the Sensible*, translated by Gabriel Rockhill. London: Continuum, 2004. Originally cited in the Spanish version: *La División de lo Sensible* (Salamanca: Consorcio Salamanca, 2002).
Ratliff, Ben. "Samba Nation." *Lingua Franca* (Spring 1999), B13–B14.
Reis, Paulo. "Di Cavalcanti," *Jornal do Brasil* (Rio de Janeiro), July 6, 1994.
Ribeiro, Júlio. *A Carne* [The Flesh]. São Paulo: Martin Claret, 1999.

Risério, Antonio. *Caymmi, uma Utopia de Lugar* [Caymmi, a Utopia of Place]. São Paulo: Perspectiva, 1993.

Roberts, Jon. "After Adorno Art, Autonomy, and Critique." Available online at <http://www.apexart.org/residency/roberts.htm>.

Romano, Eduardo. "Introducción" [Introduction]. In *Don Segundo Sombra*, by Ricardo Güiraldes. Buenos Aires: Colihue, 1985.

Rossi, Vicente. *Cosas de Negros* [Black People's Matters]. Buenos Aires: Taurus 2001.

Rouquié, Alain. "Manuel Gálvez, Écrivain Politique (Contribution a l'Étude du Nationalisme Argentine)" [Manuel Gálvez, Political Writer (Contribution to the Study of Argentine Naitonalism)]." *Cahiers des Amériques Latines*, Série Arts et Littérature 3/4, (1969), pp. 93–110.

———. "La Genèse du Nationalisme Culturel dans l'Oeuvre de Manuel Gálvez" [The Genesis of Cultural Nationalism, in the Work of Manuel Gálvez]. *Cahiers du Monde Hispanique et Luso-Brésilien (Caravelle)* 19 (1972).

Sá, Lúcia. *Rainforest Literatures: Amazonian Texts and Latin American Culture*. Minneapolis: University of Minnesota Press, 2004.

Said, Edward. *Culture and Imperialism*. New York: Vintage Books, 1994.

Sant'Anna, Affonso Romano de. *Análise Estrutural de Romances Brasileiros* [Structural Analysis of Brazilian Novels]. Petrópolis: Vozes, 1979.

Santiago, Silviano. "Permanência do Discurso da Tradição no Modernismo Brasileiro" [The Permanence of the Discourse of Tradition in Brazilian Modernism]. In *Cultura Brasileira: Tradição/Contradição* [Brazilian Culture: Tradition/Contradiction], edited by Adauto Novaes. Rio de Janeiro: Jorge Zahar, 1987.

———. "Fechado para Balanço (Sesenta Anos de Modernismo)" [Closed for Inventory (Sixty Years of Modernism)]. In *Nas Malhas da Letra* [In the Text's Web]. São Paulo: Companhia das Letras, 1989.

———. "História de um Livro" [History of a Book]. In *Macunaíma*, by Mário de Andrade. Brasilia: Archives, 1988.

———. "Liderança e Hierarquia em Alencar" [Leadership and Hierarchy in Alencar]. In *Vale Quanto Pesa* [Worth Its Weight]. Rio de Janeiro: Paz e Terra, 1982).

———. *Ora Direis, Puxar Conversa!* [And Now You Will Say, Spark Conversation!]. Belo Horizonte: UFMG, 2006.

———. "Sobre Plataformas e Testamentos" [On Platforms and Testaments]. In *Ponta de Lança* [Spearhead], by Oswald de Andrade. São Paulo: Globo, 2004.

Sandroni, Carlos. *Feitiço Decente: Transformações do Samba no Rio de Janeiro (1917–1930)* [Decent Bewitchment: Transformations of Samba in Rio de Janeiro (1917–1930)]. Rio de Janeiro: Jorge Zahar & UFRJ, 2001.

Sarlo, Beatriz. *Borges, un Escritor en las Orillas* [Borges, a Writer on the Shores]. Buenos Aires: Ariel, 1995.

———. *Una Modernidad Periférica: Buenos Aires 1920–1930* [A Peripheral Modernity: Buenos Aires 1920–1930]. Buenos Aires: Nueva Visión, 1988.

———. "Vanguardia y Criollismo: La Aventura de 'Martín Fierro'" [Avant-Garde Movements and *Criollismo*: The "Martin Fierro" Adventure]. In *Ensayos Argentinos: De Sarmiento a la Vanguardia* [Argentine Essays: From Sarmiento to the Avant-Garde], by Carlos Altamirano and Beatriz Sarlo. Buenos Aires: Centro Editor de América Latina, 1983.

Savigliano, Marta. *Tango and the Political Economy of Passion*. Boulder, CO: Westview Press, 1995.

Schreiner, Claus. *Música Brasileira: A History of Popular Music and the People of Brazil*. New York and London: Manon Boyars, 1993.

Schwartz, Lilia Moritz. *O Espetáculo das Raças* [The Spectacle of Races]. São Paulo: Companhia das Letras, 1993.

Schwarz, Jorge. *Las Vanguardias Latinoamericanas: Textos Programáticos y Críticos* [The Latin American Avant-Garde Movements: Programmatic and Critical Texts]. Madrid: Cátedra, 1990.

———. *Vanguardia y Cosmopolitismo del Veinte: Oliverio Girondo y Oswald de Andrade* [Avant-Garde Movements and Cosmopolitanism in the 1920s: Oliverio Girondo and Oswald de Andrade]. Rosario: Beatriz Viterbo, 1993.

———. (ed.), *Caixa Modernista* [The Modernist Box]. São Paulo, Minas Gerais: EDUSP, UFMG Imprensa Oficial, 2003.

Schwarz, Roberto. "Adequação Nacional e Originalidade Crítica" (National Adequation and Critical Originality). In *Seqüencias Brasileiras* [Brazilian Sequences]. São Paulo: Companhia das Letras, 1999.

———. "A Carroça, o Bonde e o Poeta Modernista" [The Cart, the Tram, and the Modernist Poet]. In *Que Horas São?* [What Time Is It?]. São Paulo: Companhia das Letras, 1997. (Included in English in *Misplaced Ideas*.)

———. "A Importação do Romance em Alencar" [The Importing of the Novel in Alencar]. In *Ao Vencedor as Batatas* [The Potatoes to the Winner]. São Paulo: Editora 34, 2000.

———. "O Psicologismo na Poética de Mário de Andrade" [Psychologism in the Poetics of Mário de Andrade]. In *A Sereia e o Desconfiado* [The Siren and the Incredulous Man]. Rio de Janeiro: Paz e Terra, 1981.

Scott, Joan Wallach. *Only Paradoxes to Offer: French Feminists and the Rights of Man*. Cambridge, MA: Harvard University Press, 1997.

Segalen, Victor. *Essai sur l' exotisme: Une esthétique du divers* [Essays on Exoticism: An Aesthetics of Diversity]. Cognac, Fontfroide: Bibliothéque artistique et littéraire, 1994.

Selles, Roberto. "El Tango y Sus Dos Primeras Décadas (1880–1900)" [The Tango and Its First Two Decades (1880–1900)]. In *La Historia del Tango*, vol. 2. Buenos Aires: Corregidor, 1980.

Sevcenko, Nicolau. *Orfeu Extático na Metrópole: São Paulo, Sociedade e Cultura nos Frementes Anos Veinte* [Orpheus Ecstatic in the Metropolis: São Paulo, Society and Culture in the Bustling Twenties]. São Paulo: Companhia das Letras, 1992.

Sierra, Luis Adolfo. *Historia de la Orquesta Típica* [History of the Autochthonous Orchestra]. Buenos Aires: Corregidor, 1997.

Souza, Eneida Maria de. *A Pedra Mágica do Discurso* [The Magic Stone of Discourse]. Belo Horizonte: UFMG, 1999.

———. *Crítica Cult* [Cult Criticism]. Belo Horizonte: Editora da Universidade Federal de Minas Gerais.

Spivak, Gayatri. *Death of a Discipline*. New York: Columbia University Press, 2003.

Stam, Robert. *Tropical Multiculturalism: A Comparative History of Race in Brazilian Cinema and Culture*. Durham, NC: Duke University Press, 1997.

———. "Samba, Candomblé, Quilombo: Black Performance and Brazilian Cinema." *Journal of Ethnic Studies* 13, no. 3 (1985).

Süssekind, Flora. *O Brasil Não É Longe Daqui* [Brazil Is Not Far from Here]. São Paulo: Companhia das Letras, 1990.

———. *O Negro como Arlequim* [The Negro as Harlequin]. Rio de Janeiro: Achiamé, 1982.

Terán, Oscar. "Modernos Intensos en los Veinte" [Intense Moderns in the Twenties]. *Prismas* 1 (1997), pp. 91–104.

Thomson, Robert Farris. *Tango: The Art History of Love*. New York: Pantheon Books.

Tinhorão, José Ramos. *História Social da Música Popular Brasileira* [Social History of Brazilian Popular Music]. São Paulo: Editora 34, 1998.

———. *Música Popular: Um tema em Debate* [Popular Music: An Issue of Debate]. São Paulo: Editora 34, 1997.

———. *Pequena História da Música Popular: Da Modinha à Canção de Protesto* (Brief History of Popular Music: From *Modinha* to Protest Song). Petrópolis: Vozes, 1975.

Tota, Antonio Pedro. *O Imperialismo Sedutor* [The Seductive Imperialism]. São Paulo: Companhia das Letras, 2000.

Treece, David. "Melody, Text and Luiz Tati's *O Cancionista*: New Directions in Brazilian Popular Music Studies." *Travesía: Journal of Latin American Cultural Studies* 5, no. 2 (1996).

Valdez, María. "La Radio en el Cine" [The Radio in Film]. In *Cine Argentino: Industria y Clasicismo* [Argentine Cinema: Industry and Classicism], by Claudio España. Buenos Aires: Fondo Nacional de las Artes, 2000.

Valença, Rachel. *Carnaval* [Carnival]. Rio de Janeiro: Rio Arte & Relume Dumará, 1996.

Vasconcellos, Ary. *Panorama da Música Popular Brasileira na "Belle Epoque"* [Panorama of "Belle Epoque" Brazilian Popular Music]. Rio de Janeiro: Sant'Anna, 1977.

Veloso, Caetano. *Verdade Tropical* [Tropical Truth]. São Paulo: Companhia das Letras, 1997.

Ventura, Roberto. *Estilo tropical: História Cultural e Polêmicas Literárias no Brasil, 1870–1914* [Tropical Style: Cultural History and Literary Polemics in Brazil, 1870–1914]. São Paulo: Companhia das Letras, 1991.

Vianna, Hermano. *O Mistério do Samba* [The Mystery of Samba]. Rio de Janeiro: Jorge Zahar & UFRJ, 1995.

Viñas, David. *Literatura Argentina y Política: De Lugones a Walsh* [Argentine Literature and Politics: From Lugones to Walsh]. Buenos Aires: Sudamericana, 1996.

Wallenstein, Sven Olov. "Object-Form and Commodity Form (Art for Art's Sake, Money for God's Sake)." *Subsol 2*. Available online at <http://subsol.c3.hu/subsol_2/contributors3/wallensteintext.htm>.

Wechsler, Diana. "Portinari en la Cultura Visual de los Años Treinta: Estéticas del Silencio, Silenciosas Declamaciones" [Portinari in the Visual Culture of the Thirties: Aesthetics of Silence; Silent Recitations]. In *Candido Portinari y el Sentido Social del Arte* [Candido Portinari and the Social Meaning of Art], edited by Andrea Giunta. Buenos Aires: Siglo XXI, 2005.

Wisnik, José Miguel. *O Coro dos Contrários: A Música em Torno da Semana de 22* [The Chorus of Adversaries: Music in Relation to the Week of the 22nd]. São Paulo: Duas Cidades, 1977.

Xavier, Imail. "Introdução" [Introduction]. In *Revolução do Cinema Novo* [The Revolution of Cinema Novo], by Glauber Rocha. São Paulo: Cosac & Naify, 2004.

———. *O Cinema Brasileiro Moderno* [Modern Brazilian Cinema]. São Paulo: Paz e Terra, 2001.

Zilio, Carlos. *A Querela do Brasil: A Questão da Identidade na Arte Brasileira; a Obra de Tarsila, Di Cavalcanti e Portinari* [The War for Brazil: The Question of Identity in Brazilian Art; the Work of Tarsila, Di Cavalcanti and Portinari]. Rio de Janeiro: Relume Dumará, 1997.

Žižek, Slavoj. *Looking Awry: An Introduction to Jacques Lacan through Popular Culture*. Cambridge, MA: MIT Press, 1991.

Zucchi, Oscar. *El Tango, el Bandoneón y sus Intérpretes* [Tango, the Bandoneón, and Its Musicians], vols. 1 & 2. Buenos Aires: Corregidor, 1998.

DISCOGRAPHY

Canaro, Francisco, and J. Caruso. "Sentimiento Gaucho" [Gaucho Feeling]. *Los Clásicos Argentinos* [Argentine Classics], vol. 4 (1996).

Gardel, Carlos. *Gardel Interpreta a Cadícamo* [Gardel Performs Cadicamo], Página 12, 2005.

Miranda, Carmen. *O Que É Que a Baiana Tem?* [What Does the Bahian Woman Have?]. Odeon, 1966.

———. *A Nossa Carmen Miranda* [Our Carmen Miranda]. EMI, 1995.

Soares, Elza. *Do Cóccix até o Pescoço* [From the Coccyx to the Neck]. Maianga, 2002.

Veloso, Caetano. *Fina Estampa* [Fine Figure]. Polygram, 1994.

———. *Fina Estampa ao Vivo* [Fine Figure, Live]. Polygram Latino, 1995.

———. Sinhô. *Revivendo* [Reliving]. Revivendo Músicas, 1999.

FILMOGRAPHY

Notas de Tango [Notes on the Tango] (2000), directed by Rafael Filipelli.

With Carlos Gardel

Luces de Buenos Aires [Lights of Buenos Aires] (1931), directed by Adelqui Millar.

Melodía de Arrabal [Melody of the Poor Outskirts] (1932), directed by Louis Gasnier.

With Carmen Miranda

Banana da Terra [Banana from the Land] (1939), directed by João de Barro.

Bananas Is My Business (1997), directed by Helena Solberg.

Down Argentine Way (1940), directed by Irving Cummings.